Financial Control for Your Foodservice Operation

Michael M. Coltman

VNR VAN NOSTRAND REINHOLD
—————— New York

Library of Congress Catalog Card Number 90-12812
ISBN 0-442-00448-6

Van Nostrand Reinhold
115 Fifth Avenue
New York, New York 10003

Chapman and Hall
2-6 Boundary Row
London, SE1 8HN, England

Thomas Nelson Australia
102 Dodds Street
South Melbourne 3205
Victoria, Australia

Nelson Canada
1120 Birchmount Road
Scarborough, Ontario MIK 5G4, Canada

16 15 14 13 12 11 10 9 8 7 6 5 4 3 2 1

Library of Congress Cataloging-in-Publication Data

Coltman, Michael M., 1930-
    Financial control for your foodservice operation / Michael M. Coltman.
        p. cm.
    Includes index.
    ISBN 0-442-00448-6
    1. Food service—Finance. I. Title.
TX911.3.F5C63 1991
647.95′068′1—dc20   90-12812
                                                                          CIP

Contents

Preface

The term *foodservice operation* in the title of this book includes many different kinds of restaurants. For example, the following are some of the many types of foodservice operations that make up the restaurant industry:

Cafeterias

Coffee shops

Delicatessens

Dining rooms

Fast-food operations

Hotel foodservices (including banquets)

Institutional feeding

On-premise catering

Off-premise catering

Transportation feeding

Each type of foodservice operation has unique characteristics. Nevertheless, with reference to financial control most of the same principles apply regardless of the type of operation.

Even though this book is entitled *Financial Control for Your Foodservice Operation* and is primarily concerned with the financial aspects of your restaurant business, it should be emphasized that financial controls alone are not sufficient to ensure a successful business.

Before financial control can be practiced, you must first have effective management of your operation. The term *management* in this context covers all aspects of your business, such as operational control, employee relations, public relations, marketing, and financial control. In other words, financial control is just one function of management.

The title might lead you to believe that you must be an accountant to understand it. You do not have to be an accountant, have an accounting background, or become an accountant to understand and put into practice the principles, procedures, and techniques outlined throughout this book.

Further, although this book provides you with many different tools to use, you should not try to use all of them. Consider this book like your restaurant's menu: It shows customers what is available and allows them to make their own selection from soups, salads, entrees, desserts, beverages, and other products. In other words, you must be selective with this book's "menu" and choose the techniques that fit your needs and can be applied in your operation.

Finally note that, for the sake of simplicity throughout this book, the word *restaurant* (rather than *foodservice operation*) is used.

ONE

Introduction

Many people describe the restaurant business as a *service* business. However, in many ways a restaurant is more like a manufacturing concern because it buys raw food products, processes them, and sells them. Nevertheless, there are some significant differences between restaurants and manufacturing companies that make the restaurant business more complex. Some of these are the following:

- The restaurant operator has to clean up after the customers have consumed and paid for the products.
- Restaurant production is generally for immediate sale on a daily (or even meal period) basis. The restaurant operator thus has to purchase most products daily in anticipation of immediate demand. Also, what customers actually order each meal period from a variety of menu items offered is not known until they are seated. This makes the planning of food purchasing and preparation difficult. A manufacturing company can generally produce its finished products far in advance of actual sales.
- Most restaurants have an unpredictable daily sales volume. This makes sales forecasting difficult, means that facilities are frequently underused on some days and overburdened on others, and makes it difficult to know how many production, service, and other employees to have on duty at any one time. Therefore, at times more labor hours are paid for than are really necessary, and at other times there are not enough employees and customers may not receive the service they normally expect. Most manufacturing firms do not have this type of daily sales forecasting problem.
- Most restaurants have a high level of fixed costs (such as rent) relative to variable costs (such as food). Because fixed costs are those that cannot be reduced when sales decrease, an unanticipated decline in sales can have a serious effect on profits. On the other hand, most manufacturing businesses have a low level of fixed costs compared to variable costs. (There is a more in-depth discussion of fixed and variable costs in Chapter 14).

- Most manufacturing businesses can automate their production processes and minimize their labor cost. Restaurants cannot, and this means that they have a relatively high labor cost (most of which is fixed) because a minimum number of employees must be on duty at any one time to cope with unpredictable sales demand. This fixed cost cannot easily be reduced. Thus, if anticipated sales do not materialize, profits can be impaired.

- The product (food) that restaurants sell is highly perishable. Although some foods (such as canned items, dried products, and frozen foods) can be stored for several months until used, many products (such as fresh fruit and vegetables, dairy items, and bakery goods) have a very short shelf life and must be discarded if not used within a few days. Spoiled products add to costs and again reduce profits. In most manufacturing businesses, the products are not perishable and can be inventoried for months or even years until they are sold.

- Sales in a restaurant are generated from hundreds, if not thousands, of individual transactions every day. Each transaction has to be recorded and tracked to ensure that the proper amount of cash is received from both cash and charge (credit) sales. Most manufacturing companies have few customers, each of whom buys infrequently and in large volume, thus minimizing the sales recording problem.

- Most restaurants are open seven days a week, and many of them for twenty-four hours a day. This makes the management process far more complex than for most manufacturing businesses that operate only eight hours a day and five days a week.

MANAGING MONEY

Running a restaurant, just like running any business, is about managing money. Without this management, a business cannot be successfully operated and will probably eventually fail. This is more true of the restaurant business than many other types, because when you compare the failure rate of various types of businesses, restaurants rank among the highest.

To generate and manage money, you must have enough profit to stay in business and ensure that this profit produces enough cash to make all payments when they are due. Thus, it is just as important to plan for cash as it is for profit. Note that profit and cash are *not* the same, as you will discover as you read this book.

What Does Financial Control Mean?

Profit and cash availability will only result if you have good financial control. Financial control means

- Knowing where you are at any time from a profit and cash perspective. (This is really the basis of all financial control.)
- Planning where you are going through the use of budgets and other tools.
- Ensuring you reach where you plan to go through regular financial reports that monitor your progress.

Knowledge of Accounting

In order to exercise any form of financial control, you must know something about accounting. You can obtain this knowledge without becoming an accountant. If you are the owner or operator of a restaurant you probably question why you need to understand anything about accounting because you employ an accountant with whom you can have regular meetings and discussions.

Even if your restaurant is not large enough to employ a full-time accountant, it is likely that you have an "outside" accountant who handles your "books," prepares your accounts, and looks after regulatory requirements such as filing annual income tax returns. He or she can also meet with you regularly to discuss your business. Indeed, this accountant probably knows a lot about many different businesses, such as small manufacturing firms, retail stores, and motels, and can gauge your results with those of other businesses. But those other businesses are not like the restaurant business, and comparison of your results with theirs is meaningless. Further, an external accountant cannot possibly know everything about each of these different businesses, cannot be a specialist at each of them, and can thus discuss your business with you only in general terms.

Knowledge of Restaurant Problems

For example, does an external accountant know anything about managing labor cost in a restaurant operation, about menu pricing, about food and beverage costs and gross profits, and about the problems inherent in operating a seven-day-a-week business? The answer is, Probably not. You, however, know all about these day-to-day problems but probably know little about accounting. This book has, therefore, been written to

- Discuss restaurant operations and relate them to what your accountant does so that *you* can better understand what your financial statements tell you about your business.
- Explain how you can interpret accounting information to improve both the effectiveness of your restaurant and its profits and cash flows.

Inadequate Records

Unfortunately, many small restaurant owners fail to keep adequate records and make no attempt to understand the basics of accounting. As a result, they often do not know whether the business made a profit or a loss until weeks after the end of each financial period (month, quarter, half year, or year) because they have not provided their accountant with sufficient information to prepare proper financial statements. Although these "official" financial statements are important (and necessary in such matters as filing income tax returns), there is no reason why any restaurant owner, given adequate accounting records, cannot prepare interim financial statements that will give at least some indication of how the restaurant is doing on a monthly basis.

As various methods, tools, and techniques of financial control are explained throughout this book, you will probably wonder why your accountant does not do all this for you. If your accountant is a full-time employee, it is likely that he or she either does not know how to do this or does not have the time. If the individual does not know, then a little investment of your time in explaining what you want produced (in addition to the regular financial statements) will provide the needed information. If your accountant does not have the time, then you will have to invest your own time to do the work or hire somebody else (such as an outside accountant) to produce the information desired.

On the other hand, if you use an outside accountant you will be paying that accountant a fee based on the time involved each month to produce your financial statements. That accountant probably has the knowledge to produce a great deal of other information if instructed to do so. But since that will entail more time, there will be an additional cost, unless you again do the work yourself.

Regardless of the situation, there is going to have to be an extra investment of time (and thus money) by someone to produce the desired additional financial information. However, that investment is sure to result in improved profits and cash flow and, therefore, generate a higher return on your investment in your restaurant.

BASIC ACCOUNTING INFORMATION

Accounting was developed to identify and record financial information about a business. It provides information about a company's assets, liabilities (debts), owners' investment, sales (revenue), and expenses. An accounting system allows you or your accountant to prepare basic financial statements (balance sheet and income statement) and other financial reports and analyses that will help you in decision making and in running an efficient, effective, and profitable business. Any restaurant needs to have records that include the following:

- Sales (sometimes called revenue) by meal period, day, week, month, or quarter and further broken down into cash or credit sales (by type of credit card, if necessary) and (in a large restaurant) by department (such as coffee shop, dining room, and beverage operation). Electronic sales registers can readily provide much of the required sales detail without requiring extensive paperwork.
- Operating expenses by type (for example, food and beverage purchases, labor, supplies, and other operating costs) in total by month and by department in a large operation. Payroll (labor cost) is a major expense for most restaurants and there are legal requirements concerning the detail that you must record. In particular, payroll withholdings (for unemployment insurance, income tax, and others) must be properly documented.
- Inventory. Inventory should be taken at least monthly. It must be classified by type (such as food and alcoholic beverages). Electronic sales registers can often be used to record adjustments to inventory as a result of sales.

It is important that you keep documents supporting all transactions. Documents include sales checks, sales register tapes, purchase invoices, cancelled checks for all purchases, and receipts or memos for cash payments not otherwise supported by an invoice or cancelled check.

Decision Making

Restaurant managers are constantly making decisions. These decisions can be improved by using various kinds of accounting information. Promptly produced accounting information can be used to

- Measure your current performance against established objectives, such as achieving a desired percentage of food cost relative to sales.
- Provide answers to questions such as the following: How much money is in the bank? What payments are due to lenders in the next year? How much can the operation afford to spend on needed new furnishings or equipment?
- Analyze sales and cost trends to make more effective plans about future trends of sales and costs.
- Help in producing forecast accounting information (such as budgets) to chart the strategies that you can use in future periods to meet your

financial objectives. In other words, financial forecasts can provide a profit plan for the future.

Decision Principles

In your restaurant, effective decisions based on financial information can only be made if this financial information is gathered and presented using certain basic principles. The most important principles are the following:

- Accuracy. For accounting information to have any validity, it must be as accurate as possible. This accuracy, however, must be balanced with practicality. For certain types of information, the more accurate it is the more time it takes to gather—and time costs money. There is a point beyond which the extra cost of accuracy is not worth the benefit. For example, it takes considerable time to take a food inventory and cost it accurately. Therefore, it makes sense in the case of certain inventory products to estimate their cost (for example, what is the cost of a half-prepared sauce or soup?) rather than spend valuable time trying to be too accurate).

- Timeliness. For example, if food cost is measured each month against a desired standard, then the actual food cost must be prepared within a few days of each month-end so that you can make a timely comparison with the standard. If the actual food cost is not known until, let us say, thirty days after the end of the month and comparison shows that corrective action should have been taken, then an entire month's time has been lost. You must recognize this timeliness limitation (as many restaurant operators do) and organize your information-gathering system accordingly. As far as sales information is concerned, electronic sales registers can provide extremely timely information, not only about dollars of sales by meal period each day but also about the quantities sold of individual menu products; this information allows more effective daily food purchasing to replace products sold.

- Consistency. For reasons of comparability of financial information from one accounting period to the next, consistency should prevail. In other words, the method of recording accounting information should not be changed without good reason. For example, at each month-end a value must be placed on the inventory of unsold food products. There are a number of different methods for pricing (valuing) this inventory. The method selected should be used consistently unless there is a good reason to change it.

Routine Decisions

Two broad types of decisions made by most restaurant operators can be identified. The first type is routine decisions made on a day-to-day basis related to ongoing operations. An example of this type of decision concerns how many employees to have on duty in each area (for example, kitchen production and dining room service) for each meal period each day to cope with anticipated volume of business. Historic accounting information concerning sales by meal period each day can help in this type of routine decision making.

Another example is the need to take corrective action in a certain area. For example, is the beverage cost of sales too high for the sales generated? Again, timely accounting information about the actual beverage cost that allows comparison with a standard can be used in such a decision.

For these routine decisions, you need to establish systems that allow the necessary decision-making information to be provided promptly and accurately.

Nonroutine Decisions

The second type of decision is a nonroutine (or infrequent) one. This type of decision concerns questions such as the following:

- Should I invest in redecorating the dining room?
- Should the menu be drastically revised?
- Should I open a second restaurant operation?

This type of decision is much more difficult to make than a routine one and involves a far more serious situation if the wrong decision is made. For example, if you make a routine decision to have more employees on duty than are actually needed for a particular meal period, labor cost will be higher than it should be, but it affects only that meal period (as long as the same mistake is not continually made). In contrast, if you decide to change your entire menu and later discover that regular customers do not like the change and stay away, business will decline, there will be an inventory of food products on hand whose cost may not be recoverable, and if the menu is changed back to the way it was before, it may take a long time to convince the "lost" customers to return.

FINANCIAL STATEMENTS

Regularly each month you should prepare, or have prepared, a set of financial statements to monitor your operation's progress. The basic documents in this set of financial statements are an income statement (also known as a profit and loss statement) and a balance sheet.

The income statement shows revenues (sales) less expenses to arrive at profit. The profit (or loss, if expenses exceed revenues) is transferred to the balance sheet and becomes part of the owners' equity. If all accounting entries have been made correctly, the balance sheet will then "balance." The balance sheet equation, as it is known, is

$$\text{Assets} = \text{Liabilities} + \text{Owners' equity}.$$

Assets are items owned by your restaurant (for example, cash, inventory, and furniture and equipment). Liabilities (debts or obligations) are items owed by your restaurant (such as unpaid accounts, bank loans, or other payments due in the future). Owners' equity (also sometimes referred to as "net worth") is the difference between the assets and the liabilities. It comprises the money you, and any other owners, have invested in the restaurant, plus the profits (less any losses) since the business began.

It perhaps makes more sense, from an owner's perspective, to state the balance sheet equation as

$$\text{Assets} - \text{Liabilities} = \text{Owners' equity}$$

because, if the restaurant were liquidated, the assets would be sold for cash, the cash used to pay off liabilities, and whatever was left returned to the owner(s). Logical as this view of the balance sheet is, however, accountants prefer to express the equation in the traditional way since an even "balance" is then maintained.

Transactions

A balance sheet is prepared from accounts in which business transactions are recorded. A business transaction is an exchange of goods or services (for example, the sale of food and beverages). In accounting, each transaction affects two or more accounts (this is why it is frequently referred to as double-entry accounting). No transaction can affect only one account. In this way, the balance sheet is always kept in balance (and your accountant eternally happy) because every transaction causes increases and/or decreases in asset and/or liability and/or owners' equity accounts. This is illustrated very simply by considering what happens if Harry Haddock starts a new seafood restaurant by investing $25,000 of his own savings in it. The balance sheet would look like this:

Assets		Owners' Equity	
Cash	$25,000	Investment	$25,000

If Harry then purchases from a supplier $5,000 of fish on credit so that he has an inventory of goods to sell in his restaurant, the balance sheet will now reflect the fact that assets have increased (because of the inventory) and so have liabilities (because the supplier must be paid for the fish). It will look like this:

Assets		Liability	
Cash	$25,000	Accounts payable	$ 5,000
Inventory	5,000		
		Owners' Equity	
		Investment	25,000
Totals	$30,000		$30,000

The balance sheet balances because the left-hand side (totaling $30,000) equals the right-hand side (also totaling $30,000).

Let us now assume that Harry uses up $3,000 of fish (thus reducing his inventory to $2,000) and makes cash sales of $5,000 (increasing the cash account by that amount). As a result, he makes a profit of $2,000 ($5,000 sales less $3,000 use of inventory), causing his equity to increase by $2,000. The balance sheet will now look like this:

Assets		Liability	
Cash	$30,000	Accounts payable	$ 5,000
Inventory	2,000		
		Owners' Equity	
		Investment	25,000
		Profit	2,000
Totals	$32,000		$32,000

In practice, transactions such as making sales or incurring expenses are not recorded immediately onto the balance sheet (because the balance sheet just would not have enough room on it and would be continuously changing). Instead, they are entered into accounting records called journals and then into accounts in a ledger or (in a small business with fewer transactions) directly into the accounts in the ledger. It is the ledger, supported by the journals, that is commonly called the books of account. Only at the end of an accounting period (such as the end of the month) is a new balance sheet created.

Further, when it is time to prepare the balance sheet, all the transactions relating to sales and expenses are first summarized on the income statement. As a result, even though the income statement is a separate document, it can be considered as an extension of the balance sheet's owners' equity section, and the balance sheet equation can be illustrated as follows to reflect this:

$$\text{Assets} = \text{Liabilities} + \underbrace{\text{Owners' Equity}}_{\text{Sales} \quad \text{Expenses}}$$

Accounts

In a business's ledger, there is usually one account for each type of asset, liability, owners' equity, sale (revenue), and expense. At the end of each accounting period only the account balances at that time are transferred, either to the balance sheet or to the income statement then to the balance sheet.

In accounting, each account is considered to have a left-hand side and a right-hand side. The left-hand side is where debit (usually abbreviated *Dr*) entries are made, and the right-hand side is where credit (*Cr*) entries are made:

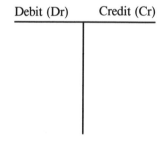

Debit (Dr)   Credit (Cr)

Because of their shape, these simply illustrated types of account are referred to as "T" accounts. In practice, you will never see accounts that look like this, but they are very useful for understanding and learning the basic "rules" of accounting.

When transactions are entered in the accounts, the entries in the debit side of the accounts must always equal the entries in the credit side. If this does not occur, the balance sheet will not balance. At the end of each accounting period, as the accounts are closed (totaled up), the difference between the debit and credit entries in each account provides the balance figure for that account.

You should not view debits as increases in the balance of accounts, and credits as decreases. Debits can either increase or decrease the balance, and credits can also either increase or decrease the balance. The rules for this are illustrated in the following T accounts:

Assets		Liabilities		Owners' Equity	
Debits	Credits	Debits	Credits	Debits	Credits
increase	decrease	decrease	increase	decrease	increase
balance	balance	balance	balance	balance	balance

Because sales increase owners' equity, sales account entries have the same effect as those for the owners' equity account, and because expenses decrease owners' equity, expense account entries are the reverse of those for sales. This is illustrated as follows:

Sales		Expenses	
Debits	Credits	Debits	Credits
decrease	increase	increase	decrease
balance	balance	balance	balance

The normal account balance for each of the five types of account would be

Account	Normal Balance
Asset	Debit
Liability	Credit
Owners' Equity	Credit
Sales	Credit
Expenses	Debit

and an example of each would be

Asset:

Cash

15,000	

Liability:

Accounts Payable

	8,000

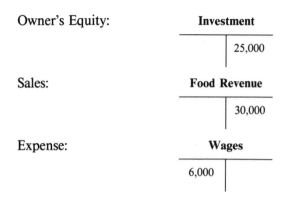

Owner's Equity: **Investment**

| | 25,000 |

Sales: **Food Revenue**

| | 30,000 |

Expense: **Wages**

| 6,000 | |

IMPORTANCE OF MATCHING PRINCIPLE

In most restaurants there can be hundreds, if not thousands, of individual sales transactions (and often as many expense transactions) each day. At the end of each period when financial statements are desired, it is likely that some transactions have not yet been recorded. If they are not recorded, then the income statement does not reflect the true profit that the restaurant has.

In order for the profit to be correct, any unrecorded transactions must be adjusted for by an important concept in accounting known as the matching principle. The matching principle simply states that transactions should be recorded at the time they occur and not necessarily at the time cash is exchanged. For example, consider the following situations:

- Assume that a regular customer of your restaurant is allowed to charge his restaurant meals to an account that is mailed out after the end of the month. Under the matching principle, the sales to that customer are shown as revenue for the month even though you may not receive the cash for several weeks. Similarly, a customer might use a credit card. At that time, the sale is still recorded as a sale, even though payment is not received from the credit card company until two weeks or more after the credit card voucher is sent to them.

- Food may be delivered to your restaurant by suppliers on a day-to-day basis as needed without your having to pay cash on delivery. In other words, suppliers sell to you on credit. At each month-end, all purchases made must be recorded even though you may not make payment to suppliers until several weeks after the end of the month.

- The amount of unused food you have on hand (inventory) is not a constant figure. From one month-end to the next, the inventory can either increase or decrease. Therefore, at each month-end (assuming that you want monthly financial statements), you must take inventory so that purchases made and still in inventory can be adjusted for and purchases used accurately matched against actual sales.

- Assume you pay the insurance premium on your restaurant's premises for the entire year in January. If you show this full payment as an expense on the January income statement, that statement will be distorted (the insurance expense will be higher than it should be) and the income statements of the other eleven months in the year will also be wrong (because they will show zero for insurance). Therefore, when the insurance is paid in January, the full amount is recorded as "prepaid insurance" (and shown as an asset on the balance sheet), and one-twelfth of that expense is transferred each month from the prepaid account to the expense account. Other expenses that are prepaid (such as rent) are handled in the same way.

- Assume that you normally pay your employees each Friday for time worked up to that Friday and that the last day of a particular month falls on the following Monday. In the three days (Saturday, Sunday, and Monday) since payday, the employees who have worked will have earned money that you will not be paying them until the following Friday. Nevertheless, in order for your income statement to reflect the correct labor cost for that month, the wages earned must be recorded in a liability account (such as "accrued wages" or "wages payable") and also as a labor expense that appears on that month's income statement.

Adjustments

When your accountant prepares your month-end financial statements, he or she makes sure that adjustments are made for all these types of transaction. The correct recording of these adjustments (and likely many others in most restaurants) at each month-end will match all sales with all expenses incurred to generate those sales. It is not necessary that you understand the mechanics of adjustments, but it is important that you understand the need for them in order that your stated monthly profit is as accurate as possible. Using adjustments to match sales and expenses is known as *accrual accounting*, as opposed to *cash accounting*, under which entries are made in the books only when cash is received or given out.

This does not suggest that cash-based accounting is never used. In fact, it might be quite a good idea to use it in some situations. For example, a small restaurant that sells meals only on a cash basis and pays cash for all wages and supplies might well use a cash-based accounting system or a combination cash/accrual system. However, because most restaurants usually have some purchases and sales (as well as other transactions) that are not on a cash basis, the matching concept of accrual accounting is assumed to be used throughout the remainder of this book.

TWO

Understanding Your Balance Sheet

In order to understand financial statements, you do not have to be able to prepare them. However, if you understand how financial statements are put together, you have the advantage of being able to analyze the information presented by them in greater depth.

INCOME STATEMENT VERSUS BALANCE SHEET

The two major financial statements are the balance sheet and the income statement. Although the balance sheet and the income statement are prepared as separate documents, the close relationship between them must be kept in mind. This is clear when you compare the definitions of the two types of statement:

- The balance sheet gives a picture of the financial position of a business *at a particular time.*
- The income statement shows the operating results of the business *over a period* of time.

The period of time referred to for the income statement usually ends on the date of the balance sheet:

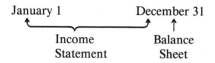

The balance sheet is discussed in this chapter, and the income statement in Chapter 3.

THE BALANCE SHEET

On the left-hand (or debit) side of the balance sheet are listed the assets or resources that your restaurant has. On the right-hand (or credit) side are listed its liabilities (or debts) and the owners' equity. Total assets always equal total liabilities plus owners' equity (this is the balance sheet equation discussed in Chapter 1).

The asset side of the balance sheet is generally broken down into three categories: current assets, fixed or long-term assets, and other assets. The breakdown of assets into these categories is not for balancing reasons but for the sake of convenience when analyzing the balance sheet.

Current Assets

Current assets are cash or items that can or will be converted into cash within a short period of time (usually a year or less). The following accounts for a restaurant generally appear under current assets:

Cash.   Cash includes not only cash in various bank accounts (such as a general checking account and a payroll account) but also cash on hand in sales register cash drawers, cash not yet deposited in the bank, and cash held as a basic on-site fund for change-making and paying for cash-on-delivery purchases.

Accounts Receivable.   Accounts receivable includes any amounts due from customers. If your restaurant operates on a cash-only basis, then it will have no accounts receivable. However, most restaurants accept credit cards that allow customers to charge their accounts. These credit card sales are accounts receivable until payment is received. Some restaurants also offer billing privileges to certain clients. An example of this might be a restaurant that does business with nearby firms who allow authorized employees to charge their meals to the company, with the company's being sent an invoice once a week or once a month. These invoiced amounts are accounts receivable until paid. Another example of an account receivable might be a restaurant that leases out part of its premises to another business (for example, a gift shop or newsstand) and receives rent for that space and/or commissions on sales of merchandise. Any unpaid rent and/or commissions are accounts receivable.

Allowance for Doubtful Accounts.   If your restaurant includes in accounts receivable any accounts that may not be collectible, an allowance for doubtful accounts should be established for the total amount of these doubtful accounts. This amount is shown as a separate amount on the balance sheet and is *deducted* from the accounts receivable to arrive at their net realizable amount. Some small restaurants that have only nominal amounts of accounts receivable do not bother with setting up an allowance for doubtful accounts.

Marketable Securities.   At times, your restaurant may have excess cash on hand. Instead of leaving these excess funds in the bank at little or no interest, it would be a good idea to place them in short-term investments (such as government bonds that pay better-than-bank interest) that can be quickly sold and converted back into cash when needed. Because these investments are readily convertible to cash, they are known as marketable securities.

Inventory.   The two major inventories for most restaurants are food and alcoholic beverages. At each balance sheet date, these inventories are physically counted and costed to provide a total value for all unused products on hand. This value appears as an asset on the balance sheet. Some large restaurants might also have a considerable amount of supplies on hand (for example, paper and plastic supplies used by fast-food restaurants). In such cases, these supplies should also be valued at each balance sheet date and the amount included in the inventory account.

Prepaid Expenses.   Many restaurants prepay certain expenses at the beginning of the year. These expenses might include rent, licenses, property taxes, and insurance. In each case, at each balance sheet date the amount that is still prepaid should be included on the balance sheet. For example, if a restaurant's annual insurance premium of $4,800 is prepaid at the beginning of each year and a balance sheet is prepared halfway through the year, the balance sheet's prepaid expense account should show at that time $2,400 for insurance along with any other prepaid amounts.

Fixed (Long-term) Assets

Fixed (or long-term) assets are those of a relatively permanent nature, not intended for sale, that are used in generating revenue. This category of assets might include the following.

Land.   If your business owns the land on which the restaurant sits, the land account will reflect the cost of this land, including expenditures such as legal costs and title fees for purchasing it and the cost of clearing it to make it usable. This cost would be reduced by any cash recovered subsequent to the purchase, such as the salvage value of any materials sold from a building that was previously there and torn down to prepare the site for your restaurant.

Building.   A restaurant that owns its own building would show that building's cost in this account. Cost includes all costs to construct the building if it is a new one or to purchase (including renovating) an existing building. "Cost" includes all items: materials, labor, architect and designer fees, building permits, construction or renovation financing expenses, and taxes during the construction or renovation period. Note that, if land and an existing building are purchased as a package for your restaurant, at the time of purchase the total purchase cost must be realistically allocated to the land account and the building account. The purchase contract may show this breakdown. If not, a professional appraisal may be required. This cost allocation is needed for income tax purposes because building costs can be depreciated, whereas land costs cannot be.

Furniture, Fixtures, and Equipment.   The furniture, fixtures, and equipment (FFE) account includes all furniture in dining, drinking, and other areas (such as reception and office); fixtures (such as carpets, drapes, and display cases); and all kitchen, service, and office area equipment (including cleaning equipment and sales registers). Cost of these items includes actual purchase cost, including taxes, import duties, freight, shipping insurance charges, and installation. If your restaurant owns any automotive equipment (for example, some restaurants deliver food to private residences and may own their own delivery vehicles), that equipment may be included with FFE or may be shown in a separate fixed asset account.

Accumulated Depreciation.   Long-term assets are shown on the balance sheet at their cost. From the cost figures for building and FFE (but not land) is deducted accumulated depreciation. Accumulated depreciation reflects the estimated decline in value of the assets due to wear and tear, passage of time, changed economic conditions, or other factors. (Depreciation is discussed in more detail in the next chapter.)

The difference between the asset cost figure and the accumulated depreciation is referred to as net book value. Net book value does not necessarily accurately reflect the current market or replacement value of the assets in question. For example, if your restaurant building is in good condition and you plan to sell your business and move on to some other endeavor, to a purchaser the building might be worth far more than its depreciated value on your balance sheet.

Linen, China, Glassware, Silver, Utensils, and Uniforms.   The value of all these items, either in reserve in inventory or in actual use at balance sheet date, is shown in this account. Items in reserve are valued at their cost, whereas those in use are valued at less than cost because usage reduces their value below cost.

Other Assets

If your restaurant has any other assets that do not fit into either the current or fixed categories they are included here. Some examples follow.

Leasehold Improvements.   Many restaurants do not own land or a building but operate in leased (rented) premises. If your restaurant is in a leased building that you have had to spend money on to "improve" or renovate to make it operable for your style of restaurant, the cost of those improvements is recorded in this account. Leasehold improvements might include redesign of the restaurant (for example, installation of additional walls or partitions) or paving of a parking lot. These improvements are of benefit during the life of the business or the remaining life of the lease. The costs should be spread over this life. This spreading of costs is much like depreciation for building and FFE, except that in the case of leasehold property it is generally called amortization.

Deposits.   Many leased restaurants are required to pay a deposit equivalent to one or more months' normal rent. This deposit is held by the landlord and is allocated to the last month or months of the lease contract. Another type of deposit might be one paid to a gas, electricity, or other type of utility company. Such deposits are assets, but not current assets, because they cannot be readily converted into cash.

Goodwill.   Goodwill is the price you pay in excess of the value of the tangible assets (land, building, FFE) when you purchase an existing restaurant. Goodwill is shown on the balance sheet at cost and is then amortized (written off) over the restaurant's life or forty years (whichever is shorter).

Franchise Fees.   Many restaurants today are franchised operations. If your restaurant is franchised, you have probably had to pay an up-front fee to the franchisor for that franchise right. This fee (including any legal and other costs to obtain the right to the franchise) is shown on the balance sheet and is amortized over the franchise life.

License Fees.   Many restaurants have to pay a fee to a local government to obtain a license to operate. For example, this is sometimes the situation to acquire an alcoholic beverage license. The license cost should be shown on the balance sheet and amortized over a reasonable number of years.

Investments.   Investments are differentiated from some other assets (such as marketable securities) because they cannot be readily converted into cash and thus cannot be used in the day-to-day operations of your restaurant. For example, you may have invested in a piece of land adjacent to your restaurant for future expansion or in a piece of land in another location to start a second restaurant some time in the future. Investments are normally shown on the balance sheet at their cost.

Total Assets

The total of all the asset categories (current, fixed, and other) gives the total asset value, or total resources, of your restaurant.

Liabilities and Owner's Equity

On the right-hand side of the balance sheet are the liabilities and owners' equity sections. The liabilities and equity show how your assets (resources) have been financed, or paid for. The liability section comprises current liabilities and long-term liabilities.

Current Liabilities

Current liabilities are those debts that must be paid, or are expected to be paid, in less than a year. On a restaurant balance sheet, you are likely to see the following current liabilities.

Accounts Payable: Trade.　　The accounts payable trade account includes liabilities (unpaid accounts) for goods (for example, food, beverages, and supplies) and services (for example, a contracted piped-in music service) incurred in the normal course of business.

Accounts Payable: Other.　　The accounts payable other account is used for amounts payable other than for day-to-day purchases of goods and services. For example, if equipment has been purchased, any amount still due and payable to the equipment supplier would be shown here.

Notes Payable.　　Sometimes amounts are due and formalized by a document known as a note. This might occur when equipment is purchased or when a bank loan is received. Any unpaid amounts (including interest) on the note(s) are recorded in this account.

Taxes Payable.　　The taxes payable account includes amounts due for such items as income taxes, federal and state payroll withholding taxes (including any matching amount your restaurant must pay), and sales taxes due to a taxing authority and collected from customers on food and beverage sales. On the balance sheets of large restaurants, each individual type of tax payable may be shown as a separate account.

Accrued Expenses. Accrued expenses are those amounts due for expenses incurred but not yet paid at the balance sheet date. For example, assume that employees are paid on every second Friday and that the month-end balance sheet is prepared on the Monday following a payday. Even though employees have not been paid for three days of work at the balance sheet date, that amount is still due to them and is recorded as a liability under accrued expenses on the balance sheet. Other common accrued expenses are unpaid interest, rent, and utilities. In large restaurants, the balance sheet may show accrued salaries and wages as an account separate from other accrued expenses.

Deposits on Group Business. Your restaurant may handle group business such as bus tours or banquets. It is common practice when a customer books group business for a deposit to be collected at the time the contract is signed by the customer. If any deposits are still being held at the balance sheet date for future group business, the total of these deposits is recorded as a liability because, if the business is cancelled within a reasonable time prior to the event, the deposit amount is likely refundable to the customer. If the business does occur, at that time the deposit amount is taken out of the liability account and shown as sales revenue.

Dividends Payable. If your restaurant is an incorporated one it may have declared (decided to pay) dividends but not yet paid them out at the balance sheet date. If so, they are recorded as a liability (just like unpaid employee salaries and wages).

Current Portion of Long-Term Debt. If your restaurant has arranged a mortgage from a lender to buy the land and/or build the restaurant, that mortgage will probably be repayable year by year over a long number of years and be shown as a long-term liability. However, any amount of that long-term debt payable within the next twelve months is shown as a current liability.

Long-term Liabilities

Long-term liabilities are the debts of your restaurant that are payable more than one year beyond the balance sheet date. Included in this category would be mortgages and any similar long-term loans such as notes or bonds, less the current portion shown under current liabilities. In a large restaurant, each type of long-term liability might be shown separately on the balance sheet.

Owners' Equity

In general terms, the owners' equity section of the balance sheet is the difference between the total assets and the total liabilities. It represents the equity, or the net worth, of the owner(s) of the restaurant. From a legal point of view, there are three ways for any business to operate: as an incorporated company, a proprietorship, or a partnership.

Incorporated Company.   If you are operating your restaurant as an incorporated company, the owners' equity comprises two main items: capital (shares) and retained earnings.

An incorporated company is limited by law to a maximum number of shares it can issue, known as the authorized number of shares. Shares generally have a par, or stated, value. It is this par value, multiplied by the number of shares actually issued up to the authorized quantity, that provides the total value of capital on the balance sheet.

Most small restaurants that operate as incorporated companies issue common shares. However, some restaurants also issue another type known as preferred shares. Preferred shares rank ahead of common shares, up to certain limits, as far as dividends are concerned. Preferred shareholders may also have special voting rights, and they normally rank ahead of common shareholders in the event that the restaurant is liquidated.

The other part of the owners' equity section of the balance sheet for an incorporated business is retained earnings. Retained earnings are the link between the income statement and the balance sheet. For that reason, the retained earnings part of the owners' equity section of the balance sheet is covered in the next chapter, where the income statement is discussed.

Proprietorship.   If your restaurant is a proprietorship in which you are the sole owner, the owners' equity section of the balance sheet will normally have a single line on it, as follows

Owner capital $xxx.xx

showing the value of your equity (net worth) in the business at the balance sheet date. This capital is made up of the amount originally invested in the business, plus any profits (less any losses) since it began, less any funds withdrawn by you from the business.

Partnership.   If your business is a partnership (two or more owners), there will be a line in the owner equity section for each partner. For example:

Partner A   capital $xxx.xx

Partner B   capital $yyy.yy
Partner C   capital $zzz.zz

Each partner's capital amount at the balance sheet date is calculated in the same way as for a proprietorship, with each partner's share of profits (or losses) allocated to his or her capital account according to the agreement drawn up when the partnership was formed.

Balance Sheet Presentation

The amount of detail shown on your restaurant's balance sheet depends on the amount of information desired and the size and complexity of the restaurant and on whether the business is a proprietorship, partnership, or incorporated company. For example, a large restaurant's balance sheet might show each type of cash account as a separate item, whereas a small restaurant's balance sheet might combine all the various cash accounts into a single figure on the balance sheet.

Some operators want their balance sheets simplified as much as possible because this makes them easier to "read" at first glance. Where more detail about an account is needed, this might then be shown as an addendum, or footnote on an adjoining page. For example, a restaurant's inventories might be shown in total only on the balance sheet and be supported by a separate schedule that shows inventories broken down into categories, such as food, beverages, supplies, and others.

The balance sheet is sometimes presented with assets on the left and liabilities and capital on the right. This method of presentation is known as the account form or method and is the one most commonly used.

Another common method is the report form. This method is vertical, rather than horizontal as in the account form. In the report form, the balance sheet is considered to have a top half and a bottom half. The top half is for the assets and the bottom half for liabilities and owners' equity, as illustrated in the balance sheet in Figure 2.1.

IMPORTANCE OF BALANCE SHEET

The balance sheet is important because it can provide information about such matters as

- Your restaurant's liquidity, or ability to pay its debts when they have to be paid.
- How much of your restaurant's past profits have been retained in the

BALANCE SHEET AS OF DECEMBER 31, 19X1		
ASSETS		
Current Assets		
Cash	$ 25,400	
Accounts receivable	15,200	
Marketable securities	32,000	
Inventory	14,700	
Prepaid expense	4,900	$ 92,200
Fixed Assets		
Land	$ 60,500	
Building	882,400	
Furniture and equipment	227,900	
China, glass, silver, linen	18,300	
	$1,189,100	
Less: Accumulated depreciation	(422,000)	767,100
Total Assets		$859,300
LIABILITIES AND OWNERS' EQUITY		
Current Liabilities		
Accounts payable	$ 16,500	
Accrued expenses	4,200	
Income taxes payable	20,900	
Credit balances	800	
Current portion of mortgage	26,000	$ 68,400
Long-term Liability		
Mortgage payable		486,800
Total Liabilities		$555,200
OWNERS' EQUITY		
Common shares	$ 200,000	
Retained earnings	104,100	304,100
Total Liabilities and Owners' Equity		$859,300

Figure 2.1 Sample balance sheet.

business to help it expand and/or reduce the amount of outside money (debt) that has had to be borrowed.

- The breakdown of your restaurant's assets into current, fixed, and other, with details about the amount of assets within each of these broad categories.

- Your restaurant's debt (liabilities) relative to owners' equity. In general, the greater the amount of debt relative to equity, the higher the restaurant's financial risk.

Balance Sheet Limitations

There are some aspects of your restaurant's business that the balance sheet may not disclose. For example:

- Because transactions are recorded in the value of the dollar at the time the transaction occurred, the true value of some assets on the balance sheet may not be apparent. Suppose your restaurant owned the land on which the building sits and that the land was purchased several years ago. Because of inflation and demand for limited land, it is likely that the land is worth far more today than was paid for it. This may also be true of some other assets. The balance sheet normally does not show these assets at today's market value.

- If you purchased your restaurant from a previous owner who had built up a successful business and you paid an amount for that business beyond the actual market value of the purchased assets, that amount would have been recorded on the balance sheet at the time of purchase as "goodwill." Goodwill that a restaurant has is normally recorded only at the time a business is purchased. Therefore, if you started your restaurant from scratch, have a good location compared to your competitors', and/or have a good reputation and faithful clientele, and/or have a superior work force with a good morale, your restaurant is probably worth far more than the balance sheet assets show, simply because the goodwill you have built up is not reflected on the balance sheet.

- Another value similar to goodwill that is not shown on the balance sheet is your restaurant's investment in its employees. This investment takes the form of time and money spent on recruiting, training, evaluating, and promoting motivated employees. Obviously, it is difficult to assign a value to these human resources, but they are, nevertheless, an asset to your restaurant.

- Many items recorded on balance sheets are a matter of judgment or estimates. For example, in recording depreciation for assets such as equipment and furniture, a number of different depreciation methods may be used. What is the best depreciation method and rate to use? Similarly, which is the best method to use of several available for the valuation of inventories? Because you must thus use judgments or estimates to decide, your balance sheet may not reflect correct values for all assets. If the judgments or estimates used are wrong, then the balance sheet is incorrect.

- Balance sheets also reflect the financial position of your restaurant at only one moment in time. After that moment passes, the balance sheet is constantly changing, yet these changes will not be reflected until another balance sheet is produced a month or more later. If your current balance sheet showed a healthy cash position at that time and a week later you spent most of that cash on new furniture, the balance sheet tells nothing about the impending use of most of the cash available.

THREE

Understanding Your Income Statement

There are a number of different names used for what in this book will be referred to as the income statement. Some of the alternatives are income and expense statement, profit and loss statement, statement of operations, and earnings statement.

The income statement shows the operating results (sales less expenses) of your restaurant for a period of time (month, quarter, half year, or year). Many restaurant operators consider the income statement to be more valuable than the balance sheet. However, in order to have complete understanding of your restaurant's operations you should be able to understand both the income statement and the balance sheet, plus any supporting statements and/or schedules that might be useful for your particular operation. No single statement or schedule can alone provide complete information. For example, an income statement can show that your restaurant made a profit for the year (always a good idea), but the related balance sheet may show there is insufficient cash in the bank to pay current liabilities (not a good idea).

QUESTIONS THE INCOME STATEMENT CAN ANSWER

The income statement, nevertheless, can provide answers to some important questions:

- What were the sales last month? How does that compare with the month before and with the same month last year?
- Did last month's sales keep pace with the increased cost of food, beverages, labor, and other expenses?
- What were the sales by department for the operating period?
- Which department is operating most effectively?

- Is there a limit to maximum potential sales? Have we reached that limit? If so, can we increase sales in the short run by raising menu prices or in the long run by expanding the premises?
- What were the food and beverage cost and gross profit percentages? Did these meet our objectives?
- Were operating costs (such as for labor and supplies) in line with what they should be for the sales level achieved?
- How did the operating results for the period compare with budget forecasts?

SALES (REVENUE)

Sales can be defined as increases in assets (cash or accounts receivable) from selling goods and/or providing services as part of your restaurant's normal operations. Thus, selling food and beverages in your restaurant (either for cash or on credit) produces sales or revenue. On the other hand, a bank lending your restaurant money may be increasing the restaurant's bank account but is not producing any revenue. Similarly, if a deposit is received by your restaurant for a banquet, that deposit is not recorded as a sale until the function is actually held. In the interim it is recorded on the balance sheet as a liability: deposits payable.

Revenue is, therefore, only recorded at the time an exchange of goods or services for "money" takes place. That money can be in the form of cash (selling a meal with the customer's paying cash), a credit card voucher that a customer signs at the end of a meal, or a promise to pay money (a banquet customer's signing an invoice at the end of a banquet and agreeing to pay the invoice within thirty days). In the latter two cases, the restaurant receives "money" (in the form of accounts receivable) and revenue is earned even though no cash has yet been exchanged.

Revenue Detail

Most restaurants separate food revenue (sales) accounts from those for alcoholic beverage sales. Where there is more than one food department (for example, a coffee shop and a dining room) sales should be recorded separately by department. Similarly, if there is more than one alcoholic beverage outlet (for example, a cocktail lounge and a separate dining room bar) sales should also be recorded separately for each. If your restaurant does banquet or group catering, there should be a separate account for those sales.

The main reason for separating sales for each food and beverage outlet is so that sales trends for each can be followed and statistics (such as average customer spending) for each can be calculated and trends analyzed.

Separate revenue accounts will also be required for interest income, commission income (for example, from vending machines), and any other type of revenue that is not directly related to food or alcoholic beverage sales.

Note that some restaurants automatically add a service charge (such as 10 percent) to each guest check for gratuities or tips. The total gratuities collected from customers are subsequently distributed to employees. The gratuities are not revenue and, until distributed, should be recorded in a separate account (such as service charges) until paid out to employees.

EXPENSES

The amount of detail concerning expenses shown on your income statement depends on the type and size of your business and your need for more or less information.

Expenses are defined as the use of cash or the incurrence of liabilities, or a combination of both, to purchase goods or services in the normal course of your restaurant's operation. Clearly, paying cash for employee labor is an expense, as is the cash purchase of operating supplies. In the case of other items, however, the point at which a purchase becomes an expense is not so clear.

For example, when food and beverages used in the normal course of business are purchased, these purchases are placed in inventory (a balance sheet asset) and only become income statement expenses as the goods are taken out of storage and used.

Similarly, the purchase of an item of furniture, fixtures, or equipment is not recorded as an expense at the time of purchase. For example, when a new item of kitchen equipment is purchased, it is recorded at that time on the balance sheet as a fixed or long-term asset. As the equipment is used over its useful life, its value declines (depreciates). Only as that value declines is the amount of decrease recorded as depreciation expense on the income statement.

Cost of Sales

A major expense item in any restaurant is the cost of food sales, or food cost. If your restaurant has alcoholic beverage sales, then cost of beverage sales (or beverage cost) will also be a major expense item.

Food cost and beverage cost should always be kept as separate expense accounts so that they can be matched against the related sales and so that food cost percentage and beverage cost percentage can be calculated. Because of the importance of food cost and beverage cost to any restaurant, there is further detailed discussion about these costs in later chapters.

Food cost should be deducted from food sales on the income statement to arrive at food gross profit and beverage cost deducted from beverage sales to arrive at beverage gross profit.

Gross Profit

Gross profit is important. If you do not have the right gross profit, you cannot then achieve an adequate net profit. Suppose gross profit is 60 percent of sales and net profit 10 percent. If gross profit drops to 59 percent, net profit declines to 9 percent. In other words, a one point decline in gross profit represents about 2 percent (1/60) of gross profit, but the one point decline in net profit represents a 10 percent (1/10) decline in that profit.

Let us have a look at gross profit in terms of some dollar figures. Suppose, for the sake of simplicity, that you operate a restaurant that serves a buffet at a fixed price of $10 per customer and food cost is 40 percent, or $4, leaving a gross profit of 60 percent, or $6 per customer. If you sell on average 200 meals a day, total gross profit is 200 × $6 = $1,200. If the other costs of operating your buffet restaurant are $1,100, then your net profit per day is $1,200 − $1,100 = $100. In the form of an income statement this is:

Sales	$2,000
Cost of sales 40%	800
Gross profit 60%	$1,200
Other expenses	1,100
Profit	$ 100

What happens if you increase your sales to 220 customers per day? Your gross profit will increase by 20 × $6 = $120 per day, but so will your net profit on the assumption that the only expense to increase will be the food cost (with possible nominal increases in other costs such as additional utilities to prepare the extra food). In the form of an income statement this is:

Sales	$2,200
Cost of sales 40%	880
Gross profit 60%	$1,320
Other expenses	1,100
Profit	$ 220

In other words, sales have increased by $200 from $2,000 to $2,200 or

$$\frac{\$200}{\$2,000} \times 100 = 10\%$$

Gross profit has increased by $120 from $1,200 to $1,320 or

$$\frac{\$120}{\$1,200} \times 100 = 10\%$$

Net profit has increased by $120 from $100 to $220 or

$$\frac{\$120}{\$100} \times 100 = 120\%$$

This demonstrates how small changes in sales or in gross profit (through control of food cost) can have a significant impact on your restaurant's profitability. The reason is that most of a restaurant's expenses are fixed (that is, they do not change with a change in sales) and only food cost (and beverage cost in the case of beverage sales) increases. Of course, this is true only up to a certain level of sales increase. At some increased level of sales, labor cost is likely to increase to cope with the additional sales volume.

Direct Expenses

After gross profit on an income statement, the direct expenses (other than food cost and beverage cost) are listed, totaled, and then deducted from gross profit to produce profit before indirect expenses. Direct expenses are defined as those that are controllable by and the responsibility of a department manager. For example, the food department manager would be responsible for direct expenses of the food department, and the beverage department manager for direct expenses of the beverage department. These expenses will increase or decrease to a greater or lesser degree as sales increase or decrease. Typical direct expenses for most restaurants are the following:

— Payroll (including employee benefits and payroll taxes)
— China and glassware
— Silverware
— Laundry
— Linen rental
— Menus
— Uniforms

_Kitchen fuel

Cleaning supplies

Paper supplies

Flowers and decorations

Wherever possible, these direct expenses should be separated by sales outlet. This is often difficult to do in practice because many of them are shared (or joint) costs and it is not easy to break them down by sales area.

Indirect Expenses

The final category of expenses are defined as indirect. These generally exist and stay fixed regardless of the sales volume. They are not normally controllable by or the responsibility of an operating department head and are often described as fixed costs or overhead costs. Typical of these costs are the following:

Automobile expense

Parking

Licenses and permits

Advertising

Utilities

Garbage removal

Office and administration

General manager salary

Insurance

Franchise fees

Maintenance and repairs

Rent

Real estate taxes

Interest

Depreciation and amortization

On some income statements the last four expenses listed are not included with the other indirect expenses. Instead, after the other indirect expenses are listed they are totaled and deducted to arrive at profit before occupation costs, and then rent, real estate taxes, interest, and depreciation and amortization are listed as occupation costs before they are totaled and deducted.

(One of the major items of expense that appears on most income statements as an indirect expense is depreciation. Because depreciation is a special kind of expense, a more detailed discussion of it is given later in the chapter.)

After these indirect expenses and occupation costs have been deducted on the income statement, they provide the amount of profit before income tax. Income tax is then deducted to arrive at net profit. Income tax includes taxes for all levels of government (federal, state, and city). Income tax is only shown on your income statement if your restaurant is an incorporated business. Proprietorship and partnership restaurants do not show any income tax because any profits of the business are taxable and payable by the individual owner(s)—and not by the organization—at personal tax rates.

A sample income statement for a restaurant operating as an incorporated company is illustrated in Figure 3.1.

Profit Centers

When a restaurant has more than one department, each department is sometimes referred to as a profit center. If your restaurant is a family or

INCOME STATEMENT FOR YEAR ENDING DECEMBER 31, 19X1		
Food Sales		$1,175,200
Food Cost of Sales		419,400
Gross Profit		$ 755,800
Operating Expenses		
Payroll and related expense	$319,200	
Operating supplies	101,400	
Administration and general	57,900	
Marketing	20,700	
Maintenance and repairs	15,400	
Energy	25,100	
Property taxes	28,800	
Insurance	13,100	
Interest	51,900	
Depreciation	41,900	675,400
Profit before tax		$ 80,400
Income tax		40,200
Net profit		$ 40,200

Figure 3.1 Sample income statement.

fast-food one serving no alcoholic beverages, then there is only one profit center. However, in the typical restaurant serving both food and alcoholic beverages there is normally more than one profit center: for example, the food department is a profit center, and the bar is another. If your restaurant handles group business (such as banquets or off-premise catering) these could be additional profit centers.

Sales revenue and cost of sales (food cost and beverage cost) should be separated by profit center. If possible, all direct expenses should be separated by profit center so that each department's profit can be identified. In practice, however, it is difficult to show these expenses separately. The reason is that in the typical restaurant the food operation works very closely with the bar operation, and they probably have many common costs that cannot be easily identified as belonging to one or the other.

For example, a food waiter will pick up a cocktail from the bar to be served to a customer having a meal. How much of that waiter's labor cost is attributable to food service and how much to beverage service? Arbitrary expense allocations may be possible in some situations, but the results of cost allocations are only as good as the allocation method selected. In other words, a poor allocation will provide misleading results that in turn lead to faulty decision making.

However, as long as food sales and food cost are kept separate from beverage sales and beverage cost, more information will be provided than if sales and cost of sales for each of these two profit centers were lumped together.

RETAINED EARNING

Usually the balance sheet and the income statement for an incorporated company are accompanied by a statement of retained earnings. In the statement of retained earnings the net profit of the business (from the income statement) for a period of time (let us say a year) is added to the preceding year's figure of retained earnings to give the new total. If any dividends were paid out during the year, these are deducted to arrive at end-of-year retained earnings. In other words, the retained earnings are the accumulated net profits (less any losses) sustained by the business since it began, less any dividends.

The retained earnings are not necessarily represented by cash in the bank because the money may have been used for other purposes, such as purchasing new equipment or expanding the size of the building.

The following is a completed statement of retained earnings. Note how the $40,200 of net profit from the income statement (Figure 3.1) has been transferred to the statement of retained earnings and the year-end retained earnings figure of $104,100 transferred to the balance sheet (Figure 2.1).

Statement of Retained Earnings for Year Ending December 31, 19x1

Retained earnings December 31, 19x0	$ 63,900
Profit for year 19x1	40,200
Retained earnings December 31, 19x1	$104,100

Proprietorship or Partnership

For a proprietorship or a partnership, a statement of retained earnings is not used. Instead, there is a statement of capital that is similar to a statement of retained earnings but uses different terminology. For example, the statement of capital for a proprietorship might show the following:

Capital January 1, 19x0	$ 83,900
Net profit for year	40,200
	$124,100
Withdrawals	(20,000)
Capital December 31, 19x1	$104,100

Withdrawals are funds taken out of the business by the proprietor for personal use (similar to dividends for an incorporated company). The closing capital figure is then transferred to the balance sheet. Alternatively, all the information from the statement of capital could be shown directly on the balance sheet, thus eliminating the need for a separate statement of capital.

In the case of a partnership, the statement of capital is similar to that for a proprietorship, except that for each partner the beginning-of-the-year capital is shown, and his or her share of net profit is added and withdrawals deducted to arrive at end-of-the-year capital, which is then transferred to the balance sheet. Again, if space permits, the full information for each partner can be shown directly on the balance sheet, eliminating the need for a separate partnership statement of capital.

DEPRECIATION

When long-life assets (such as building and equipment) are purchased by your restaurant, they are recorded on the balance sheet as assets at their original cost price. If at the time of purchase these assets were shown as expenses on the income statement, that income statement and future ones would show a distorted net profit because they would not be conforming to the matching principle (discussed in Chapter 1).

To prevent these distortions, in each accounting period that benefits from the use of a long-life asset a portion of the cost of that asset is recorded on the income statement and at the same time deducted from the balance sheet by way of accumulated depreciation, as discussed in Chapter 2. The portion of cost on the income statement is known as depreciation expense and reduces profit for that period. This has cash flow advantages because depreciation is not a cash expense. That is, it does not require an outlay of cash at the time you record the depreciation expense. It simply reduces on your books the value of the related asset(s). However, by recording it as an expense you reduce taxable profits and save on income tax, which means you save cash or increase cash flow. For that reason, most businesses claim the maximum depreciation allowable for tax purposes.

What is the useful life of an asset for depreciation purposes? This is often a matter of opinion influenced by such factors as inadequacy, obsolescence, and economic changes. In the case of a building, useful life could be thirty, forty, or fifty years or more. In the case of a piece of equipment, it could be as much as ten years or as short as a couple of years if a new and better piece of equipment becomes available.

There are a number of different methods for calculating depreciation, such as straight-line, declining balance, and units of production. Each of these is discussed.

Straight-line Method

Straight-line depreciation is probably the simplest of all methods because it spreads the cost of the asset, less any estimated trade-in or scrap value at the end of its useful life, equally over each year of the asset's life. The equation for calculating the annual amount of depreciation is

$$\frac{\text{Cost of asset} - \text{Trade-in value}}{\text{Service life of asset in years}}$$

In this equation, note that cost is a known and exact figure. The other two figures are estimates, but through experience and discussion with suppliers they can be fairly realistically estimated, thus making the depreciation expense calculation reasonably accurate. Let us assume the following concerning the purchase of a piece of equipment: initial cost $32,000 and trade-in value $2,000 at the end of its five-year life. Annual depreciation will be

$$\frac{\$32,000 - \$2,000}{5 \text{ years}} = \frac{\$30,000}{5} = \$6,000 \text{ per year}$$

To obtain the monthly depreciation expense, you simply divide the annual rate by 12.

Declining Balance Method

With the straight-line method (assuming a five-year life) one-fifth (or 20 percent) of the cost of the asset less its trade-in value was the annual depreciation. Using the same facts, with the declining balance method the straight-line depreciation rate of 20 percent is doubled to 40 percent and 40 percent is then multiplied by the undepreciated balance (book value) of the asset each year to obtain the depreciation expense for that year. With this method, you ignore any trade-in or scrap value.

In other words, in year one the depreciation expense is 40% × $32,000 (the cost of the asset) = $12,800. The book value of the asset is now $32,000 − $12,800 = $19,200. Year two depreciation expense is 40% × $19,200 = $7,680. If this information is set up in the form of a schedule for all five years, it appears as follows:

Declining Balance Depreciation

Year	Annual Depreciation	Net Book Value
	Initial cost	$32,000
1	40% × $32,000 = $12,800	19,200
2	40 × 19,200 = 7,680	11,520
3	40 × 11,520 = 4,608	6,912
4	40 × 6,912 = 2,765	4,147
5	40 × 4,147 = 1,659	2,488

The declining balance method of depreciation is sometimes referred to as an accelerated method. You will note that the depreciation expense is high in the early years and decreases as the years go by. The reasoning behind this accelerated method is that maintenance costs are low in the earlier years of an asset's life but increase with age. Therefore, in theory, the sum of depreciation plus maintenance should be approximately the same each year.

There are also tax advantages to using accelerated depreciation. Because depreciation expense is higher in the early years, the taxable profit will be lower and thus income taxes reduced. Over the long run the total tax will be the same, but, by reducing income taxes in the early years, cash flow can be increased in those years.

Units-of-Production Method

The equation for the units-of-production depreciation method is

$$\frac{\text{Cost of asset} - \text{Trade-in value}}{\text{Estimated units of production during asset's life}}$$

To illustrate, assume a catering company purchases a delivery vehicle for $8,000. It is estimated that this vehicle will be driven for 50,000 miles before it is traded in for $800 at the end of its useful life. The cost of depreciation per unit of production (mile) is

$$\frac{\$8,000 - \$800}{50,000} = \frac{\$7,200}{50,000} = \$0.144$$

Annual depreciation expense is then based on the mileage driven in that year. Assuming 10,000 miles in year one, annual depreciation is $10,000 \times \$0.144 = \$1,440$. Subsequent years' depreciation is calculated in a similar manner.

The units-of-production depreciation method has the advantage of equitably spreading total depreciation over each period of the asset's useful life. Disadvantages are that it does not easily allow calculation of each period's depreciation expense in advance (useful, for example, in budgeting, to be discussed in Chapter 16); nor is it likely to give higher depreciation amounts in the early years of the asset's life, which, as mentioned earlier, are useful for reducing income taxes and increasing cash flow.

Depreciation and Income Tax in the United States

A number of times in this chapter the topic of depreciation in relation to income tax has been mentioned. Some additional comments about depreciation and income tax are now in order.

Generally, the U.S. Internal Revenue Service (IRS) regulates the amount of depreciation that may be claimed for tax purposes for depreciable assets purchased after 1980. The concept of depreciation, according to the Economic Recovery Tax Act of 1981, was replaced with the concept of cost recovery (referred to as the accelerated cost recovery system [ACRS]).

Under the ACRS, the useful life of an asset and its salvage value are no longer relevant. The cost of an asset can be recovered (depreciated) over an allowed period of time, regardless of the asset's life.

Four time periods are allowed: three, five, ten, and fifteen years, depending on the type of asset. In general terms, the cost recovery amount allowed for depreciation expense is based on statutory percentages that are similar to those for declining balance depreciation.

As long as you are in business for a full year, it does not matter when you purchase an asset during that year. A full year's cost recovery (depreciation) may be claimed. In other words, if you purchase a new item of kitchen equipment for your restaurant on the last day of your accounting year, you may still claim a full-year's cost recovery. This is useful to know, because if you were planning to buy a new fixed asset early next year, it might be a good idea to advance the purchase to the end of the current year to benefit now from that additional depreciation allowance.

Depreciation and Income Tax in Canada

In Canada, the Income Tax Act states that declining balance depreciation must be used and stipulates the maximum percentage rate of depreciation (called capital cost allowance [CCA] by the tax department) that may be used for each class or type of asset (for example, 5 percent on buildings, 20 percent on most items of equipment, 30 percent on automotive equipment).

As long as you are in business for a full twelve months (which would be the normal situation unless your business is just starting up) it does not matter when you buy an asset during the current fiscal year; you may claim only a half-year's depreciation in the asset's year of purchase. In other words, even if you buy an asset on the last day of your fiscal year you may still claim a half-year's depreciation. Thus, if you intend to buy an asset next year, by buying it late in the current year you will be able to reduce the current year's tax payable by claiming the equivalent of a half-year's depreciation.

Which Depreciation Method to Use?

Even though for tax filing purposes you may only claim depreciation using allowable rates, this does not mean that you cannot use a different method or different rate of depreciation on your books. However, when you file your annual tax return you cannot deduct on your income statement for tax reduction purposes any depreciation in excess of the allowable amount.

A difficult decision for the restaurant operator is the choice of depreciation method to use. Regardless of the method selected, one fact is quite clear: you can never record more depreciation for an asset than its cost. Whether the asset is depreciated by an accelerated method or not, total depreciation expense cannot exceed the investment in that asset. Generally, it is wise to show on your income statement the maximum depreciation that can be claimed to minimize income tax.

Note also that it is possible to use one depreciation method for one type of asset and a different method for another. However, once a particular method has been selected for an asset, you should use it consistently during that asset's life.

Also, if you eventually sell all your assets and receive more for them than their written down or net book value, you run into a recapture of depreciation situation. This means that you now pay tax on the excess amount of depreciation you previously claimed. For example, if you had a small catering business with one truck with a book value of $4,000 that you sold for $5,000, you are likely to be liable for tax on the recaptured depreciation of $1,000.

Finally, note that in no case can you claim any depreciation on land that your restaurant owns. Land is a nondepreciable asset as far as the tax department is concerned.

Because the subject of depreciation can be quite complex and the regulations concerning it are changed by the government from time to time, it is best to consult your accountant in any matters concerning depreciation. This is particularly true if you are expanding your operation by buying the assets of another restaurant and you wish to maximize the total depreciation that you can claim in future years on those purchased assets.

FOUR

Internal Control

In a very small restaurant very few internal controls are required since the owner/operator generally handles all the cash coming in and going out and, by being present, ensures a smooth and efficient operation. In large restaurants, one-person control is no longer possible and it is necessary for the owner/operator to implement a system of internal control.

PRINCIPLES OF INTERNAL CONTROL

A good system of internal control incorporates the following two broad requirements:

1. Methods and procedures for the employees in the various jobs to follow to ensure they
   - act according to your policies.
   - achieve operational efficiency.
   - protect assets (such as cash and inventory) from waste, theft, or fraud.
2. Reliable forms and reports that measure the efficiency and effectiveness of the restaurant and provide accounting and other information that, when analyzed, indicates problem areas. This information must be accurate and timely if it is to be useful. It must also be cost effective; in other words, the benefits (cost savings) of your internal control system must be greater than its cost. Information produced must also be useful. If it is not used then you have wasted effort and money.

Management Attitude

Most employees are honest by nature but, because of a poor internal control system or (worse still) complete absence of controls, are sometimes tempted to be dishonest. If you do not care, why should your employees?

Management Supervision

By themselves, control systems solve no problems. They do not guarantee protection against fraud or theft. Even with a good control system, collusion (two or more employees' working together for dishonest purposes) may be undetected for a long time. For this and other reasons, your control system must be supervised by you or a delegated manager.

Employee Selection

Important aspects of effective internal control are employee competence, trustworthiness, and training. This means that you should have a good system of screening job applicants, selecting employees, providing employee orientation and on-the-job training, and making periodic employee evaluations. Obviously, supervisory personnel must also be competent, with skills in maintaining your operation's standards, motivating employees they supervise, preparing staffing schedules, maintaining employee morale (to reduce the cost of employee turnover), and implementing procedures to control labor and other costs. A poor supervisor will fail to extract the full potential from employees and will thus add to your restaurant's operating costs.

Job Responsibilities

One of the requirements for good internal control is a clear definition of job responsibilities. For example, in the case of food deliveries who will do the receiving? Will it be a clerk/receiver, the maintenance person, or you? And once that is determined, how is receiving to be handled?

Written Procedures

Once job responsibilities have been determined, you should establish written job procedures so that employees responsible will know what the procedures are. Written procedures are particularly important where employee turnover is high (often the case in the restaurant industry) and continuous employee training to support the internal control system is required.

It is impossible in this chapter to provide procedures that will fit every possible restaurant situation because of the wide variety of types, sizes, and styles of restaurant and their differing needs. Even in two restaurants of similar type and size, the procedures for any specific control area may differ because of management policy, type of customer, layout of the establishment, or numerous other reasons. However, a sample of a set of written procedures for receiving food products is given in Chapter 5.

Adequate Records

Once procedures have been established and employees given detailed written guidelines about how to perform tasks, you need to establish standards of performance. This requires designing forms and reports to provide information about all your restaurant's operations. Properly designed forms and reports provide you with the information you need to determine whether standards are being met. They also allow you to make decisions that will improve the standards, increase productivity, and ultimately produce higher profits.

For example, for food deliveries there should be a written record on a daily order sheet of what is to be delivered, from which suppliers, and at what prices. In this way, the receiver can check invoices (which accompany the delivered goods) both against the actual goods and against the order form.

The larger your restaurant, the more records may be necessary, such as a market quotation sheet so that some responsible person can be designated to obtain quotes from two or more suppliers before any orders are placed.

Without good records, employees will be less concerned about doing a good job. The forms, reports, and other records that are part of the internal control system depend entirely on the size and type of your establishment.

Standards and Results

Another important aspect of a good internal control system is to establish standards and evaluate results. For example, one of the many benchmarks used in a restaurant to measure its effectiveness is the food cost percentage. You need to know whether the foot cost percentage you actually achieved is close to the standard desired. In later chapters you will see how cost control standards can be established and actual results evaluated for food, beverages, and labor.

System Supervision and Review

One of your major responsibilities in internal control is continuous system supervision and review. This supervision and review are necessary because any system becomes obsolete as business conditions change. Also, without continuous supervision your control system can break down.

For example, one of the important control techniques in a food service operation is to ensure each day that there are no missing prenumbered checks on which sales are recorded. Suppose an employee (after having served food and beverages, presented the sales check, and collected the cash from a customer) personally retains both the sales check and the cash and is subsequently not questioned about the fact that the sales check has not been turned in. He or she will realize that the control system is not working effectively and is then free to continue to hold back further sales checks and pocket the cash.

In small restaurants, the supervision and review of the internal control system are the owner/operator's responsibility. In a larger restaurant, the supervision and review responsibility may be turned over to a manager.

CONTROL OF CASH RECEIPTS

Good cash handling and internal control procedures are important not only to you as owner but to the employees involved because a good cash control system will show that employees have handled their responsibilities correctly and honestly.

All cash receipts should be deposited intact each day in the bank. A deposit slip (receipt) stamped by the bank should be retained by you. If all cash received each day is deposited daily, no one who handles it will be tempted to "borrow" cash for a few days for personal use.

Employees who handle cash (and other assets such as inventories) should be bonded. In this way, losses are less likely to occur because the employee knows he or she will have to answer to the insurance company if shortages occur.

Separate Record Keeping and Asset Control

One of the most important principles of good cash control is to separate the functions of recording information about cash and actual cash handling.

Consider the accounts of the people or companies to whom you sell meals on credit. These accounts are an asset (accounts receivable). Checks received in payment are given to the bookkeeper, who records the payments on the accounts. These checks, along with other cash and checks received from customers, are deposited each day in the bank. There is nothing wrong with this procedure as long as the bookkeeper is honest.

A dishonest bookkeeper could practice a procedure known as *lapping*. Company A owes you $150 on account. When it receives its statement at the month-end it sends in a check for $150. The bookkeeper does not record the payment on Company A's account. Instead, the check is simply put into the cash drawer and $150 in cash is removed for personal use by the bookkeeper. The bookkeeper's remittance at the end of the shift will balance, but Company A's account will still show an unpaid amount of $150.

When Company B with an account for $170 sends in its payment, the bookkeeper records $150 as a payment on Company A's account, puts the $170 check into the cash drawer, and removes a further $20 in cash for personal use.

A few days later Company C's payment of $200 on its account is received. The bookkeeper records $170 on Company B's account, puts the $200 check into the cash drawer, and takes out $30 more in cash.

This lapping of accounts will eventually increase to the point where the bookkeeper can no longer cover a particular account and the fraud will be discovered. However, the outstanding account may be so large that the misappropriated cash cannot be recovered from the dishonest bookkeeper.

To aid in preventing this type of loss, separation of cash receiving and recording on accounts should be instituted. Checks or cash received in the mail in payment of accounts should be deposited directly into the bank by you or a responsible employee. The employee looking after the accounts receivable is simply given a list of account names and amounts received, and the appropriate accounts can be credited without that person's handling any money. In order words, the responsibilities for handling cash and recording payments on accounts are separated.

The separation of asset control and asset recording does not only pertain to cash. For example, inventories of food and beverage in a storeroom may be controlled (received and issued) by a storekeeper, but it is often a good idea to have the records of what is in the storeroom (for example, perpetual inventory cards, to be discussed in Chapter 5) maintained by some other person.

Divide the Responsibility for Related Transactions

The responsibility for related transactions should be separated so that the work of one person is verified by the work of another. This is not to suggest duplication of work—that would be costly—but to have two tasks that must be carried out for control reasons handled by two separate employees.

For example, many restaurants record menu items sold and their prices on handwritten sales checks. When the customers pay, these checks are inserted into a cash register that prints the total amount paid on the sales check and on a continuous register audit tape. At the end of the shift or day the machine is cleared—that is, the total sales are printed on the audit tape—and the audit tape is removed by you or a delegated responsible person. The total cash turned in by the restaurant cashier or manager should agree with the total sales on the audit tape. But even if there is agreement, there is no guarantee that the audit tape figure is correct. Overrings or underrings may occur or a sales check may be rung up more than once, not be rung up at all, or be rung up without being inserted into the register.

Because of all these possibilities, further control over sales checks is needed. First the prices, extensions, and additions of all sales checks should be verified by you or a delegated responsible person (if time does not allow this to be done each day, then it should at least be done on a spot-check basis). The sequence of numbers of sales checks turned in should then be checked to make sure there are no missing ones. Finally, an adding machine listing of sales checks should be made. Assuming no errors on this adding machine listing, it will be the total against which cash turned in should be reconciled. If no errors were made, the register audit tape will also agree with the adding machine listing.

The job of verifying sales checks for prices, extensions, and additions; of ensuring there are no missing sales checks; and of preparing the adding machine tape should be carried out by a person other than the bookkeeper. In this way the responsibility for sales control is divided and one person's work is verified by another. The cost of the second person's time will probably be more than recovered in increased profit as a result of reduction of losses from undiscovered errors.

Use Machines

Whenever possible machines should be used for control. Although machines cannot prevent all possibilities of theft or fraud, they can considerably reduce these possibilities. The installation of a machine may also reduce labor cost if an employee is no longer required to perform a task manually. For example, an electronic preset-precheck sales register will eliminate many of the losses resulting from the types of errors mentioned in the preceding section. Also, the saving in labor (because manual verifications will no longer be required) will contribute to the cost of the equipment.

CONTROL OF CASH DISBURSEMENTS

For minor disbursements that have to be handled by cash, you should establish a petty cash fund. You should put enough cash into this fund to take care of about one month's transactions. The fund should be the responsibility of one person only. Payments out of it must be supported by a receipt, voucher, or memorandum explaining the purpose of the disbursement. When the cash fund is almost used up, the supporting receipts, vouchers, and memoranda can be turned in and the fund replenished with cash up to the original amount. Receipts, vouchers, or memoranda turned in should be stamped "paid," or cancelled in some similar way, so that they cannot be reused.

All other disbursements should be made by check and supported by an approved invoice. All checks should be numbered sequentially and be used in sequence. Checks should be prepared by you or a responsible person, but that other person should have no authority to sign the checks. As checks are prepared, the related invoices should be cancelled in some way so that there is no possibility of their being fraudulently reused. Any checks spoiled in preparation should be voided so that they cannot be reused.

Bank Reconciliation

One control that is necessary in a good internal control system is a monthly bank reconciliation. This reconciliation should be handled by you or your accountant. At each month-end, you should obtain a statement from your bank showing each daily deposit, the amount of each check paid, and other items added to or subtracted from the bank balance. The cancelled (paid) checks should accompany this statement. The steps in the reconciliation are as follows:

1. Compare and mark off on the statement the amount of each check received back with your bank statement.
2. Arrange your cancelled (paid) checks in number sequence.
3. Verify the amount of each cancelled check with the amount on your check register or journal. Make a note of any outstanding checks. An outstanding check is one made out by you but not yet paid by the bank.
4. To the bank statement balance, add deposits made by you and not yet recorded by the bank and subtract any outstanding checks.
5. To your bank balance amount add any amounts added by the bank on its statement but not yet recorded by you (for example, bank interest earned on deposits) and subtract any deductions made by the bank (such as automatic payments on loans and interest or service charges).
6. Once steps 1 to 5 have been completed, the two balances should agree. If they do not, the work should be rechecked. If the figures still do not agree, then errors have been made either by the bank or on your books. These errors should be discovered and corrected.

To illustrate how a reconciliation is carried out, consider the following hypothetical figures:

Bank statement balance	$4,456
Company bank balance	6,848

Deposit in transit	2,896
Outstanding checks	
#355	372
#372	40
Interest earned on deposits	98
Bank service charge	6

The reconciliation would be as follows:

Bank Balance	Your Balance
$4,456	$6,848
2,896	98
(372)	(6)
(40)	
$6,940	$6,940

METHODS OF THEFT OR FRAUD

The remainder of this chapter lists ways in which theft or fraud has happened in restaurants. These lists are not exhaustive. They include the more common ways in which misappropriations of assets have occurred. The lists can never be complete because, regardless of the improvements that you make to your internal control system, there is always a method of circumventing the system (particularly if there is collusion between employees).

Deliveries

Methods that suppliers or delivery drivers can use to defraud a restaurant when they observe that control procedures for receiving are not being used include the following:

- Invoicing for high-quality merchandise when poor-quality goods have been delivered.
- Putting correct-quality items on the top of a box or case with sub-quality items underneath.
- Opening boxes or cases, removing some of the items, resealing the boxes or cases, and charging for full ones.

- Delivering less than the invoiced weight of meat and other such items.
- Using padding or excess moisture in items priced by weight.
- Putting delivered items directly into storage areas and charging for more than is actually delivered.
- Taking back unacceptable merchandise without issuing an appropriate credit invoice.

Receiving and Inventory

The people working in and around your receiving and storage areas, if these are not properly controlled, can defraud in the following ways:

- Working with a supplier's delivery driver by approving invoices for deliveries not actually made to your restaurant.
- Working with a supplier's delivery driver by approving invoices for high-quality merchandise when poor-quality merchandise has been delivered.
- Pocketing items and walking out with them at the end of the shift.
- Using garbage cans to smuggle items out the backdoor.
- Removing items from a controlled storeroom and changing inventory records to hide the fact.

Cash Funds

Cash funds include general reserve cash under your control, the petty cash fund, and banks or change funds established for food and beverage cashiers and/or servers for making change. Persons handling cash can cheat in various ways:

- Removing cash and showing it as a shortage.
- Using personal expenditure receipts and recording them as paid outs for business purposes.
- Removing cash for personal use and covering it with an IOU or postdated check.
- Underadding cash sheet columns and removing cash.
- Failing to record cash income from sundry sales, such as vending machines, empty returnable bottles, and old grease.

Accounts Payable and Payroll

The person(s) handling accounts payable and/or payroll can practice fraud by the following actions:

- Setting up a dummy company and making out checks on false invoices in the name of this company.
- Working in collusion with a supplier and having the supplier send padded or dummy invoices directly to the accounts payable clerk.
- Making out checks for invoices already paid.
- Padding the payroll with fictitious employees.
- Padding the gross pay amount on employee(s') checks in collusion with the employee(s).
- Carrying employees on the payroll beyond their termination date.

Food and Beverage Sales

For good sales control, a system of sales checks and duplicates should be established (although there are exceptions, as in a cafeteria). Nevertheless, even with sales checks servers or cashiers can defraud in several ways:

- Obtaining food and beverages from the kitchen or bar without recording the items on a sales check; these items are then used by employees for personal consumption.
- Collecting (and keeping) cash from a customer without recording the sale on a sales check.
- Collecting (and keeping) cash from a customer by using a sales check already presented to another customer.
- Collecting cash from a customer with a correct sales check, destroying the check, and keeping the cash.
- Overadding a sales check, collecting from the customer, and then reducing the total of the check to the correct amount and keeping the difference.
- Purposely underadding a sales check (or omitting to include an item on it) to influence the amount of a tip.
- Collecting cash with a correct sales check and recording the sales check as a cancelled or voided one.
- Collecting cash with a correct sales check and recording it as a charge (with a false signature) to a credit card number.
- Using sales checks obtained elsewhere to collect from customers and not recording the sale.

- Not returning a customer's credit card after a sale is complete and subsequently using this stolen card to convert cash sales to charge sales using a false signature.
- Since the customer in the preceding situation will eventually discover this fact and report it to the credit card company, exchanging this stolen card after a few days with one from another customer (since customers seldom check to see whether they are getting the correct card back) can prolong this fraud for some time.
- Collecting a credit card from a customer for an authentic charge transaction but (before returning the card to the customer) running additional blank charge vouchers through the imprinter and subsequently using the vouchers to convert cash sales to ficticious charge ones.
- Collecting cash but recording the sale as a "customer walkout." You and your employees should always be alert to actual walkouts (both intentional and unintentional) in all sales areas.

Bar Sales

There are many methods of fraud that can be used in bar areas, particularly where bartenders also handle cash from sales. These methods are listed and discussed in Chapter 8, where bar control methods are discussed.

FIVE

Food Purchasing, Receiving, and Inventory Control

PURCHASING

Your restaurant's reputation and success depend to a large degree on good food (and good service), and good food depends on high-quality purchases. The financial success of your restaurant, however, also depends on control over the amount of money spent on food purchases.

At the time that you purchase your initial inventory, a cost is incurred. Everytime you reorder to replenish that inventory, further costs are incurred. Therefore, to minimize these costs, more attention should be paid to the purchasing function than is probably paid in most restaurants.

Indeed, large restaurants and restaurant chains frequently have separate purchasing departments with one or more employees solely involved in purchasing. These large companies consider a purchasing department necessary in order to contribute to profits through effective purchasing to reduce overall costs. To illustrate, consider the following:

Sales	$1,000,000
Cost of sales	400,000
Other costs	550,000
Net profit	$ 50,000

If the restaurant in this situation could save 5 percent through more effective purchasing, this would be $20,000 (5% × $400,000). Profit would thus increase from $50,000 to $70,000: an increase in profit of 40 percent.

The purpose of purchasing, whether carried out by you or by a delegated person, is to make sure needed inventory and other supplies and services are available in quantities appropriate to predetermined standards, at the right price, and at a minimum cost to meet those standards.

By following established purchasing procedures you can prevent purchasing pitfalls such as panic buying, over- or short-purchasing, buying by price rather than by a combination of quality and price, pressure buying, or, what is probably quite common, satisfied buying. With satisfied buying, the purchaser operates under the assumption that no improvements in either quality or price can be achieved.

Knowledgeable Purchaser

The first step in effective food purchasing is to have a knowledgeable person responsible for this function. For any food product there can be wide extremes in quality. The food purchaser must, therefore, know what quality is needed. This does not always mean buying the highest quality if a lower quality at a lower price will do. The food purchaser must also be familiar with the availability and seasonality of products, aware of weather and transportation problems that can affect product supply and cost, and alert to new products that are introduced onto the market.

Product Grading

Even though government standards for many food products guarantee that they will be wholesome and properly labeled and measured, the purchaser still has the responsibility for identifying available products for freshness and potential yield (because that determines the cost per portion). Many food products (such as meat, poultry, fresh produce, and groceries) are government graded for quality. The processor does this grading voluntarily, and many ungraded products are on the market. This does not mean the food purchaser should only buy products that are graded; many suitable ungraded products that represent excellent value for money can be found.

Some processors forego voluntary government grading so that they can sell their own products labeled under their own brand names. For large processors, the product's brand name is an indication of quality level. Processors label one quality of a product with one brand name and another quality of the same product with a different brand name. It is the purchaser's job to find out what quality level is indicated by each brand name.

Perishable and Nonperishable Items

Generally, food products can be classified as perishable and nonperishable. Perishable items are those that have a relatively short storage life, such as dairy and bakery goods, fresh fruit and vegetables, and fresh meat, poultry, and seafood products. Perishable food products are generally put into production and consumed within a day or so of being purchased. Nonperishable items, on the other hand, have a much longer shelf life that could conceivably run into years (although locking up money in food inventory for several years may not be wise).

Nonperishable items are frequently also called groceries, or staples, and are received in sealed cans, packages, or other types of containers. Some frozen products could also be classified as nonperishable. Because most nonperishables are not usually put immediately into production, they can be stored in a separate, lockable storeroom and can be controlled with a system of perpetual inventory cards and requisitions (discussed later in this chapter).

Who Orders?

If you operate a small restaurant, you will likely do all the purchasing. You will know best which menu items sell, what you have in inventory, what market conditions and prices are, and which special items you can add to your menu. You are, therefore, in the best position to recognize the need to purchase specific goods.

If your restaurant is a large one, the purchasing task may be delegated to others, such as the chef or the dining room manager. For example, the chef might be responsible for some or all of the perishable items, because he or she is usually most knowledgeable about freshness and other important qualities, and the storekeeper might order nonperishable items that he or she is responsible for controlling in the storeroom.

Alternatively, the chef might delegate the ordering of certain perishables (such as dairy and bakery goods) to the storekeeper or another qualified assistant. In a fairly large restaurant, the chef might be too busy with other tasks to spend time ordering and checking perishables. In such cases, all perishable ordering will have to be delegated to an assistant.

In a very large organization, with a separate purchasing department, the responsibility for all food purchasing and ordering might be centralized in that department along with all other products needed by the organization.

Purchasing Perishables

Because perishables are usually purchased daily, it is recommended that you use a system of standing orders for bakery, dairy, and fresh fruit and vegetable products.

A standing order is an arrangement with a supplier to provide a predetermined quantity of a particular item or items on a daily or other periodic basis without having to contact the supplier each time. One type of standing order allows a supplier to deliver, at an agreed price, a fixed quantity of a specific item each day. For example, a dairy supplier might be asked to deliver a specified number of dozens of eggs daily. This quantity remains fixed until there is a need to change it.

Another type of standing order requires the supplier each day to replenish the stock of a certain item up to a predetermined or par level. You must establish the par stock level for each separate item handled this way, according to your restaurant's needs. To prevent replenishing beyond the par level, a par stock form is recommended. This form requires a designated employee to take stock of each item covered by this system daily in order to calculate the quantity required and so advise the supplier. A form that could be used for this is illustrated in Figure 5.1.

If you have large fluctuations in daily volume of business or if you cater to banquets and similar functions, it will probably be necessary to adjust the daily standing orders to take care of these fluctuations. One way to do this is to establish a minimum par stock or standing order for each item and to add to it each day the additional quantity required for that day's banquet business. Good internal communication is necessary. For example, the person doing the ordering must know what special functions are being held each day and be familiar with daily fluctuations in normal volume caused by the day of the week, special events, holidays, or the weather. Sales forecasts based on historical records are useful for this purpose.

For perishable items not purchased on a standing order or par stock basis, or in restaurants where standing orders and/or par stocks are not used, the chef may prepare a daily list of perishables required. In other

Item	Par stock	On hand	Required
Apples, cooking			
Apples, baking			
Apples, crab			
Apples, table			
Apricots			
Bananas			

Figure 5.1 Par stock form.

cases, this list may be prepared by the storekeeper after discussion with the chef. As another alternative, the storekeeper will ensure that there is a sufficient supply on hand of bakery and dairy items as well as fresh fruits and vegetables; this means that a daily perishables list will only be needed for meat, poultry, and fish items.

Purchasing Nonperishables

Purchasing nonperishables is simpler than purchasing perishables. Because nonperishables do not have to be ordered daily, you can limit the ordering process to once a week or once every two weeks. However, whenever you reduce the frequency of purchasing, more of each item must be ordered each time and carried in inventory. You must consider the added costs of carrying a larger inventory.

If your restaurant has a storekeeper, even if only part-time, to receive nonperishable items and later issue them from the storeroom by requisition, perpetual inventory cards are recommended. (Perpetual inventory cards and requisitions are discussed later in this chapter.) As will be seen, perpetual inventory cards are very useful for food inventory control, but they are also valuable because they considerably reduce the time required to determine how much of each item to order. Without them, all storeroom items would have to be counted each order day and compared with a par stock list to find out how much to reorder.

Preparing Specifications

Whenever practical, you should prepare purchase specifications for major items or for items that are being ordered for the first time. A specification is a detailed description of the item(s) desired, such as the quality of seafood you want or the cut of steaks you use.

You should send a copy of the specification to each potential supplier and copies to appropriate employees, such as the department head involved and the person responsible for receiving the goods.

The language of specifications must be sufficiently precise so that there is no misunderstanding between you and the supplier. However, this does not mean that specifications cannot be changed. Indeed, as market conditions or the needs of your restaurant change, new specifications should be prepared. The main advantages of specifications are that they do the following:

- Require you to think carefully and document exactly what your product requirements are.
- Leave no doubt in suppliers' minds about what they are quoting on,

thus reducing or eliminating misunderstandings between you and your suppliers.

- For frequently purchased items, eliminate the time that would otherwise have to be spent repeating descriptions over the telephone (or directly to salespersons) each time the goods are needed.
- Permit competitive bidding.
- Allow the person responsible for receiving to check the quality of delivered goods against a written description of the quality desired.

Market Quotation Sheet

An important consideration in selecting suppliers is to contact as many of them as is practical to ensure that enough quotations are received so that the right quality of food is purchased at the lowest possible price.

A minimum of three quotations is recommended for each separate product or service (although this may not be necessary or possible in every case) to ensure that competitive pricing prevails. In some cases, you might ask for written quotations. In other cases, they might be taken over the telephone.

A market quotation sheet is a good idea. Standard quotation sheets are available from stationers who deal with the restaurant business, and these forms usually have space to list the special requirements of your restaurant. If your restaurant purchases a lot of unusual food products, you may have to design your own form. On the market quotation sheet, it is common industry practice to circle the quoted price from the supplier from whom the product is ordered, as illustrated in Figure 5.2.

You should buy the items you need that have the quality you desire at the lowest cost. This does not mean always buying at the lowest price since the items at the lowest price may be of poor quality. Reliability of the supplier and frequency of shipping can be considerations. Also, if a supplier's quotation is the lowest only for one or two items, he may not be willing to pay for the shipping cost if his order totals only a few dollars.

Food Tests

The "yield" of an item may be important and can be determined by tests. For example, a cut of meat from one supplier may be lower-priced than that from a second. However, when meat is trimmed and fat removed, the second supplier's price may, in fact, be lower in terms of yield. Consider the following:

Item	Quantity required	Suppliers		
		Jang	Tobin	Louie
CHEESE American	25 lb.	2.10	2.30	2.28
Bel Paese				
Camembert	2 lb.		4.20	4.30
Cheddar, Mild	10 lb.	2.22	2.22	2.15
Cheddar, Medium				
Cheddar, Strong	5 lb.	2.50	2.50	2.60
Cottage				

Date __February 2__

Figure 5.2 Market quotation sheet.

	Purchase weight	Price per lb.	Weight after trim	Net price per lb.
Supplier A	10 lb.	$2.00	8 lb.	$2.50
Supplier B	10 lb.	2.05	8.25 lb.	2.48

Even though Supplier A's price appears initially lower, butchering tests indicate that Supplier B's net price per pound after trim is in fact lower.

Tests can also be carried out on other food products to ensure that they provide value for money. For example, you can test canned food to ensure that the best net-weight yield is obtained after draining the liquid in which the food is packed. The count, uniformity, and quality of canned food contents should also be evaluated. If the liquid is to be used, its quality might also be important. Similar tests can be made on packaged products that are not packed in liquids, and fresh fruit and vegetable tests ensure that the best weight or count of product is received for money spent.

Order Form

Because the person receiving food items may not be the same as the one doing the ordering, it may be useful to summarize all items ordered each

Order Date	February 2		Delivery Date		February 3		
Item	Supplier	Quantity ordered	Price	Total	Received	Comment	
American	Jang	25 lb.	2.10	52.50	✔		
Camembert	Tobin	2 lb.	4.20	8.40	✔		
Cheddar, Mild	Tobin	10 lb.	2.22	22.20	✔		
Cheddar, Strong	Jang	5 lb.	2.50	12.50	✔		

Figure 5.3   Order form.

day on a food order form. A sample order form is illustrated in Figure 5.3. Even if all ordering and receiving are carried out by the same person, an order form can still be a useful control because you can record on it whether the products were actually received. If not, a note or explanation should be placed in the Comment column for later reference or for reordering the products the next day. Where the receiving function is separate from the ordering function, it is important that the receiver be given a copy of this form each day so that he or she knows what should be delivered, at what prices, and in what quantities.

Food Deliveries

If it is necessary to restrict hours when shipments can be received (this is likely the case where the receiving function is combined with some other job), you should make these limited delivery hours known to suppliers to see whether some mutually acceptable time can be established. In a large restaurant with a full-time receiver, this would not be a problem. Suppliers should also be advised to provide fully priced invoices with the goods because, as you will see later in this chapter, invoices are necessary for preparing a daily food receiving report.

RECEIVING

Those responsible for receiving must be skilled in the job. Some suppliers, knowing that the receiver does not have the skills, might substitute a lower grade than the grade ordered, a practice known as upgrading. For example, if porterhouse steaks are specified from the top end of the USDA choice grade with moderate marbling, does the person receiving this product have the ability to determine whether the delivered goods are average choice or top choice?

Upgrading is often difficult to prove, because with some products quality is often a matter of opinion and the supplier can always claim that the correct quality grade was delivered as specified. This is particularly true with fresh produce (such as fruit and vegetables) but also applies to brand-name items such as bacon, sausages, and canned or frozen products. Some suppliers have also been known to upgrade canned products by removing the label from a cheap brand and replacing it with a high-quality-brand label, even though this practice is illegal.

Methods of Fraud

Apart from upgrading, there are various methods suppliers or delivery drivers can use to defraud a restaurant when they observe that control procedures for receiving are not being used. These methods include the following:

Failing to meet specifications.   Suppliers sometimes fail to meet required specifications in order to increase their own profit or to compensate for having deliberately underbid to obtain your business (in which case they can only now make a normal profit by doing such things as failing to meet size or trim specifications). For example, a supplier could deliberately leave more fat on a roast than the specifications require, charge for boneless cuts and deliver cuts still containing the bone, include preportioned cuts that are of short weight, or send a shipment that is incomplete (short weight or count). To control these problems, you, your chef, or a qualified and trained receiver must be on hand to verify quality against specifications and against purchase order quantities and to prepare credit memoranda for short-count or short-weight shipments.

With size specifications, you should allow some tolerance. For example, if specifications call for 10-ounce prime rib, bone-in steaks, you might allow individual steaks to vary from 9.5 to 10.5 ounces, as long as the overall average is 10 ounces. Where these items are shipped by weight and by count, they should be taken out of their cases to be counted and weighed. For example, 100 10-ounce steaks = 1,000 oz./16 oz. = 62.5 lb. There should be both 100 items and 62.5 lb. of steak in this delivery.

It is also necessary to spot-check portioned meats for their weights. For example, suppose portioned hamburgers are specified in 2-ounce weights and are charged for by the supplier by the pound. If 2.25-ounce hamburgers are regularly delivered, the invoiced total weight will be 12.5 percent more than required and your food cost on this item will also increase by 12.5 percent.

Watering and icing products shipped by weight or adding excess packaging. Another fraudulent method suppliers may employ is to water moisture-retaining vegetables (for example, head lettuce) excessively or to use too much packing ice for items (such as poultry) that are shipped in crushed ice. The receiver must examine goods for excessive watering (a water-stained container may signal this) and must weigh items after first taking them out of their ice packing. In all situations where items are shipped by weight, verifying the weight should be a matter of routine after removing items from their packaging materials.

Invoicing high-quality products for low-quality products delivered. A supplier may invoice at a quoted price but deliver products of a lower quality than the price specifies. Again, a qualified receiver will be able to catch this type of fraud. Some suppliers, however, have been known to pack a case with correct quality on the top to cover up lower-quality items underneath. Spot-checking the entire case is necessary to control this. Alternatively, one or more cases could be opened and inspected from the bottom! Quality (as well as count and weight) of packed products should always be verified against the actual products—not against what is printed or stamped on the outside of the case. Suppliers have been known to repack containers with lower-quality products, or products of short weight or count, when they notice that only the case-printed information is verified by the receiver. A supplier might also open containers or cases prior to delivery, remove some of the items, reseal and deliver the partially full boxes or cases, and charge for full ones.

Shipping overweight or overcount. A supplier may also ship more products than were ordered to add to its sales and profits. Accepting more products than are actually desired can lead to excessive inventories and eventual spoilage of goods. Products not ordered should be returned to the supplier, accompanied by a supporting credit memorandum.

Invoice overcharging. Normally, you should require food suppliers to send a priced invoice with delivered goods. In this way, the priced invoice can be compared with prices on market quotation sheets and/or order forms. Any overpricing should immediately be corrected on the invoice by the receiver and a credit memorandum prepared. Where suppliers only mail an invoice some time later, particular care should be taken to verify prices at that time to ensure that a supplier is not deliberately attempting to overcharge; if any invoice prices have been changed, these changes should also be carefully checked. Such suppliers should be instructed to send a priced invoice with the goods in the future.

Bulk weighing. A supplier noticing that certain deliveries are bulk-weighed may be tempted to defraud by substitution. This could occur with a meat order in which various cuts are delivered and are weighed in total rather than by individual cut. For example, a delivery may call for 100 pounds of meat broken down into 50 pounds of hamburger at $2.00 per pound (total $100) and 50 pounds of sirloin at $4.00 per pound (total $200) for a total invoice cost of $100 + $200 = $300. If these two items are not separately weighed, the supplier could actually ship 55 pounds of hamburger (total $110) and only 45 pounds sirloin (total $180), for a total value of $110 + $180 = $290, while still invoicing for $300 and thus making an extra $10 profit. Bulk weighing by a receiver should never be allowed, particularly with expensive items such as meat and seafood.

Putting products directly into storage areas. You should insist and ensure that no products are put into storage areas by delivery drivers, either before or after the goods have been inspected by the receiver. If direct storage is allowed, a driver may eventually bypass the inspection and fail to deliver the proper quantity or quality of merchandise.

Delivering products outside normal receiving hours. A delivery driver who is allowed to deliver outside the hours when the qualified receiver is available may simply obtain the signature of another employee acknowledging that the products have been received, without any count, weight, or quality checks. Indeed, the driver may simply leave the goods without having anybody check them at all. Both these cases encourage fraud.

Honest Suppliers

The comments in the preceding sections are not meant to imply that all suppliers are dishonest. Most are quite honest. Nevertheless, it is sensible in your restaurant to follow recommended receiving practices carefully at all times, not only to ensure that fraud does not occur but also to catch honest errors. Also, even though the supplier might be honest, the delivery driver may be dishonest and doing things that cost your restaurant money without the supplier's being aware of it.

Standard Practices

To eliminate potential losses, a set of standard receiving practices should be prepared in writing for your operation so that those involved in receiving food products will be aware of them. A set of standard receiving practices (to be amended to suit your restaurant's particular needs) could include the following:

- Count each product that can be counted (number of cases or number of individual items).
- Weigh each product that is delivered by weight, such as meat. (Appropriate weighing scales must be provided for this purpose. Scales that print out a tape showing the weight of each item are available. Tapes should be attached to the related invoices to indicate that this important aspect of receiving has been properly carried out.)
- Check the count or weight figure against the count or weight figure on the invoice accompanying the delivery.
- Confirm that the products are of the quality desired; quality control tests may have to be performed to ensure that the quality of delivered items meets the specifications.
- If specifications were prepared and sent to the supplier, check the quality against these specifications. Specifications should also state acceptable production or quality expiration dates on perishable goods. These dates should be checked to ensure that they are not being breached by a supplier. In this regard, wherever possible all products received should be dated with the time of receipt. New stock must be put behind old stock. Dating allows this process to be verified and ensures proper stock rotation.
- For perishable produce that is sensitive to temperature, receipt at the proper temperature should be verified. For example, items to be received frozen should be completely frozen, not partially thawed.
- Spot-check case goods to ensure that cases are full and all items in the case are of the same quality. Where two or more cases of a particular product are delivered, it is not a good idea to remove all items to be sampled from the same case. For example, if three samples are needed, they should be taken from separate cases.
- Check prices on invoices against prices quoted on the market quotation sheet (Figure 5.2).
- If products are delivered without an invoice, prepare a memorandum invoice listing name of supplier, date of delivery, count or weight of items, and, from the market quotation sheet, price of the items.
- If goods are short-shipped or if quality is not acceptable, prepare a credit memorandum listing the products returned and obtain the delivery driver's signature acknowledging that the items were taken back or were short-shipped. This signature is your proof that the goods should not be paid for and ensures that the supplier will issue you an appropriate credit invoice. A sample credit memo is illustrated in Figure 5.4. Staple this credit memorandum to the original

Supplier _____ Date _____			
Please issue a credit memorandum for the following:			
Quantity	Item description	Unit cost	Total
Reason for request for credit:			
Delivery driver's signature_____			

Figure 5.4 Credit memorandum.

invoice. Do not accept a short shipment without the necessary credit memorandum on the strength of a driver's promise to deliver the balance "tomorrow," because tomorrow may never come, the matter will be forgotten, and your food costs will increase as a result of products invoiced and paid for but never received.

- Store all products in proper storage locations as soon after delivery as possible.
- All invoices should be stamped and the stamp initialed in the appropriate spots to indicate that all the required checking has been completed. A typical receiving stamp is illustrated in Figure 5.5.
- Send all invoices and credit memoranda to the office so that extensions and totals can be checked and then recorded.

In addition to requiring these practices, you should carry out spot checks to ensure that the receiver is performing required duties. Complete checking of all deliveries cannot be overemphasized. When a delivery driver notices that weighing scales are not used or that quantities are not counted, he may

Date received _____
Quantity checked by _____
Quality checked by _____
Prices checked by _____
Listed on receiving report by _____

Figure 5.5 Receiving stamp.

be tempted to short-ship deliveries. If he notices that quality is not checked, he can substitute a lower quality.

STORING FOOD

There are three basic types of food storage area required by most restaurants: dry storage, refrigerated storage, and freezer storage.

Dry Storage

Dry storage is used primarily for nonperishable items. It goes without saying that products placed in a lockable storeroom should be kept under ideal conditions to reduce spoilage, wastage, or other nonrecoverable costs. Temperature, ventilation, and sanitation must be considerations in storeroom location and design.

Unfortunately, in many hospitality operations those responsible for food storage frequently do not show the same concern about nonperishable products as they do about those requiring refrigeration or freezing. This attitude probably stems from a false sense that deterioration of nonperishable products does not occur. Unfortunately, no food products last indefinitely. Even canned products deteriorate over time, though the rate of deterioration may be slower than that of perishable products.

The dry goods storeroom should be on the same level as the receiving area and as close to it as possible to reduce movement of heavy goods. For the same reason, proximity to the kitchen is ideal.

Dry storage temperature should not be too high because heat encourages bacteria that can lead to food spoilage. For the same reason, the humidity of your dry storage area should be kept as low as possible. Dry storage needs to be well ventilated, with adequate sturdy shelving so that goods are not piled on top of each other.

Food products should be placed in sectionalized compartments that can be labeled for easy identification. Heavy items that are issued in bulk (sacks of flour or sugar, for example) and products that are frequently used should be closest to the door. Once items have been placed in specific locations, those locations should be changed as infrequently as possible. Permanent locations mean increased efficiency in placing items in their locations and issuing them when needed. They also allow month-end inventory sheets to be preprinted in the same order as the items are located on the shelves, thus speeding up stocktaking and minimizing the possibility of overlooking items. As products are received and put into their right location on shelves, it is useful to date-stamp them to ensure proper stock rotation.

Refrigerated Storage

Refrigerated storage should be kept at different temperatures for different products. If you can afford the luxury of separated refrigerated areas, these temperatures are as follows:

Meat	32–36°F	0–2°C
Fruit and vegetables	35–45°F	2–7°C
Dairy products	38–46°F	3–8°C

If you have only one refrigerated area, then you will have to compromise and keep the temperature in the 35–40°F, or 2–5°C, range.

Freezer Storage

The temperature of your freezer area should, of course, be kept below freezing. The length of time that frozen food can be safely stored depends on the type of item, the way it is packaged, and the maintenance of a constant storage temperature. A fluctuating temperature reduces the shelf life of these items. Small packages are more likely to become dehydrated or suffer freezer burn than large packages that are better packaged. Items such as ham and bacon do not freeze well. Once frozen goods have been thawed they generally deteriorate in quality if refrozen and in such a situation should never be kept refrozen more than thirty days.

Direct versus Storeroom Purchases

In some cases, products might be delivered directly to sales areas; for example, bread rolls might be delivered directly to the dining area each day. Products that are put directly into production (either in the kitchen or in the sales area) are usually referred to as *direct purchases*. Items that are put into a controlled storeroom are referred to as *storeroom purchases*. To simplify the next step in the food cost control process, you should instruct the receiver to note on each invoice, where it is not obvious, that an item is either a direct or a storeroom purchase. This information is useful for completing the daily food receiving report to be used in controlling the food storeroom and in calculating a daily food cost.

Daily Food Receiving Report

A daily food receiving report summarizes each day's invoices, as shown in Figure 5.6. It is not necessary to list on the receiving report each individual item on each invoice, because this detail can always be obtained if it is

				Date	February 3
Supplier	Items	Direct purchases	Storeroom purchases	Other purchases	Invoice total
Jang	Cheese	65.00			65.00
Charlton	Groceries		113.20	13.28	126.48
Atlantic	Fresh fish	48.16			48.16
Atlantic	Fresh fish	(12.39)			(12.39)
J.G. Packing	Groceries		25.19		25.19
	Totals	216.20	157.92	13.28	387.40

Figure 5.6 Daily food receiving report.

needed later by referring to that invoice. The important point in completing this report is to assign the purchase-cost figures from each invoice to either the Direct Purchases or the Storeroom Purchases column.

In some cases, an invoice may include nonfood items. In that case, the dollar amount of those items is entered in the Other Purchases column. In still other cases, food items that are not intended for the food operation may be received. An example might be fruit (such as limes) purchased specifically for the cocktail lounge. Because one of the main reasons for having a daily food receiving report is to aid in calculation of a daily food cost, the food cost should not be charged with purchases for the bar. Therefore, the cost of those items should also be entered in the Other Purchases column. All invoices for each day should be entered on the receiving report. Note, with reference to Figure 5.6, how the credit memorandum from Atlantic has been recorded as a deduction.

Once all invoices have been entered, the columns should be totaled and cross-footed to ensure a balance, in our case,

$$\$216.20 + \$157.92 + \$13.28 = \$387.40$$

At the end of each day, the person completing the receiving report (usually the receiver) should forward it to the office together with the related invoices. The office should then verify the following:

- All invoices have been extended and totaled properly by the supplier. If any errors are discovered, the invoice and the receiving report figures should be corrected and the supplier notified.
- Invoice amounts have been properly entered on the daily food receiving report.

Later in this chapter you will see how the daily food receiving report figures can be used for storeroom inventory control and in the next chapter how it can be used in calculating a daily food cost.

INVENTORY CONTROL

You need to have control over items in your food storage areas. The objectives in control are to minimize losses, avoid running out of items, and minimize the amount of money tied up in inventory. In other words, you need both physical and financial control of your inventory. Funds needlessly tied up in inventory are not earning a profit (in fact, carrying an inventory costs money). If you kept the money in the bank rather than putting it into inventory, it would be earning you a profit: the interest rate paid by the bank.

For refrigerated and freezer items, control may be difficult because there may be several people working in food production who must have constant access to these storage areas. Management supervision is often the only method of control for those areas.

Perpetual Inventory Cards

A good way of keeping track of the inventory you have on hand in your dry goods storeroom, particularly if you do not carry hundreds of different items, is to use a system of perpetual inventory cards maintained by you or a delegated person.

An individual card is required for each item carried in inventory. A sample card is illustrated in Figure 5.7. The In column figures are taken from the invoices delivered with the goods. At the same time, the price of the item on the invoice is recorded in the Requisition Cost Information column. The figures in the Out column are for items that have been issued from the storeroom.

Obviously, if all In and Out figures are properly recorded on the cards by the person who completes them, the Balance figure on the card should agree with the actual count of the item on the storeroom shelf. Thus the cards are useful in inventory control.

The cards also help ensure that items are not overstocked or understocked because they can show the maximum inventory level for each individual item and the minimum point to which that level can fall before the item needs to be reordered.

Without having to count quantities of items actually in stock, you only have to go through each of the cards in turn once a week, or however frequently it is practical to reorder, and list all items for which the Balance

| Item _____ Supplier _____ Tel. # _____ |
| Minimum _____ Supplier _____ Tel. # _____ |
| Maximum _____ Supplier _____ Tel. # _____ |

Date	In	Out	Balance	Requisition cost information

Figure 5.7 Perpetual inventory card for a single item.

figure is at or close to the minimum point and then order the quantity required to bring the inventory up to maximum or par stock.

Note that the cards can also be designed to carry the names and telephone numbers of suggested suppliers.

Even though perpetual inventory cards can be valuable for storeroom control, in quite small restaurants there is just no practical way in which a storeroom can be completely supervised. In such cases, perpetual inventory cards are not practical. In that case, only one person (such as the chef) should have a key to the storeroom so that other employees are not tempted to remove items for personal use.

Requisitions

If your restaurant is large enough, you should also use requisitions so that those authorized to receive items from the storeroom will record their requests on this form. A typical requisition is illustrated in Figure 5.8. Requisitions are prepared by authorized employees and are presented to the storekeeper, who uses them as his authority to issue goods. Depending on the size of your restaurant, you might want to handle the stores issuing job yourself or delegate it to an employee, part of whose job is to issue items during restricted hours. The rest of the time the storeroom is kept locked.

At the end of each day the requisitioned goods quantity figures are recorded from requisitions in the Out column of the appropriate perpetual inventory cards (if you use them) and the new Balance figure calculated and recorded. At the same time, the cost of the item is copied from the

Department _____ Date _____ #6329			
Quantity	Item description	Item cost	Total
Authorized signature_____			

Figure 5.8 Requisition.

perpetual inventory card to the requisitions. Requisitions can then be extended (quantity of each item times its cost) and totaled.

In small restaurants, it may also be impractical to use requisitions, but it may still be desirable to know what has been taken out of the storeroom. This can be done by having the person with the storeroom key record on a sheet each day a list of items issued and their unit costs. The unit cost has to be recorded on the case, carton, package, can, or bottle at the time the products are received and put into the storeroom. At the end of each day, this "master" requisition can be extended and totaled so you know the daily total value of food issued from the storeroom.

Taking Storeroom Inventory

Food inventory in your restaurant should be taken monthly or more frequently if desired. This type of inventory is known as an actual, periodic, or physical inventory. A person other than the storekeeper should do it. In a large restaurant, it is easier and faster if two people (preferably from the office) perform this task.

One person counts the quantity of each item on the shelves, and the second verifies that this count agrees with the perpetual inventory card balance (assuming you are using perpetual inventory cards). If the figures do not agree, a recount should be made. If they still do not tally, the figures recorded from invoices and requisitions on the cards should be traced back to their invoices and requisitions and the arithmetical accuracy of the card balance checked. However, this checking of items whose count does not match should not be done during the actual inventory taking because it slows the process. If discrepancies between actual counts and card counts cannot be resolved, then the card balance figure should be changed to the actual figure so that the card is correct from that point on.

Discrepancies between actual count and card balance can also occur if deliveries have been made to your storeroom on that day but have not yet been recorded on cards, or if the invoice information has been recorded on the cards but the products have not yet been put into the storeroom. Similar situations can arise with items requisitioned on stocktaking day. These possibilities should preferably be checked and corrected before inventory is taken.

To speed the inventory-taking process, perpetual inventory cards and the listing of the items on the inventory sheets should be in the same order as that of items on the shelves. This reduces the possibility of missing items and is, obviously, more efficient. Figure 5.9 illustrates a partial inventory sheet.

If the storekeeper is also the same person who completes perpetual inventory cards from invoices and requisitions, then it would be possible for him or her purposely to fail to record quantity information on the cards, remove items from the shelves for personal use, and still have the card balance figure and the actual count agree. You should spot-check cards against invoices and requisitions to eliminate this possibility.

If perpetual inventory cards are not used, then stocktaking is simply a matter of recording the actual count of items directly on the inventory sheets. The process is faster and easier, but an element of control is lost without the cards.

Month of July			
Item	Quantity	Unit cost	Total
Balance forward			$3,164.38
Carrots, #10	25	$1.43	35.75
Carrots, baby, 24 oz.	12	0.85	10.20
Corn, creamed, #10	4	1.12	4.48
Corn, kernel, #10	8	1.05	8.40
Total			$4,218.76

Figure 5.9 Inventory sheet.

Once all items are listed on the inventory sheets, each item must be extended (item quantity times item cost) and the total inventory added up.

Open Stock Inventory

The storeroom inventory is not, however, the only food inventory to be considered to ensure that income statements are as accurate as possible. At any time in a restaurant, there are food products in kitchens and other areas that have not yet been used, as well as stocks, soups, sauces, and other menu items that are in a state of preparation. There are also unused food products, such as condiments, sauces, and nonalcoholic beverages, and many other items in dining room, coffee shop, and banquet areas. All of these items are part of inventory, and their value must be calculated each month-end. This part of the inventory is usually referred to as open stock.

To obtain an accurate open stock inventory, each item should be physically counted, listed on an inventory sheet, and costed out. In some cases, a cost for products that have been combined into other items (such as soups and sauces) is difficult to determine. In these cases, an estimate must be made (preferably with the help of the chef) to value them.

It may not be necessary to repeat this work every month. Because of the time required, it may be more practical to do it only quarterly. In the interim months, you can estimate how much the current month's open stock is above or below the base period. In most cases, you can assume that most open stock items do not fluctuate from month-end to month-end in total dollar value. What might fluctuate are expensive items such as meat, poultry, and seafood that constitute the major part of your food purchase dollar. Therefore, why not use only these items? Taking an inventory of them is relatively easy, and that amount can be used for adjusting total open stock for each interim month. Let us look at an example.

Assume that an accurate physical inventory of all open stock is taken on January 31 and the total is $5,400. Of this total, $2,500 is for meat, poultry, and seafood items, and $2,900 is for all other items. On February 28, an accurate inventory of the meat, poultry, and seafood items gives a new total of $2,750. This is $250, or 10 percent ($250 divided by $2,500 and multiplied by 100), more than on January 31.

At this point, there are two alternatives: With alternative one, you assume that the entire open stock value has increased from January 31 to February 28 by 10 percent:

$$10\% \times \$5,400 = \$540$$

and

$$\$5,400 + \$540 = \$5,940 \text{ open stock on February 28.}$$

With alternative two, you assume that the value of open stock items (other than meat, poultry, and seafood) on February 28 has remained the same as on January 31, or $2,900, and that the 10 percent increase applies only to the meat, poultry, and seafood part of your open stock. In this case, the total open stock value is

$$\$2,900 + \$2,750 = \$5,650 \text{ for month two.}$$

The difference between the two alternatives is $290. Whether or not this is a large difference must be decided on the basis of how it might affect your food cost percentage. Perhaps the dilemma can be resolved by suggesting that, if the 10 percent increase in meat, poultry, and seafood items were the result of overall market price increases, then it is logical to assume that all market prices have gone up and therefore you should use the first alternative. On the other hand, if the meat, poultry, and seafood open stock increase were the result of carrying more of these items in stock than might normally be the case, then the second alternative might be more realistic.

One final consideration is that open stock is normally higher if the month-end falls on a Friday, because additional purchases would have been made to carry the operation through the weekend. If the month-end falls at the end of a long weekend or holiday period, the reverse is generally true. Under normal circumstances, with daily delivery of most food items, you would expect to see the value of open stock equal to about one-and-a-half day's normal food cost. In other words, if your restaurant's food cost for a typical month were $30,000, or about $1,000 a day, then open stock would probably be about $1,500.

Inventory Investment

Finally in this section on inventory control we come to the matter of inventory investment. It has already been mentioned that to prevent tying up too much investment in inventory and thus losing interest that could otherwise be earned on these funds it is important not to carry too much in inventory. It is also important not to have too few items and risk running out. This can be controlled by recording maximum and minimum quantities on perpetual inventory cards (if you use them), adjusting them from time to time as the need arises, and ensuring with spot checks that what is in inventory is within these limits. Without drastically increasing the total value of items carried in inventory, products of individual small value can normally be ordered in large quantities, thus increasing maximum levels while reducing the frequency of ordering. These products generally also take up little storage space. The reverse is generally true of higher value items.

SIX

Evaluating Your Food Cost

ACTUAL FOOD COST

The concept of food cost percentage was developed to measure how well the cost of food sold was being controlled in comparison to a restaurant's food cost objective. The equation for calculating food cost percentage is

$$\frac{\text{Cost of food sold}}{\text{Food sales}} \times 100$$

The reason for using a percentage is that cost and sales are compared on a common basis. For example, it is difficult to compare the relative change from month one to month two if you have only the following information:

	Month 1	Month 2
Food sales	$140,000	$120,000
Food cost	63,000	52,000

When this is converted to a percentage, comparison is much easier:

	Month 1	Month 2
Food cost	45.0%	43.3%

It is strongly emphasized at this point, however, that even though the food cost percentage is a traditional yardstick for measuring a restaurant's results and even though it continues to be a major measurement tool, it should not be the only one. As will be illustrated later, emphasizing a low food cost percentage may be the complete opposite of what you should be doing. Sometimes a higher food cost percentage can be more profitable in terms of higher gross profit (sales less cost of food sold) and net profit.

Calculating a Daily Food Cost Percentage

Many restaurant operators like to calculate their food cost daily so that they can see over a month the percentage trend, rather than waiting until the end of the month to calculate an overall monthly percentage. With a system of daily food receiving reports (see Chapter 5) categorizing purchases of food into either direct or storeroom, and with a system of properly costed requisitions for items issued daily from the storeroom, it is relatively easy to calculate a daily food cost percentage. A form that will allow this is illustrated in Figure 6.1. A brief explanation of how each of the columns of this report is completed follows:

Direct Purchases.   This amount is the total of the Direct Purchases column of the daily food receiving report for that day. For example, compare the February 3 amount on Figure 5.6 with Figure 6.1.

Storeroom Issues.   This is the total amount of food issued from the storeroom according to requisitions for that day. Note, however, that this figure should only include requisitions for the cost of items to be charged to the food operation. If there are any requisitions for other departments (for example, the cocktail lounge may requisition food items such as olives, cherries, and sugar), these requisitions should be excluded when calculating the figure for this column.

Transfers In.   In your restaurant food items put into production may be transferred from one department to another. In order to authorize such transfers, a transfer memo showing the details of the movement of these products should be completed. Figure 6.2 illustrates such a form. As this form shows, on February 3 the kitchen requested wine (originally purchased and delivered to the cocktail lounge) for cooking purposes at a cost

Date	Direct purchases	Storeroom issues	Transfers In	Transfers Out	Employee meals	Cost of food sold Today	Cost of food sold Accumulated	Revenue Today	Revenue Accumulated	Food cost percent Today	Food cost percent Accumulated
1	134.92	42.08	8.16	(4.11)	(24.50)	156.55	156.55	611.95	611.95	25.6	25.6
2	116.20	84.22		(3.20)	(27.00)	170.22	326.77	650.40	1,262.35	26.2	25.9
3	216.20	176.12	9.05	(6.64)	(26.50)	368.23	695.00	994.25	2,256.60	37.0	30.8
30	118.70	42.16		(3.64)	(29.00)	128.22	6,482.20	375.50	19,446.60	34.1	33.3
31	90.16	101.90	11.08		(30.00)	173.14	6,655.34	510.75	19,957.35	33.9	33.3

Open stock inventory adjustment (150.00)
Month-end adjusted food cost   6,505.34   32.6

Figure 6.1   Daily food cost form.

Transfer from	Bar			
Transfer to	Kitchen	Date	Feb. 3	
Quantity	Item		Item Cost	Total Cost
2 bottles	Casa Bello red		3.15	6.30
1 bottle	Domestic dry sherry		2.75	2.75
			Total	9.05
Requested by	G. Jacobs — Exec. Chef			

Figure 6.2 Transfer memo.

of $9.05. Obviously, the food operation should be charged with this cost and the lounge credited.

Transfers Out. A transfer out from the food department occurs when food items are sent from the food production areas to a nonfood department. For example, it is not necessary for your bar to purchase directly the small quantities of items such as eggs and cream that it needs for some cocktails each day. Your restaurant can buy these items in bulk and the bar simply request what it needs daily by means of a transfer memo. The food department, originally charged with this cost from the invoiced amount recorded in the Direct Purchases column of the daily food receiving report, should now be credited by entering the amount in the Transfers Out column of the daily food cost form.

Employee Meals. Most restaurants allow certain employees to have meals at little or no cost while on duty. In such cases, the cost of that food has no relation to sales revenue generated in the normal course of business. Therefore, the cost of employee meals should be deducted from food cost of sales. Employee meals cost is then transferred to another expense account (for example, it could be added to payroll cost as an employee benefit). Note that, if employees pay cash for meals but receive a discount from normal menu prices, this revenue should also be excluded from regular food sales (because it will distort the food cost percentage calculation) and be transferred to a different revenue account such as "other income."

Where employees eat their meals in a regular dining area, a sales check should be made out in the same way as for regular customers. In this way, your bookkeeper can calculate the cost from the sales value of employee meals. For example, if employee meals on sales checks totaled $100 for a day and your restaurant normally operates at a 40 percent cost of food sales, the cost of employee meals will be 40% × $100 = $40. Obviously, it is preferable that sales checks be made out for all employee meals, but in practice it is recognized that this is often not possible. If sales checks are not used, then an average cost of a meal must be estimated and this cost multiplied by the number of employee meals taken each day.

Promotion Meals.   Most restaurant operators provide some customers with complimentary (free) food. This is a good practice if it is used with good customers who are likely to continue to provide your restaurant with business. The cost of promotional meals should be handled in the same way as the cost of employee meals; that is, the cost of these complimentary items should not be included in food cost of sales because, again, the food cost will be distorted. This cost should be transferred from food cost and be recorded as advertising or promotion expense. Employees who are authorized to allow promotional meals to customers should be instructed always to make out a sales check to record each item's value. From this value, cost of promotion items can be calculated using your operation's normal food cost percentage, as was demonstrated for employee meals.

For promotional purposes your restaurant may issue coupons that allow two meals for the price of one. In this case, the value of both meals should still be recorded on the sales check, even though the customer pays for only one meal.

Note that Figure 6.1 does not have a column for promotion meals. If your restaurant provides them, the form should have a Promotion Meals column added to it.

Cost of Food Sold Today.   On Figure 6.1 the cost of food sold today amount is calculated as follows:

> Direct purchases + Storeroom issues + Transfers in
> − Transfers out − Employee meals
> = Cost of food sold today

Accumulated Cost of Food Sold.   The Accumulated Cost of Food Sold figure is simply the sum of today's and all previous days' Cost of Food Sold Today amounts.

Revenue Today.   The Revenue Today figure is the total food sales for that date, excluding any revenue from employee meals (unless, of course, the employees consumed and paid for food as if they were regular customers paying normal menu prices).

Accumulated Revenue.   Accumulated Revenue is the total of today's revenue (sales) plus all previous days' revenue.

Food Cost Percentage Today. The Food Cost Percentage Today figure is calculated as follows:

$$\frac{\text{Cost of food sold today}}{\text{Revenue today}} \times 100$$

For example (with reference to Figure 6.1), the first day's food cost is

$$\frac{\$156.55}{\$611.95} \times 100 = 25.6\%$$

Accumulated Food Cost Percentage. The Accumulated Food Cost Percentage figure is calculated as follows:

$$\frac{\text{Accumulated cost of food sold}}{\text{Accumulated revenue}} \times 100$$

For example, the day three accumulated cost is

$$\frac{\$695.00}{\$2,256.60} \times 100 = 30.8\%$$

Accuracy of Daily and Accumulated Food Cost

It must be stressed that, even though you can calculate a daily food cost percentage as illustrated in Figure 6.1, this figure may be quite inaccurate. A reason for this is that direct purchases made each day may not all be used that day, yet they are included in the Cost of Food Sold Today figure, thus distorting the daily food cost percentage. This might be particularly true on a Friday when large purchases of direct items are made to carry the operation over the weekend.

The Accumulated Food Cost Percentage figure, however, particularly after the first seven-day period of the month has gone by, tends to average out these peaks and valleys of daily purchases. Therefore, if you compare your restaurant's food cost objective and the food cost percentage calculated on the daily food cost form, this comparison should be made with the accumulated figure rather than the daily one.

You might question whether it serves any purpose to have a tightly controlled food receiving, storage, issuing, and production system, if the food cost results from it are inaccurate. If the only reason for these controls were to calculate a daily food cost, the benefits would not be worth the cost. However, the various steps in the control system serve other purposes than to provide an accurate daily food cost. They are intended to control the flow of food in a way that minimizes losses, pilferage, spoilage, and other destructive factors—all of which affect your food cost not only daily but cumulatively.

Therefore, it is important that your food cost be reviewed regularly and over periods of time that are long enough to cancel out daily random variations but short enough to allow you to take corrective action, where it is needed, before it is too late.

In some situations, such as in a fast-food restaurant, where food usage each day can be very closely matched to sales and where little food inventory is carried overnight, it may be feasible to take inventory at the end of each day and achieve a quite accurate figure for daily food cost.

Month-end Adjustment for Open Stock.   At the month-end, an adjustment normally has to be made to the Accumulated Cost of Food Sold. This adjustment is for the change in the open stock inventory from last month-end to this month-end. Open stock inventory was discussed in Chapter 5.

The rule for open stock adjustment is that if this month's open stock is higher than last month's, you subtract the difference from accumulated cost of food sold. If this month's open stock figure is lower than last month's, you add the difference. Assume that January's open stock amount was $600 and February's $750. The difference of $150 has been subtracted in Figure 6.1.

Once the adjustment for open stock inventory has been made, you can then calculate the final adjusted month-end food cost. In the case of Figure 6.1, this is:

$$\frac{\$6,505.34}{\$19,957.35} \times 100 = 32.6\%$$

What Should the Food Cost Be?

You now know how to calculate a daily and an accumulated food cost percentage during the month and an adjusted food cost percentage at the end of the month. It was mentioned earlier in this chapter that you should control your actual food cost with your restaurant's food cost objective or standard. Let us now turn our attention to establishing what that standard should be for your restaurant.

STANDARD FOOD COST

One of the major problems that restaurant operators face in cost control is the perishable nature of food. This perishability occurs from the moment of receiving through storage, preparation, production, and service.

As well as "normal" perishability from such problems as frozen foods exposed too long at room temperature in a thawed state, dairy products left unrefrigerated, fish allowed to rot before it is used, vegetables and fruit that become bruised, and food that is overproduced for the number of customers, another type of perishability is "perishability" resulting from employees' temptation to steal.

You must, therefore, establish a system that allows you to know what your food cost should be (your standard food cost) and then measure how the actual cost compares with that standard. If you do not know what your food cost should be, then you will never know that your profit is lower than it should be because of food perishability.

The steps in developing a standard food cost are as follows:

1. Establish your standard recipes and portion sizes.

2. Calculate your menu item costs.

3. Set your selling prices.

4. Calculate your standard food cost and compare your actual food cost with the standard.

Establish Standard Recipes and Portion Sizes

You need to prepare standard recipes for each menu item. A standard recipe is a written formula detailing the quantity of each ingredient required in that menu item to produce the quantity and quality you want. A typical standard recipe is illustrated in Figure 6.3.

The recipe should describe the cooking procedure and temperature, where necessary, because temperature can affect the shrinkage, quality, and final cost of the menu item. Recipes should define the portion size to be served (for example, 2 ounces of shrimp in a seafood cocktail).

Portion Control. Food production employees should be provided with portion scales where they are needed, such as in weighing sliced meat for a sandwich or seafood for a cocktail. Scales do not need to be used for measuring each portion but for checking from time to time that there is no deviation from standard portions. Alternatively, measuring devices such as ladles, scoops, or spoons, or individual cooking utensils (such as casserole dishes) should be used.

Your food production employees must be trained to follow your recipes and portion sizes, not only to control cost but to ensure that customers receive a consistent size and quality of menu item.

The care taken in food production control can all be lost if food is indiscriminately plated or poorly portioned. If an 8-ounce steak is overportioned by only 0.5 ounces, this will result in more than a 6 percent

Recipe for Beef casserole							Recipe # 14	
Portion size 8 oz.								
Quantity produced 100 portions								

		Date:	Feb.	Date:		Date:		
Ingredient	Quantity	Cost	Total	Cost	Total	Cost	Total	
Stew beef	25 lb.	2.10	52.50					
Flour	2 lb.	0.30	0.60					
Tomato paste	½ lb.	1.00	0.50					
Beef stock	1 gal.	0.75	0.75					
Brown stock	1 gal.	0.65	0.65					
Fresh carrots	5 lb.	0.35	1.75					
Fresh onions	6 lb.	0.40	2.40					
Celery	3 lb.	0.20	0.60					
Green peas	5 lb.	0.40	2.00					
Seasonings			0.25					
Total cost			62.00					
Cost per portion			0.62					

Cooking procedure:

1. Brown meat; add flour and tomato paste; mix well.
2. Add beef and brown stocks; simmer for 1 hour.
3. Dice carrots, onions, and celery, and add them, with the peas; cook until tender.
4. Add seasonings.
5. Serve in 8 oz. casserole dish.

Figure 6.3 Standard recipe.

increase in your food cost. To an individual server, 0.5 ounces may not seem like much, but if every steak or every item of food is overportioned by 6 percent, your normal profit margin will quickly turn into a serious loss.

Another problem relates to customer perception and satisfaction. If one steak is overportioned by 1 ounce and is compensated for by another that is underportioned by 1 ounce, the 2-ounce difference between them when they are seen side by side is obvious, and the short-portioned customer is going to feel that adequate value for money has not been received.

If you allow employees to use their own judgment about portion sizes, then you will have no control. You need to spot check from time to time that all standard recipes and portion sizes are followed by your employees.

In a buffet or self-serve salad bar, portion control is not easy. You can decide on the size of plate that the customer is given and the size of ladle provided for soups and salad dressings, but this does little to control how much the customer piles on a plate or how many repeat visits the customer makes to the serving area. In a self-serve situation, you have to establish pricing based on what the average person will eat and on how many trips the average person will take to reload. You can do this by test observations.

In a fast-food restaurant, portion control is a lot easier because most food products are purchased and inventoried in preportioned units and employees have little or no discretion to affect the quantities served. Even in the case of an item such as french fries, the carton's serving size dictates the volume that can be served, and items such as mustard and ketchup can be dispensed through machines that serve a controlled quantity.

A final problem involves checking suppliers to ensure that preportioned sizes or weights of products purchased that way conform to specifications and that you are not paying full price for undersize or underweight preportioned products (which would also mean that the customer would be paying for value not received).

Calculate Menu Item Costs

The next step is to calculate your menu item costs. This is simply a question of multiplying the quantity of each ingredient used in each menu item by its cost, as shown in Figure 6.3.

Because it is difficult to arrive at an ingredient cost for a single portion, it is common practice to cost out recipes for, let us say, fifty portions, and then divide the total recipe cost by 50 to arrive at the individual portion cost.

The cost of seasonings and other items used in very small quantities is often estimated or included in a "safety factor." This safety factor may also include an allowance for any shrinkage or wastage that may occur. This factor might range up to 10 percent of overall recipe cost and is added to the total recipe cost before the individual-portion cost is calculated.

Trim and Cooking Loss.   The cost of the main ingredient in many menu items can frequently be obtained directly from the invoice or your supplier's current price list. For example, many restaurants purchase meat in prepared, preportioned quantities. Steaks and similar items purchased this way, ready to cook, have a definite known cost to which you only have to add the cost of other ingredients served with them to determine the total menu cost for that item.

However, if you purchase large cuts of meat and do your own on-premise butchering, you will have to make some further calculations to obtain your main ingredient cost. This is particularly true if meat is aged on site and a weight loss results during the aging process. There could also be weight losses from butchering (deboning and trimming) and further losses in the cooking process from dripping and evaporation. The true cost of a menu item in this case can only be determined when you know the net yield after all these processes.

For example, suppose that you wish to know how many portions can be served from a 20-pound purchase of meat that in butchering had a 10 percent loss (bones and fat) and a further 15 percent cooking loss. Portion size is to be 5 ounces cooked weight:

Original purchase weight	20 lb.
Loss 10% + 15% = 25% × 20 lb.	5 lb.
Yield	15 lb.

$$15 \text{ lb.} \times 16 \text{ oz.} = 240 \text{ oz.}$$
$$\text{and } 240 \text{ oz.}/5 \text{ oz.} = 48 \text{ portions}$$

If the original purchase cost were $1.75 per pound, your cost per portion served would be:

$$20 \text{ lb.} \times \$1.75 = \$35.00$$

and

$$35 \text{ lb.}/48 \text{ portions} = \$0.729, \text{ or } \$0.73 \text{ per portion.}$$

In determining losses from trimming and shrinkage from cooking, it is a good idea to purchase a number of 20-pound weights of this type of meat and subject each purchase to the same butchering and cooking tests so that the results of all tests can be averaged. In cooking, the temperature and cooking time should be the same for all tests.

Portion Cost Factor.   A useful multiplication factor, once a portion cost for a main ingredient menu item has been calculated, is a portion cost factor. Calculating the portion cost factor eliminates the need to retrace all the steps to recalculate a new portion cost if your supplier changes his price. The equation for a portion cost factor is

$$\frac{\text{Your cost per portion}}{\text{Supplier's price per lb.}}$$

In our example, this would be

$$\$0.73/\$1.75 = 0.417$$

Note that this portion cost factor is not a dollar amount but simply a multiplier. If your supplier changes his price, either up or down, you simply multiply his new price by the portion cost factor to arrive at your new portion cost. For example, if the supplier's price increased to $2.00 per pound, your new portion cost would be

$$\$2.00 \times 0.417 = \$0.834$$

Metric Weights.   If you are using metric measures or weights, the same approach to portion costing can still be used. Suppose that your supplier sells 10-kilogram-size cuts of meat for $3.50 per kilogram. If there is a 25 percent shrinkage loss in butchering and cooking, your yield would be 7.5 kilograms, or 7,500 grams. You wish to serve 150-gram portions of cooked weight. Your after-cooking yield will be 50 portions (7,500 divided by 150), and your portion cost is

$$\frac{10 \text{ kg} \times \$3.50}{50 \text{ portions}} = \frac{\$35.00}{50} = \$0.70$$

Your portion cost factor is

$$\frac{\text{Your cost per portion}}{\text{Supplier's price per kg.}} = \frac{\$0.70}{\$3.50} = 0.2$$

If the supplier's price increases to $3.75 per kilogram, your new portion cost will be

$$\$3.75 \times 0.2 = \$0.75$$

Lowest Net Cost.   One of the advantages of carrying out butchering and cooking tests is that you can analyze products from different suppliers to ensure that you buy from the supplier who can meet your specifications at the lowest net cost. For example, assume you wish to buy 20-pound cuts of a certain type of meat. Supplier A's price is $2.10 per pound; Supplier B's is $2.20. Total cost from each would be

Supplier A: 20 lb. × $2.10 = $42.00
Supplier B: 20 lb. × $2.20 = $44.00

Loss in butchering and cooking from Supplier A is 4 pounds, and from Supplier B 3 pounds. Net yield is, therefore, 16 pounds from A and 17 pounds from B. Net cost per pound, rounded to the nearest whole cent, is

Supplier A: $42.00/16 lb. = $2.63
Supplier B: $44.00/17 lb. = $2.59

Thus, you can see that the supplier with the lowest quoted price might not always have the lowest net cost based on yield.

Changing Costs.   If ingredient purchase costs change drastically, you must recalculate your menu item costs. Alternatively, to compensate for cost increases you can make a change in the portion size so that the relationship between cost and selling price remains the same.

As long as you have only a limited number of menu items, menu item cost calculations can easily be completed manually. Alternatively, if your menu is extensive and the number of ingredients used runs into the hundreds, there are today computer programs available for use on a personal or microcomputer that will automatically recalculate your menu item costs when you enter the new ingredient cost(s).

Set Your Selling Prices

When you know what your cost is for each menu item, you can then establish a selling price.

Suppose you wanted to have a food cost (cost of sales) of 40 percent. You simply take the cost of a menu item, multiply it by 100, and divide by 40. For example, if the standard recipe cost were $2.00, the selling price to give you a 40 percent food cost would be

$$\$2.00 \times \frac{100}{40} = \$5.00$$

Alternatively, the menu item cost of $2.00 could have been multiplied by 2.5 (the 2.5 multiplier is simply 100 divided by 40). If a 50 percent food cost were desired, the multiplier would be 2 (100 divided by 50). In fact, you can derive the multiplier for any specific food cost percentage by dividing 100 by the cost percentage number.

Even though you might desire an overall 40 percent food cost for your restaurant, this does not mean that all menu item costs will be multiplied by 2.5 to establish menu prices. Competition and customer acceptance of prices may dictate that some items will be marked up less (using a lower multiplier and giving a higher cost percentage) and others will be marked up using a higher multiplier (resulting in a lower food cost percentage). This means that, if you wanted an overall 40 percent food cost, some menu items might be costed at 45 or 50 percent and others at 30 or 35 percent, so that the overall average works out to your desired standard.

Also, there is nothing magic about a 40 percent food cost. Some restaurants operate with a 20 percent food cost, others with a 60 percent food cost. You must set your own goal, calculate your selling prices on the basis of cost, and then establish your final menu prices. The objective is to arrive at a menu that offers a range of prices that will, on average, result in the desired overall objective.

Influencing Factors.   Menu item selling prices can also be influenced by such factors as your restaurant's type of clientele, what they are prepared to pay, style of service, cost of interior decor, location, labor rates, competition, and similar factors. The amount of convenience foods used can also have a bearing. When you use convenience foods, much of the preparation labor is provided by the supplier, who, in turns, passes on this cost in his selling price. You thus pay more for the product but benefit from a reduction in your labor cost. The result is that your food cost percentage may be higher and your labor cost reduced, relative to selling price.

Another complication is the relationship between the selling price for an individual menu item and the volume of sales for that item. Changing your selling price can directly influence the demand for an item. Demand is never easy to determine, but, because most restaurant operators can observe what happens to demand if a menu's price is changed (and even what competitive restaurants in your area might do with their menu selling prices as a result), demand/volume changes can be documented to aid in future menu-price decision making.

Gross Profit. Remember, also, that the cost percentage of an individual menu item is not always critical. Consider the following calculation concerning two alternative menu items and their gross profits. (Gross profit is the selling price less the cost of sales, or food cost.)

Item	Cost price	Selling price	Cost percentage	Gross profit
1	$4.00	$8.00	50.0	$4.00
2	1.00	4.00	25.0	3.00

In this illustration, all other factors being equal, you would be better off to sell item 1 rather than item 2. Item 1 has a higher food cost percentage, but it also has a higher gross profit. For each of item 1 you sell with a 50 percent food cost, you will have a $4.00 gross profit, versus only $3.00 with item 2 even though it has a low 25 percent food cost. In other words, you should use cost percentages as a starting point for calculating your prices but not ignore the gross profit that results.

Calculate Your Standard Food Cost and Compare Actual and Standard

Now that you have established standard recipes and portion sizes, calculated your menu item costs, and set your selling prices with a certain overall food cost in mind, the last step is to calculate your standard food cost on the basis of how many of each menu item are to be sold (that is, your sales mix). One method of establishing a standard food cost is to base it on a historical test period for your restaurant.

Historical Test Period Percentage.   With this method, you must take a count of each separate menu item sold during a test period. The test period should generally be an entire month, or at least long enough to even out peaks and valleys. At the end of the test period, the total quantity of each menu item sold is listed on a test period standard cost form (see Figure 6.4).

Quantities of each menu item sold are multiplied by their cost and selling prices to arrive at total standard cost and total standard revenue. A division of overall standard cost by standard revenue, multiplied by 100, gives the standard cost percentage. In our case it is 29.4 percent. From now on, the actual cost percentage for each future period is compared with this standard so that deviations can be detected.

Generally, with this method the actual food cost would be allowed to deviate from standard by 1 percentage point above or below the standard. In other words, if the standard were 29.4 percent, the actual could vary from 28.4 to 30.4 percent. You have to allow a tolerance because the standard is based on perfect costing and other factors, and absolute perfection cannot be expected in practice. Differences could occur for any or all of the following reasons:

- Poor receiving practices, such as not counting or weighing items or receiving low quality and paying for high quality.
- Improper storeroom controls resulting in too much wastage or spoilage or in issuing of items to unauthorized personnel for personal use.
- Failure to follow standard recipes and portion sizes, leading again to wastage and spoilage.
- Excessive cost of employee meals.
- Pilferage.

Item	Item cost	Item selling price	Quantity sold	Total standard cost	Total standard revenue
1	$0.95	$3.00	822	$ 780.90	$ 2,466.00
2	1.22	4.75	1,340	1,634.80	6,365.00
3	2.54	6.75	319	810.26	2,153.25
			Totals	$10,111.98	$34,393.60

Standard cost percent: $\dfrac{\$10,111.98}{\$34,393.60} \times 100 = 29.4\%$

Figure 6.4   Test period standard cost calculation form.

The Sales Mix Problem. There is one other factor that can cause a deviation of actual from standard cost percentage, and that is the problem of sales mix. The sales mix is the quantity of each separate menu item that is sold during any period (a meal, a day, a week, or a month). A changed sales mix can cause a considerable change in the cost percentage and is a factor that you have very limited control over in most cases.

Customers' preferences change over time. When historical sales mix patterns are used to calculate the standard cost percentage (as illustrated in Figure 6.4), the assumption is made that this sales mix will remain the same, or relatively the same, in the future. This is highly unlikely in practice, although it is possible that, if your restaurant has an extensive menu, changes in the sales mix tend to even themselves out and might have a lesser influence than otherwise.

Illustration of Sales Mix Change. We can illustrate how a change in the sales mix affects the cost percentage using only two menu items. In Figure 6.5, Case A's overall food cost is 47.1 percent ($800 divided by $1,700 and multiplied by 100).

In Case B, there is a change in the sales mix (with no change in number of customers because 300 items in total are still sold) that causes the cost to decrease from 47.1 to 43.8 percent. The reason for this is that we are now selling more of item one (which has a much lower food cost percentage) than item two. This change in the sales mix might seem desirable because it has led to a decrease in the food cost percentage. In fact, however, it has made absolutely no difference to the restaurant's gross profit. In both cases, the gross profit is $900. And if all the other operating costs stayed the same, there would also be no change in net profit.

No one can argue, therefore, that lowering the food cost percentage

CASE A						
Item	Item cost	Item selling price	Quantity sold	Total cost	Total sales	Food cost percent
1	$2.00	$5.00	100	$200.00	$ 500	40.0%
2	3.00	6.00	200	600.00	1,200	50.0
Totals			300	$800.00	$1,700	47.1%
CASE B						
1	$2.00	$5.00	200	$400.00	$1,000	40.0%
2	3.00	6.00	100	300.00	600	50.0
Totals			300	$700.00	$1,600	43.8%

Figure 6.5 Illustration of sales mix effect on food cost percentage.

will increase profit. Indeed, in some situations lowering the percentage can *decrease* profit, and vice versa. It is for this reason that some restaurants can successfully operate with a 60 percent food cost, while others may operate with a 30 percent food cost and have financial difficulties.

Adjusting for the Sales Mix.   Since a change in your sales mix can thus cause a major change in the standard food cost from one period to the next, this can make comparison of your actual food cost with the standard food cost meaningless unless you adjust the standard food cost each period for that period's sales mix. This can be easily done.

At the end of each review period you simply multiply each menu item's cost and selling price by the quantity of that item actually sold during the period. This is illustrated in Figure 6.6.

The figures in the Actual Quantity Sold column of Figure 6.6 are your actual quantities of that item sold from your sales checks or counted automatically for you in your sales register if it has this feature.

The Total Standard Cost column is the product of the Item Cost column multiplied by the Actual Quantity Sold column.

The Total Standard Revenue column is the product of the Item Selling Price column times the Actual Quantity Sold column.

The overall Standard Cost Percentage can be calculated using information from the Total Standard Cost and Total Standard Revenue columns as shown in Figure 6.6.

Finally, on this form you can record your actual cost percentage for

Item	Item		Actual quantity sold	Total standard	
	Cost	Selling price		Cost	Revenue
1	$0.75	$2.00	143	$ 107.25	$ 286.00
2	1.25	2.75	219	278.75	602.25
3	4.00	6.50	95	380.00	617.50
4	2.10	6.00	305	640.50	1,830.00
5	1.50	5.50	142	313.00	781.00

Week ending____ February 17

			Totals	$3,249.00	$8,266.00

Standard cost $\dfrac{\$3,249.00}{\$8,266.00} \times 100 = 39.3\%$

Actual cost (adjusted) $\dfrac{\$3,275.00}{\$8,266.00} \times 100 = 39.6\%$

Figure 6.6 Comparison of overall standard cost and actual cost.

that period. The information for this can be easily obtained if you use a daily food cost form as illustrated in Figure 6.1.

Note that in the actual cost percentage calculation the denominator (sales) is the same amount as in the standard cost percentage calculation. This is because the two amounts should be the same unless errors have occurred, such as in recording sales or making change.

The difference between the standard food cost and actual food cost percentages can be calculated. You must expect some difference (usually 0.5 percent above or below would be normal). For example, if your standard food cost for this period is 39.3 percent, as shown in Figure 6.6, you could expect the actual to be somewhere between 38.8 percent and 39.8 percent.

Generally, you would expect to see the actual cost above standard cost because the standard is based on the assumption that actual menu item costs will turn out exactly as calculated when they are established. Because of wastage and other similar losses in excess of any safety factor built into menu item costs, actual costs would tend to exceed standard costs. Also, the cost of menu items purchased can vary from day to day and it is just not practical to adjust standard menu costs daily.

With this method, if a major difference exists between the standard cost percentage and the actual cost percentage, you can be absolutely sure that it is not caused by a change in the sales mix, because you have taken the actual sales mix into consideration in the calculations.

Therefore, any serious difference that occurs must be caused by one or more of the factors listed earlier in this chapter, such as poor receiving, storing, and production practices; pilferage; or wastage. Alternatively, there may have been ingredient cost changes. If these cost changes were major, you menu item cost prices should be adjusted to compensate for them in the calculations.

Standard Cost Changes Each Period.   Note that, when you calculate your standard cost percentage for the following period you will find it will change from the current period because there will likely be a change in the sales mix during the following period. However, your actual cost percentage will also change, so you are still able to compare oranges with oranges and your only concern is that the difference between the two figures is within an acceptable limit.

Fixed-Menu Establishments.   Many restaurants today have limited menus offering only a few items. These items are seldom changed, although sometimes daily "specials" may be offered. Usually, these restaurants have a relatively steady volume of business, and purchase precut, preportioned, and, frequently, frozen entree and other items that are much

Item	Opening inventory	Purchased	Closing inventory	Quantity used	Quantity sold	Difference	Comment
Filet mignon 6 oz.	18	24	8	34	32	− 2	Customers complained
Filet mignon 8 oz.	22	12	3	31	31		
New York 10 oz.	15	36	7	44	43	− 1	Spoiled

Figure 6.7   Food inventory portion cost control form.

less prone to deterioration in the short run. Often these restaurants only cook to order. For them the problem of forecasting production requirements is minimized.

For this type of restaurant, a portion control form such as that illustrated in Figure 6.7 may be useful. This type of inventory sheet is completed daily. The Quantity Used column is calculated as follows:

Opening inventory + Purchased − Closing inventory

The quantity used is compared with the quantity sold to determine any differences. In a small restaurant, this form might be completed by the chef for his or her own satisfaction to be sure that losses are not occurring. In a large restaurant, the inventory of these items would be stored under lock and key and issued daily by requisition, based on the chef's estimate of anticipated demand.

If actual demand is greater than expected, more items can be quickly requisitioned. If less, then unused portions can be returned to the storeroom to be requisitioned again on a future day. In the latter case, the form might have to be redesigned with column headings as illustrated in Figure 6.8.

Banquet Portion Control.   A restaurant that caters to banquets and similar group functions can also use a type of portion control. A typical banquet portion control form is illustrated in Figure 6.9. The figures in the

Item	Quantity requisitioned	Quantity returned	Quantity used	Quantity sold	Difference	Comment

Figure 6.8   Food inventory portion control: alternate form.

Function	Construction Association			Room	Madison	Date	Feb. 16

Server number	Appetizers	Soups	Salads	Entrees	Desserts	Guests served	Comment
1	15			15	14	15	
2	14			14	14	14	
3	16			16	13	16	
Totals	428			428	414	428	

Figure 6.9 Banquet portion control form.

various course columns can be entered on the form by a person from the kitchen production area as each waiter or waitress leaves that area with trays of menu items to be served to guests. At the end of each function, the manager's figure of guests served by each server, and in total for all servers, can be compared with the banquet portion control form figure. This should ensure that servers do not take out of the kitchen more portions than they have guests to serve. This form can also be useful for customer-invoicing purposes.

MENU ANALYSIS

Most restaurants offer a variety of menu items covering a range of prices, some with higher food costs than others. When analyzing your menu to improve gross profit, you have a number of alternatives:

- Reduce purchase costs by reducing ingredient quality.
- Reduce portion sizes.
- Increase selling prices.

Alternatively, you can change your menu by having on it only items that have a high individual gross profit. To make such a drastic move, however, might severely disrupt your restaurant's present clientele and result in an unbalanced menu as far as offering a range of prices is concerned.

A better way might be to substitute one or two items on your present menu to see what effect this has on overall gross profit. For example, Figure 6.10 lists the five entree items presently offered by Sally Sayle's restaurant. Sally is going to substitute item 5, with a $4.31 gross profit ($6.25 less $1.94) with a new item 5, with a $4.64 gross profit ($6.40 less $1.76). In anticipation of this change, Sally expects that a number of

Item	Cost	Item Selling price	Average daily quantity sold	Total cost	Total revenue
1	$1.28	$4.60	75	$ 96.00	$ 345.00
2	2.26	5.95	42	94.92	249.90
3	3.74	6.30	61	228.14	384.30
4	1.78	5.75	99	176.22	569.25
5	1.94	6.25	74	143.56	462.50
Totals			351	$ 738.84	$2,010.95
Gross profit				$1,272.11	
Cost percent				$\dfrac{\$\ 738.84}{\$2,010.95} \times 100 = 36.7\%$	
Average gross profit per guest				$\dfrac{\$1,272.11}{351} = \$3.62$	

Figure 6.10   Menu analysis to determine gross profit.

customers will switch from one item to another and produce a changed sales mix even though the total number of customers will not change.

Figure 6.11 shows these changed results. If Sally's sales mix predictions are correct, gross profit will increase from $1,272.11 to $1,301.49, or by $29.38 per day on average. In this particular case, Sally's gross profit increase is combined with a decreased food cost percentage. Depending on the circumstances, it could also be combined with an increased cost percentage. Thus, to reiterate, overemphasizing the cost percentage and ignoring its effect on gross profit can be misleading.

Item	Cost	Item Selling price	Average daily quantity sold	Total cost	Total revenue
1	$1.28	$4.60	55	$ 70.40	$ 253.00
2	2.26	5.95	41	92.66	243.95
3	3.74	6.30	65	243.10	409.50
4	1.78	5.75	120	213.60	690.00
5	1.76	6.40	70	123.20	448.00
Totals			351	$742.96	$2,044.45
Gross profit				$1,301.49	
Cost percent				$\dfrac{\$\ 742.96}{\$2,044.45} \times 100 = 36.3\%$	
Average gross profit per guest				$\dfrac{\$1,301.49}{351} = \$3.71$	

Figure 6.11   Menu analysis to determine gross profit after menu change.

Gross Profit per Customer

Sally may also find it useful to calculate her average gross profit per guest or customer. This has been done in Figures 6.10 and 6.11. The average has increased from $3.62 to $3.71. This is to be expected, because Sally's overall gross profit has increased and there has been no change in number of customers. In substituting menu items, if there is an increase in average gross profit per customer but (because of a decrease in total customers) a decline in the overall gross profit, this would not be a desirable trend.

Initially, you should make experimental menu changes on paper. Perhaps surveys of customers could also be carried out before changing your menu to improve gross profit. If you have kept sales histories, these could be very useful in forecasting the sales mix resulting from proposed menu changes.

Finally, in evaluating a change to a menu to improve gross profit, you must always be aware of a potential change in total demand for all menu items, particularly if you remove a popular (but low gross profit) item from the menu, and the potential effect on other costs (such as serving or preparation labor, and/or cooking time and its effect on energy costs).

Pricing of menu items is discussed in more detail in Chapter 11.

CONTROL OF COST OF SALES

Most competitive restaurants of the same type generally have a similar food cost (and thus a similar gross profit) because their menus offer similar products at similar prices. Their food purchase costs are also generally the same (because they often buy from the same supplier or from competitive suppliers whose products are similarly priced). If the operating and fixed costs of these restaurants are also similar, then the only explanation for the higher profitability of one over the other is control of its food cost and thus gross profit.

If a restaurant wishes to improve its profitability, assuming most or all of its costs other than food cost are fixed, then the only way to do this (other than by increasing sales or menu prices) is through gross profit, that is, by reducing the food cost through more effective purchasing, receiving, storing, issuing, kitchen production, and control of sales of food.

In actual practice, food cost and gross profit are never a constant percentage of sales. For example, as your sales increase and you have to buy more products, you should be able to buy them at a somewhat lower cost because of volume purchases. This means that your food cost should be reduced, which in turn leads to an increase in both gross and net profit.

On the other hand, if you have considerable losses from food inventory as a result of food spoilage, wastage from overproduction, or employee pilferage, your food cost will increase and both gross and net profit will decline.

Other Factors

Some of the other factors that influence food cost percentage and thus gross and net profit are the following:

- Skill of person responsible for purchasing to ensure that the right products are purchased at the right prices and in the right quantities.
- Acceptance of poor-quality food products delivered by a supplier while being charged for high-quality products.
- Failure to check food deliveries and being charged by suppliers for products not actually received.
- Menu pricing policies. For example, are you going to lower prices (thus increasing the food cost percentage) to generate more sales or establish higher prices (thus reducing the food cost percentage) that might actually reduce total sales?
- Paying invoices promptly to take advantage of a price discount offered by a supplier.

Even though the preceding comments relate to food purchases, they apply equally well to the beverage part of your operation.

Note also that if you are to analyze your gross profit intelligently you must keep the sales and costs of food and alcoholic beverages separate. Combining food and beverage sales and food and beverage costs will not provide you with clear enough information for decision-making purposes. If you do not make this separation, a money-losing food operation could be disguised by a highly profitable beverage operation, or vice versa.

SEVEN

Alcoholic Beverage Purchasing, Receiving, and Storeroom Control

PURCHASING

For most restaurants, the purchasing of alcoholic beverages is less of a problem than the purchase of food. Beverage purchasing and control are simplified because

- Brands that customers like to drink can be easily established.
- Beverages are generally purchased in sealed cases or bottles that are easy to receive and check.
- Product quality is consistent from one purchase to the next for any particular type or brand of beverage.
- Most beverages (except keg beer) have a fairly long shelf life, which means that purchases can be made on a periodic basis.
- On receipt, all beverages can be delivered to a locked, controlled storeroom prior to being issued. This is not the case with food, where control over direct purchases can be a major problem.

Control of Distribution

In most jurisdictions, the government is the sole wholesaler/distributor and prices to purchasers are controlled and fixed with few opportunities (if any) for "sales" or quantity buys at special prices. In these jurisdictions, the government may specify the liquor-ordering and invoice-paying procedures.

In the United States, states that have government distribution of liquor are known as control or monopoly states. The others are known as license or open states. The following are control states:

Alabama	Ohio
Idaho	Oregon
Iowa	Pennsylvania
Maine	Utah
Michigan	Vermont
Mississippi (wholesale only)	Virginia
Montana	Washington
New Hampshire	West Virginia
North Carolina	Wyoming

All other states are license states.

Control States

In control or monopoly states, there is generally only one price for each product and you cannot shop around among competitors for lower prices. As a result, the product cost is usually higher than in license states. There may also be a limited brand selection, because the government monopoly will usually only carry products that sell well and may be less responsive to purchasers' needs. Nevertheless, some monopoly governments are willing to bring in specialty products for you if you are willing to buy them in a specified minimum quantity of case lots.

In control states, the government normally requires purchasers to pay in cash or by certified check at the time of pickup, as well as to arrange and pay for their own pickup and delivery.

License States

In license states, prices may be lower because of competition, but this is not necessarily the case on all items. Some manufacturers grant exclusive distribution rights for some products to a particular supplier, who then has no competition.

Where there is competition, the suppliers may nonetheless be reluctant to compete on the prices of products that a bar must stock. These "must stock" items are the heavily advertised brands that customers demand. Thus, the customer dictates in most cases what your restaurant's bar will carry, and to some extent this enables the suppliers to maintain prices even in a competitive situation. Suppliers then compete only on the discretionary products that you may wish to carry or through discounts or other inducements not allowed in government-controlled jurisdictions.

In license states, the reputable restaurant operator also has access to supplier credit and will be allowed to delay paying invoices until the end of an agreed credit period. In many jurisdictions, if the invoice is not paid by that date, the supplier is required to advise the licensing authorities, who have the discretion to prevent the operator from making further purchases until the bill is paid.

Familiarity with Local Situation

It is up to you to be familiar with all the necessary legal requirements and distribution channels where your restaurant is located; even where the government is the sole supplier, there may still be importers, wholesalers, dealers, or their agents or sales representatives, trying to influence you to buy their products through the government supplier.

Suppliers are often very useful in advising about local or regional trends in the drinking tastes and habits of customers or potential customers. Of course, suppliers will be eager to tell you about any new products they have and (where this is allowed) about any discounts or other purchase incentives they are offering. But you must be wary of discounted wines and beers that may have reached the limit of their quality or freshness.

Number of Product Suppliers

In situations where there is a choice of suppliers, it is important to consider how many different suppliers you should deal with. Concentrating orders with a limited number of suppliers creates larger-size orders, and you thus become a more important customer to the supplier. In recognition of this, lower prices and/or better supplier services can be expected.

On the other hand, if you deal with a large number of suppliers, each one may be forced to compete harder, although with some products (as mentioned earlier) they may be reluctant to do this. For major-selling products, you could place an order for each separate product with a different supplier, simply because that supplier currently has the lowest price for the item and meets the quality standards desired.

The opposite extreme would be to place all product orders with a single supplier that, despite having a higher cost on one or two products, provides the *lowest overall cost* on all products. Since this simplifies purchasing, ordering, receiving, storing, and invoicing, it is often the best approach. Unfortunately, it is often rejected by restaurant operators because they think about their purchasing only on a product-by-product basis.

In general, it is best to use as few suppliers as possible, even if this means reducing the number of brands carried. Many restaurant operators use a single supplier for their basic stock and other suppliers as needed for specialty items.

Kickbacks

When you do not do the actual purchasing yourself, you should be alert to kickbacks. Kickbacks can take the form of cash or merchandise given to the purchaser for favoring a supplier, even in situations where liquor has to be purchased from a government outlet.

In other cases, a kickback can occur when a supplier sells goods to your operation but inflates the price of products, includes items on the invoice that were not actually delivered, or substitutes low-quality products when invoicing for high-quality products. The "savings" to the supplier are then split with the person responsible for purchasing.

These kinds of kickbacks can be spotted through effective supervision. You should watch for a supplier whose products seem to be favored by the person responsible for purchasing. The best protection is to ensure that the purchasing and receiving functions are separated and that proper receiving controls are implemented and practiced. (Receiving will be discussed later in this chapter.)

Dishonest kickbacks should be differentiated from honest discounts. Legal discounts (either in the form of cash or free alcoholic beverage products) should be received by the establishment and not by an employee. You should notify employees that any violation of this practice will lead to termination, and suppliers should be advised that their services will be discontinued.

Post Offs

In some states, liquor suppliers are allowed to offer a price discount known as a post off. Post offs usually range from 5 to 10 percent of the product's listed wholesale price. Post offs are generally available for various liquor brands at different times of the year, depending on the jurisdiction.

To obtain a benefit from such a discount, you need to buy post-off brands in larger quantities. You should make yourself aware in advance of the date when a post off is to occur in your jurisdiction and which products will be available at the discounted price. You should then reduce your inventory of those products prior to purchasing at the discount so that large-quantity purchases can be made. If you have to purchase more than a six-month supply to obtain the discount, you are likely to be better off buying smaller quantities more often at the regular price and not tying up too much money in inventory.

The post off is not always in the form of a price discount. For example, it can take the form of a free bottle of liquor for each full case ordered.

Supplier Services

Liquor, wine, and beer producers may be allowed in some jurisdictions to provide useful services such as supplying you with blank purchase orders, bin cards, and other control forms (the use of which will be discussed later). These "free" forms can save you money because they help control the purchase, storage, and use of alcoholic beverages.

In some cases, a wine supplier may be useful in helping create wine menus or lists, training wine service employees, providing sales and promotion suggestions, and assisting you in other matters.

You should not, however, be unnecessarily influenced to favor a particular supplier because of these services. Instead, purchasing should serve the purpose of buying the products that at a reasonable price will also satisfy your operation's customers.

Other Considerations

Other questions or considerations in purchasing from a particular supplier include the following:

- What is the frequency of delivery? A supplier that is prepared to deliver daily, even though orders are normally placed less frequently, allows you to carry less in inventory and still obtain needed supplies in an emergency.
- How large a variety of products does the supplier offer? A supplier with a large and varied inventory is more useful to you than a specialist supplier with a limited inventory.
- For beer supply, does the supplier have refrigerated premises and delivery vehicles? It may be a good idea to visit the supplier's warehouse to see how beer and wine are stored (for example, whether corked wine bottles are stored on their sides).
- Where is the supplier located? If the supplier is remote from your operation, how will this distance affect such considerations as delivery times? Will travel time and weather affect the product's quality?
- Does the supplier offer other bar supplies, such as carbonated drinks and drink mixes?
- What are minimum quantities that must be ordered at any one time?
- What are the supplier's credit terms?
- Is the supplier's representative an order taker or a sales person? With

the former, an order is simply processed; with the latter, you can obtain advice and counsel about products offered.

• Does the supplier deliver as promised? Undelivered products can translate into lost profits.

Premium and Nonpremium Liquor

In purchasing liquor, a major decision you have to make involves the premium and nonpremium liquor brands to be carried.

Most restaurant bars serve a house brand (sometimes known as "well" liquor) to customers who do not specify a particular brand but merely the generic type of drink desired (for example, scotch). On the other hand, premium or "call" liquor refers to specific brand names, such as Chivas Regal scotch.

Well Liquor

Well liquors are usually the largest-selling items of the basic types of liquor (rye, gin, rum, scotch, vodka, and bourbon) in a typical beverage operation. Because they usually provide the best (lowest) cost to you, they are also the cheapest for the customer to buy. And because they are generally serviced with other ingredients (such as a carbonated mixer) little taste discrimination by the consumer is possible.

Despite the fact that you should seek the best possible price with well liquors, some judgment may be needed because distillers do sometimes produce brands that are unacceptable and there is a limit to what the customer should be expected to tolerate. In other words, you should not buy Rotgut Rum just because it is 10 cents less per bottle than better brands. Where the government controls the purchase and distribution of liquor, unacceptable brands are less likely to be available.

You should select well brands that offer value for money and stay with those brands for drink consistency. By purchasing a higher-quality product at slightly more money, you will not pay an appreciably higher cost per drink. For example, consider two liquors, one costing $10 and the other $9 per bottle. From each bottle you can obtain 35 drinks. On the $10 bottle the cost per drink is $0.2857, and on the $9 bottle it is $0.2571. Thus the difference is less than 3 cents per drink.

Call Liquor

In the case of premium or call liquor, you have less control over cost, because you generally have to carry the brands that customers ask for regularly. Drink selling prices will be dictated primarily by what the customer is prepared to pay. Thus, because you cannot substitute cheap brands for call brands, liquor cost cannot be reduced as it can through selection of low-priced well liquor.

A rule of thumb with call liquors (including liqueurs) is that if the product sells it should be carried in inventory; otherwise it should not. An inventory of unsold call liquors and liqueurs represents money tied up and not earning any income. One good inventory operating method is never to add a new product without deleting an old one.

If a particular type of call liquor is tied up and not selling, it might be a good idea to sell it as house or well liquor. At least that way, even if the liquor costs you a little more per drink than normal well liquor, money from dead inventory will be freed. Because the same selling flexibility does not apply to liqueurs, you should carry them in inventory only if it is clear that customers want them.

One good idea to reduce inventory is to put strict limits on the number of brands carried and to print a list of the limited brands offered. Most customers will choose from the list, and the problem of customers' having an open-ended choice disappears. What to carry depends on type of restaurant, volume of business, type of clientele, cash available for investment in inventory, and customers' preferences.

Cost per Ounce

Good beverage cost control begins with knowing what your drinks cost. This is most easily established on a cost-per-ounce basis, because it makes comparison easier between brands and between containers of different sizes. Generally, the larger the container in which liquor is purchased, the lower the cost per ounce. This is not always so, however, providing another reason to convert the bottle cost to a per-ounce cost before making the purchase decision.

Nevertheless, although cost per ounce is important, it may not be the only factor to consider. Other significant factors include volume of business and availability of a container size that is convenient for pouring. Also, the quantity that you are required to buy to obtain desirable savings might necessitate a considerable investment in inventory that may not be used up for several months, or even longer. You must then consider the resulting loss of interest on money that could otherwise be left in the bank.

Metric Equivalents

Cost per ounce is calculated by dividing the bottle price by its size in ounces. Because alcoholic beverage bottles today are in metric sizes, it is necessary to convert metric volumes to an equivalent ounce size. The following table can be used:

Metric size	United States Ounce equivalent	Canada Ounce equivalent
4 liters	134.8	140.8
3 liters	101.0	105.6
1.75 liters	59.2	61.6
1.5 liters	50.7	52.8
1 liter	33.8	35.2
750 milliliters	25.4	26.4
375 milliliters	12.7	13.2
200 milliliters	6.8	7.0
187 milliliters	6.3	6.6
100 milliliters	3.4	3.5
50 milliliters	1.7	1.8

ORDERING

You should try to limit ordering to once a week because this lessens the demands on time, reduces the possibility of errors, and simplifies the paperwork and bookkeeping.

If your restaurant is a small one, you should handle the ordering function yourself because it is a key element in beverage cost control. However, if your restaurant is a large one, you may have to delegate this function, in which case you should be alert to the possibility of supplier/ purchaser kickbacks or bribes.

For items used in quantity, about ten days' supply should be on hand after each order is received. These items are usually ordered in case lots. For slow-moving items, quantities may be ordered in multiples of bottles, unless the supplier refuses to break open cases, at which point you may have to order a full case of an item that may take a year to sell.

Alternatively, your supplier may be willing to sell a split case, or a case of several different brands totaling to a normal case lot of twelve bottles. For example, a supplier may be willing to sell four bottles of each of three wines at the case-discounted price. This is an additional service by a supplier that provides value to you.

How Much to Order?

A problem in beverage purchase control involves knowing (without having to take a physical inventory of what you have on hand) how much of each product to order to carry you through until the next order date. An easy way to control this is to use storeroom perpetual inventory cards (discussed in Chapter 5 with reference to food storeroom control). From each card, you can quickly determine at any time what you have on hand of each item in stock.

Because each card can also have recorded on it the maximum quantity normally carried of that product, the order quantity is the amount required to increase the present stock to the maximum level, allowing (if necessary) a safety margin for any time delay between ordering and receiving the goods.

It is desirable to develop your ordering system as precisely as possible. Liquor is expensive, and when too much is purchased and sitting idle on a shelf, that money is not earning a profit. Further, a large inventory requires more space, more paperwork, and more security, and there may be a problem with deterioration of quality in beer and some wines; in addition, changing customer tastes may leave you with inventory that cannot be sold. However, if your restaurant specializes in fine wines, it may be necessary to buy high-quality wines in large quantities when they are available; otherwise, that opportunity will disappear.

Order Form

Where many different items are ordered, a purchase order form is useful because it helps the person responsible for receiving to know what is to be delivered from each supplier and at what prices. Figure 7.1 illustrates an order form.

RECEIVING

In receiving alcoholic beverages, you should break down products received into three separate categories: beer, wine, and liquor. Any nonalcoholic beverages received (such as carbonated beverages) are generally included in

Order Date _Dec. 28_   Delivery Date _Dec. 30_

Supplier	Item	Size	Ordered	Received	Price	Total
H & J	Old Kentucky	1.75 L	36	36	8.10	291.60
H & J	Chivas Regal	1.75 L	12	12	17.50	210.00
Vintage	Kressman red	750 ML	12	12	4.75	57.00

Figure 7.1 Order form.

the liquor category, because the revenue derived from drinks in which these nonalcoholic beverages are used is generally liquor revenue.

Sales Mix

Three separate categories are used because the markup for each category is generally quite different and distortions, false assumptions, and erroneous decisions could result if cost analysis were not made by category. Figure 7.2 illustrates this. Notice that from month one to month two the overall beverage cost has declined from 36.6 percent to 36.3 percent. This might seem desirable. However, analysis of the cost percentage by category shows that, in each case, the cost percentage has increased, despite the decline in the overall percentage.

The decline in the overall percentage was caused entirely by a change in the sales mix. There has been a major shift in month two in the amount of beer sold relative to wine (with little change in liquor revenue). Because beer has a lower cost percentage than wine, this shift has influenced the overall percentage downward, even though the cost percentage of all three categories has gone up. Only analysis by category will show the underlying trend.

Again, as with food cost percentages, beverage cost percentages by themselves can be misleading. For example, in Figure 7.2, despite the decline in overall cost percentage from month one to month two, the gross profit has also decreased from $91,600 to $90,000—and this would not normally be a desirable trend.

	Month 1			Month 2		
	Cost	Revenue	Cost Percent	Cost	Revenue	Cost Percent
Beer	$ 4,800	$ 12,200	39.3%	$ 9,600	$ 24,200	39.7%
Wine	23,600	48,000	49.2	16,400	33,200	49.4
Liquor	24,400	84,200	29.0	25,200	83,800	30.1
Totals	$52,800	$144,400		$51,200	$141,200	
Overall cost	$\dfrac{\$52,800}{\$144,400} \times 100$ $= 36.6\%$			$\dfrac{\$51,200}{\$141,200} \times 100$ $= 36.3\%$		
Gross profit	$144,400 - $52,800 $= \$91,600$			$141,200 - $51,200 $= \$90,000$		

Figure 7.2 Sales mix analysis by cost category.

Receiving Checks

Because alcoholic beverages are prone to "evaporation" (or removal by unauthorized persons), it is important that the person responsible for receiving and checking be there at the time of delivery. It may be necessary to instruct suppliers to deliver only during hours when a person who combines the beverage-receiving function with some other job is available. The receiver should check that

- Quantities received agree with quantities listed on the order form and with the invoice. This requires counting all bottles or other types of container or counting the number of cases where items have been delivered in case lots. In the latter event, cases should be opened to ensure that no bottles have been removed prior to delivery. Alternatively, where the correct full weight of the case is known, cases can be weighed. If bottles are supposed to be sealed, spot checks should be carried out to ensure seals are not broken.
- Prices on invoices agree with prices listed on the order form.
- Quality of products is acceptable (proof of liquor, vintages of wines, freshness of keg beer) where this type of check is appropriate.

In the event that bottles have been broken prior to receipt, that the wrong product has been delivered, or that items have been short-shipped, a credit memorandum (Figure 7.3) should be prepared by the receiver. If an invoice does not accompany the shipment, a memorandum invoice should be prepared by the receiver using actual quantities delivered and obtaining pricing information from the order form.

Once all receiving checks have been carried out, each invoice should be stamped with the receiving stamp (Figure 7.4) and initialed in the appro-

Supplier _Vintage Imports_ Date _Sept. 4_			
Please issue a credit memorandum for the following:			
Quantity	Item Description	Unit Cost	Total
2 L	Haut Villages	7.10	14.20
Reason for request for credit:			
Bottles broken			
Delivery driver's signature _____			

Figure 7.3 Credit memorandum.

```
┌─────────────────────────────────────────────────────────┐
│  Date received _____       │
│  Quantity checked by _____       │
│  Quality checked by _____       │
│  Prices checked by _____       │
│  Listed on receiving report by _____       │
└─────────────────────────────────────────────────────────┘
```

Figure 7.4   Receiving stamp.

priate places. Finally, beverages should be immediately moved to the locked storeroom.

Beverage Receiving Report

The final step in receiving is completion from invoices of the beverage receiving report. A sample weekly beverage receiving report is illustrated in Figure 7.5. In a very large restaurant with several daily deliveries it may be better to produce a daily receiving report. In that case, each day's beverage total would be subsequently transferred to the beverage receiving summary form illustrated in Figure 7.6.

How this beverage purchase cost information can be used to aid in beverage storeroom control will be explained later in the chapter.

STOREROOM CONTROL

In a beverage operation, the storeroom is ideally located adjacent to the bar. In some restaurants, the beverage storeroom might be part of the food storeroom, although this is not recommended. Because of the "perishable"

Week ending March 9				
Supplier	Liquor	Wine	Beer	Invoice Total
Atlantic Brewers			$214.60	$214.60
Vintage Imports		$125.40		125.40
H & J Agency	$375.48	75.90		451.38
Totals	$375.48	$201.30	$214.60	$791.38

Figure 7.5   Weekly beverage-receiving report.

Week ending _March 9_				
Date	Liquor	Wine	Beer	Total
March 5	$ 114.10	$213.10	$ 72.35	$ 399.55
6	893.21		315.95	1,209.16
7	132.18	128.06	371.60	631.84
Totals	$1,321.10	$782.16	$1,851.40	$3,954.66

Figure 7.6 Weekly beverage-receiving summary form.

nature of the product, a separate beverage storeroom is preferable. In a large restaurant with a number of different bars, each bar may have its own small storeroom in addition to the main storeroom. In this case, for control purposes it is recommended that all beverage purchases be processed through the main storeroom before any of the products are distributed to the individual bar storerooms.

In some situations, it is not possible to centralize beverage storage. For example, in the case of keg beer that must be kept refrigerated the storage location may have to be separate from that for other products. Also, high-quality wines should be stored at below room temperatures. If properly cooled storage cannot be provided for these wines in the liquor storeroom, an area elsewhere may have to be set aside for them.

Regardless of the number and type of beverage storage areas, only one person should have access to them. In a small restaurant, this might be you as owner or manager. In a large operation, it might be the task of the food storekeeper to handle beverage storeroom responsibilities as well. In a very large operation, the volume of business might require a separate beverage storekeeper. In order to have control and define responsibility for losses if they occur, only one person should have a storeroom key.

Perpetual Inventory Cards and Requisitions

In Chapter 5, a system of food storeroom control using perpetual inventory cards and requisitions was discussed. The information in that chapter is also relevant to alcoholic beverages, because all beverage purchases should be recorded on individual perpetual inventory cards as the items are placed in storage. Items should be issued only by properly authorized requisitions.

If your restaurant has a number of bars, each requisitioning its own requirements from storage, a specially designed perpetual inventory card is

			Out				
Date	In	Main Bar	Bar 1	Bar 2	Bar 3	Balance	Requisition Cost Information
March 1	24	6	2		4	12	$17.10
2			2	2	3	5	17.10
3	24	4		2		23	16.85

Item _Chivas Regal_   Supplier _J & H_   Tel. # _432–1981_
Maximum _30_   Supplier _Savory_   Tel. # _436–2732_
Minimum _6_   Supplier _____   Tel. # _____

Figure 7.7 Perpetual inventory card for an establishment with several bars.

useful. This card will show for each requisition recorded the bar to which the items were transferred. Figure 7.7 illustrates such a perpetual inventory card.

Par Stock

To aid in knowing how much of each item to requisition each day, your bar(s) should be provided with a par stock list. The list shows how many of each item should be on hand to start each day's business. Par stock lists must be changed when necessary (for example, if customers' drinking habits change with a change of season). The lists may also have to be adjusted if there is a special event on any particular day or for some other reason. You should verify from time to time that par stock lists are being followed.

Full-bottle Replacement

It is not usually possible for a bar to replenish its stock each day exactly to the par stock list because there may be partly used bottles in the bar. Therefore, a system of full-bottle replacement for each empty bottle on hand is often used. Empty bottles should be returned to the storeroom and be destroyed (unless, of course, a refundable deposit is available from the supplier or the bottles are recyclable).

Bottle Coding

Some restaurants issue full bottles with coding devices that are difficult or impossible to duplicate (such as an ink-stamped logo or symbol) or with marks only readable with an infrared light. These coding devices identify bottles before they are issued. If your restaurant has only one bar, all bottles can be coded as they are received and put into storage. If there are two or more bars, it is recommended that bottles be coded just prior to issuing so that each bar can receive a separate and unique code identifying that bar. Obviously, empty bottles returned for replacement should still have the code on them.

This control does not prevent a bartender from bringing in his or her own privately purchased bottles, selling the contents, not recording the sale, and pocketing the cash. It does reduce the possibility, however, because your spot checks can show whether all bottles at the bar are properly coded. You must also be alert to a bartender's transferring the contents of a privately purchased bottle to a coded empty one before selling the liquor and pocketing the cash.

Storeroom Inventory Reconciliation

Each day or week, you should verify that the invoices for beverage purchases have been properly recorded on the beverage receiving report (Figure 7.5). At the end of each beverage storeroom control period, an actual count of each item in inventory should be taken. The procedures for taking food inventory were described in Chapter 5 and apply equally well to taking beverage inventory, particularly with regard to reconciling differences between the perpetual inventory card and actual count figures.

When inventory taking has been completed, the final inventory value figures for the period can be recorded on the beverage storeroom inventory reconciliation form (Figure 7.8). On this form, the Opening Inventory figure is the actual inventory from the previous period. The Purchases for Period amount is transferred from the beverage receiving report(s) for that period. The Requisitions for Period figure is the total cost information

Period ending _April 15_	Beer	Wine	Liquor	Total
Opening inventory	$241.40	$305.79	$ 659.60	$1,206.79
Add: Purchases for period	807.80	492.73	1,378.24	2,678.77
Deduct: Requisitions for period	(716.10)	(516.05)	(1,288.18)	(2,520.33)
= Closing inventory	333.10	282.47	749.66	1,365.23
Actual inventory	335.40	281.10	752.90	1,369.40
Difference	2.30	(1.37)	3.24	4.17

Figure 7.8 Beverage storeroom inventory reconciliation.

Period ending	February 28					
		Quantity on Hand				
	Size	Storeroom	Bar	Total	Item Cost	Total Value
Ballantine	L	6	2.2	8.2	$10.28	$ 84.30
Bell	L	8	3.9	11.9	11.10	132.09
Red Label	L	4	1.5	5.5	10.76	59.18
Black Label	L	1	4.1	5.1	13.87	70.74

Figure 7.9 Storeroom and bar inventory sheet.

from all relevant requisitions completed for that period. Opening Inventory plus Purchases for Period less Requisitions for Period provides the Closing Inventory amount. This can be compared with the Actual Inventory for the end of the period. You can expect minor differences between the two sets of figures because the item cost figures taken from invoiced amounts are rounded to the nearest cent on the perpetual inventory cards and requisitions. Differences of more than a few dollars should be investigated to try to determine the cause.

Bar Inventory

As far as beverage inventory is concerned up to this point, only the storeroom inventory and control have been discussed. At the end of each accounting period, you must include in total inventory the value of all items in each of the bars in your establishment. At each bar, there will be an inventory of items previously requisitioned from the storeroom that have not yet been used. Those items should be inventoried and costed so that your periodic beverage cost of sales can be calculated. A combined storeroom and bar inventory form is illustrated in Figure 7.9.

EIGHT

Bar Control Methods

METHODS OF THEFT OR FRAUD

As discussed in the preceding chapter, control of your beverage storeroom is relatively easy using the procedures outlined. Unfortunately, control of the bar is not so straightforward. This is particularly true where your bartenders are also responsible for handling cash from sales. There are many opportunities for theft or fraud if a bartender or beverage server is dishonest:

- Underpouring five drinks by, let us say, one-sixth the normal measure; not recording the sale of each sixth drink; and pocketing the cash from that drink; or using personal drink measuring devices (shot glasses or jiggers) that are smaller than the house ones, with the objective of achieving the same result.

- Diluting liquor with water and keeping the cash from the additional drinks sold. This is particularly easy to do with gin, vodka, and tequila because there will be no color change. With the "brown" liquors any color change can be reversed by also adding a little tea. If the bartender only uses diluted brands with mixed drinks, customers are highly unlikely to notice any taste change. The only effective way to check for this is by chemical analysis.

- Bringing in liquor bottles purchased personally, selling the contents, not recording the sales, and pocketing the cash.

- Not recording the sales of individual drinks until they add up to the normal number of drinks from a full bottle, recording the sale as a cash sale of a full bottle, and disposing of the bottle. Because the full-bottle sale price is normally less than the accumulated sales of individual drinks, the bartender can pocket the difference.

- Substituting a house brand for a call brand (that usually sells at a higher price), charging for the call brand, and pocketing the difference. A more serious substitution occurs when an empty call-brand bottle is filled with a house brand. In this case, the substituted brand can be poured with no one aware that the wrong bottle is being used.

- Selling drinks; recording them as spilled, complimentary, or "walk-outs"; and pocketing the cash.
- Overcharging the number of drinks served to a group of customers who are running up a tab to be paid later.
- If automatic drink measuring and dispensing devices are used, obtaining the contents for (let us say) five drinks, spreading this content into six glasses, and pocketing the cash from the sixth drink.
- Overpouring drinks (and underpouring others to compensate) to influence a larger tip or induce a guest to "buy" the bartender a drink.
- Using private sales checks rather than those authorized by your restaurant.
- Reusing an already paid sales check.
- "Losing" sales checks after the guest has paid.
- Changing sales check items and prices after the customer has paid.
- Bringing in empty bottles, exchanging them from the storeroom for full ones, and selling from the full ones without recording the sales.
- Using a fraudulently obtained credit card to convert cash sales to charge sales and pocketing the cash.
- Using a customer's legitimate credit card, running through some blank charge vouchers with that card, and later converting cash sales to those vouchers. (A bartender doing this will eventually be caught as a result of complaints from the credit card issuing company about the fraudulent charges.)
- At banquet functions that are "hosted" functions (a "hosted" function is one in which the hosting organization pays for all drinks that customers consume), removing unsold bottles for personal use or transferring them for sale at the regular bar and pocketing the cash, and charging the hosting organization for those bottles.
- Recording the sale of every drink, but from time to time registering the sale as a beer (rather than a more expensive highball or cocktail) and removing the difference in cash.
- Prerecording and registering the sale of drinks that have not actually been sold at lower than normal prices during the "happy" hour and pocketing the cash difference when these drinks are actually sold at higher prices after the happy hour. Alternatively, unsold drinks can be recorded as sales during normal periods, and when they are actually sold at higher prices during an entertainment period a bartender can again pocket the difference in cash. Use of differently colored guest checks during these special periods may help prevent this.

- Not recording sales of straight soft drinks because the sales revenue from them is often not controlled in many bars.
- Breaking a "used" empty bottle, claiming it was an accidental breakage of a full one, and receiving as a replacement a full one that can be sold to the benefit of the bartender.
- Short-pouring cocktails that contain a number of different alcoholic ingredients and filling them up with extra amounts of nonalcoholic ingredients, such as cream, egg white, or lemon juice.

Management Awareness

Your awareness of these and other dishonest practices and supervision to ensure they do not occur can be preventive measures. In particular, you should watch for collections of toothpicks, matches, small coins, or any similar items that a bartender may have at the working station to keep track of how much to remove in cash at the end of the shift.

But even implementing all possible control procedures cannot guarantee that nothing will go wrong. For example, consider the par stock control procedure outlined in Chapter 7. If a par stock policy is in effect and personal bottles were brought in by bartenders, this would mean that there were more bottles of that brand at the bar than there should be. But you will not discover this unless you check the par stock from time to time by randomly counting and verifying it against the par stock list. Without this spot check, the par stock policy will not provide an effective control. Similarly, for bottle coding to be effective, bottles at the bar need to be spot-checked to ensure that they have your restaurant's proper code on them.

You may choose to use one of the many security firms who have trained "spotters" expert at posing as regular bar customers and observing common forms of bartender theft. If such people are employed to help determine whether your bar is being properly run, make sure that they are familiar with your operation's policies, systems, rules, and prices so they know what to look for.

CONTROL REQUIREMENTS

The control methods that follow concentrate on control of liquor, rather than beer or wine, because in the typical bar liquor sales account for the greatest part of total sales, and losses, theft, or fraud are more likely to occur with liquor than with other alcoholic beverages.

The control techniques described for liquor, however, can be applied equally well — often in a simplified form — to control wine and beer. Make sure that your sales register breaks down sales into the three basic categories: liquor, beer, and wine.

Standard Recipes

Regardless of the type of bar and control methods used, you must first establish standard recipes for each type of drink. It may seem strange to talk about recipes for liquor, but even defining the amount of liquor to be served in a standard measure constitutes a "recipe."

Because most drinks in the typical bar are simply a standard portion of liquor, usually measured by some type of pouring or measuring device, recipes are generally easy to prepare. Standard recipes should include the amount of ice, water, carbonated beverage, or juice to include.

For cocktails, the recipes will be more lengthy because they will include the quantities of all liquid ingredients used and, where required, the garnish (such as cherry, olive, or fruit slice). Cocktail food ingredients are usually considered part of beverage cost and must be included in the recipe.

The type and quantity of ice in cocktails and the mixing method used are quite important (and, therefore, should be included in the recipe) because they affect the quantity and quality of the drink served.

The type and size of glass for each type of drink offered on your drink list should also be part of the recipe. Drink appearance is important. Drinks must appear attractive, and a 2-ounce martini served in a 6-ounce serving glass could appear to be a short measure to a customer. Alternatively, a highball drink served in too small a glass with insufficient mixer may taste too strong.

When all recipes are developed, you should provide a copy of them to each bartender. It is important that all your bartenders be familiar with and follow these recipes.

Costing Drinks

Your standard recipes control the quantities of liquor used and thus your beverage cost. From recipes, you can calculate the cost of each drink. The standard cost of each drink is what it should be if all procedures are correctly followed. Drink standard costs should be updated when ingredient purchase costs change.

Only by calculating drink costs can you establish selling prices that will yield an appropriate beverage cost percentage. A typical costed recipe showing the standard cost for a Rye Alexander is illustrated in Figure 8.1. Note that the procedure for making the drink is incorporated in the recipe.

A simplified method of costing drinks is to cost only the main alco-

Drink: Rye Alexander					
Ingredient	Quantity	Cost	Cost	Cost	Cost
House rye	3/4 oz.	$0.25	$0.28		
Crème de cacao, dark	3/4 oz.	0.30	0.32		
Cream	3 oz.	0.10	0.11		
Total cost		$0.65	$0.71		
Selling price		2.50	2.75		
Cost percentage		26.0%	25.8%		
Method: Shake all ingredients with small-cubed ice. Pour through strainer into 6 oz. champagne glass. Sprinkle with nutmeg.					

Figure 8.1 Drink recipe.

holic ingredient or ingredients (house rye and crème de cacao in Figure 8.1) and then add an allowance (for example, 10 percent) for other ingredients. Obviously, this method is easier than costing each ingredient, but it may not provide the true cost for your drinks and could provide misleading information when actual performance at your bar is evaluated by one or more of the control methods to be outlined later in this chapter.

Measuring Devices

Bartenders must be provided with appropriate measuring devices. Allowing them to free-pour liquor is asking for trouble even if they complain that it is slowing them down.

There are two types of measuring device (apart from those attached to automatic or electronic dispensing equipment). These are shot glasses and jiggers. The shot glass is primarily used for basic "highball" drinks, for example, 1 ounce or 1¼ ounces (or the equivalent in metric). Shot glasses can be purchased with or without engraved lines below the top rim. It is preferable to use lined glasses because you can then see whether a full measure is served.

The jigger measures smaller quantities of ingredients, for example, ¼ ounce or ⅓ ounce (or their equivalent in metric) for cocktails. Because the jigger is usually made of stainless steel it is not very effective for controlling underpouring. Jiggers are also often an inverted cone shape, and it is easy for a dishonest bartender to fill the jigger to just below the rim and quickly pour the contents into a serving glass. Because most of this volume is at the wide top of the cone, even a slight underpour can provide significant extra liquor for the bartender's profit.

You must check measuring devices from time to time to ensure that bartenders have not substituted devices containing a smaller measure.

Keep Full-Bottle Sales Separate

In some jurisdictions, bars are allowed to sell full bottles of liquor for off-premise consumption. The price to the customer of the full bottle is generally considerably less than the price of an equivalent number of individual drinks. For this reason, sales revenue derived from full-bottle sales should be distinguished from revenue from individual drink sales. The reason for this will become clear later in the chapter.

Interbar Transfers

In some restaurants, there may be more than one bar. In such situations it is sometimes necessary to transfer bottles of beverages from one to another. In such cases, an interbar transfer form is useful, because it will ensure that each bar's costs can be separated for later analysis. An interbar transfer form is illustrated in Figure 8.2.

Spillage Allowance

You may want to permit a spillage allowance. This allowance recognizes that it is not practical (in the absence of mechanical or electronic dispensing/measuring devices) to expect each bottle's contents to be accounted for to the last drop. Also, drinks may be wrongly mixed and have to be discarded. Some inadvertent overpouring may also occur.

To compensate for these types of error, a spillage allowance for each bottle of liquor used may be permitted. For example, if there were normally thirty-four standard drinks in a bottle of liquor if all drinks were correctly measured, a spillage allowance of one drink per bottle may be

From Main bar				
To Service bar		Date March 10		
Item	Size	Quantity	Unit Cost	Total Cost
House rum	L	3	$10.20	$30.60
Ordered by _____		Filled by _____		

Figure 8.2   Interbar transfer form.

established, and you would expect to account for only thirty-three drinks per bottle.

Remember, however, that if a generous spillage allowance is made known to bartenders they may be tempted to take advantage of it for individual gain.

In this chapter we will take a look at four of the most frequently used liquor control methods:

Requisition control

Standard cost control

Quantity (ounce) control

Standard revenue control

REQUISITION CONTROL

One of the easiest "control" methods to use is based on daily requisitions that the bartender completes to obtain full bottles from the beverage storeroom. Daily requisitions are costed, extended, and totaled to arrive at the total cost of beverage sales for the day. That cost can then be divided by sales and multiplied by 100 to arrive at a cost percentage.

As illustrated in Figure 8.3, each daily cost and sales figure can be accumulated to give the To-date figure. For example, on June 2 the To-date Cost figure is the accumulation of the Today amounts for both June 1 and June 2, or $252.75 + $201.76 = $454.51. On June 3, the June 2 To-date Cost figure is brought forward and added to the June 3 Today Cost figure of $384.58 to give the June 3 To-date amount of $839.09. The To-date Sales figures are calculated in the same way.

	Cost		Sales		Cost (%)	
Date	Today	To-date	Today	To-date	Today	To-date
June 1	$252.75	$ 252.75	$1,001.50	$1,001.50	25.2%	25.2%
2	201.76	454.51	963.10	1,964.60	20.9	23.1
3	384.58	839.09	1,401.90	3,366.50	27.4	24.9
4	280.25	1,119.34	1,096.55	4,463.05	25.6	25.1
5	651.06	1,770.40	2,711.05	7,174.10	24.0	24.7
6	503.78	2,274.18	2,118.75	9,292.85	23.8	24.5

Figure 8.3 Requisition cost and sales record.

The Today Cost Percentage figures are calculated by dividing the Today Cost figure by the Today Sales figure and multiplying by 100, or by dividing the To-date Cost figure by the To-date Sales figure and multiplying by 100. For example, on June 6 the Today Cost Percentage figure is

$$(\$503.78/\$2,118.75) \times 100 = 23.8\%$$

and the To-date Cost Percentage figure is

$$(\$2,274.18/\$9,292.85) \times 100 = 24.5\%$$

Advantages and Disadvantages

The advantage of the requisition control method is that it is fast and simple and does not require that an inventory be taken. A major disadvantage is that it may not be accurate because it assumes (unless this is adjusted for) that there are no partly full bottles of liquor in the bar at the end of each day. Because that is highly unlikely, the cost figure could be considerably wrong (either too high or too low) on a daily basis.

Over time, however, the daily highs and lows tend to even out, and the accumulated average by the end of a week should fairly accurately reflect your bar's actual cost of sales for each period. The actual cost can be compared with previous periods' costs to see whether it is within "normal" limits.

Another major problem with this method is that, despite its simplicity and the fact that it shows what the cost actually was, it provides no information about what the cost should be! In other words, you have no means of comparing the actual result with a standard. The standard cost control method rectifies that problem.

STANDARD COST CONTROL

A standard cost (based on accurate costing of recipes) is what the cost should be for a given level of sales. The standard cost control method compares the standard cost for a period of time with the actual cost for that same period. The cost comparison can be either in dollars of cost or in percentage of cost (cost of sales as a percentage of revenue). If your restaurant has more than one bar, cost information should be separated for each bar. To use this method, you need to have a record of the number of each drink sold. With the electronic sales registers presently available, a tally of drinks by type is easy to maintain. The actual count of each type of drink sold during the period is multiplied by its recipe (or standard) cost and by its selling price.

Drink	Drink Cost	Drink Selling Price	Quantity Sold	Total Standard Cost	Total Standard Sales
House rye	$0.35	$1.80	830	$ 290.05	$1,494.00
House gin	0.30	1.50	420	126.00	630.00
House rum	0.32	1.80	315	100.80	567.00
Totals				$1,218.10	$4,937.70

Standard cost percent $\dfrac{\$1,218.10}{\$4,937.70} \times 100 = 24.7\%$

Actual cost percent $\dfrac{\$1,237.80}{\$4,937.70} \times 100 = 25.1$

Difference $\quad\quad\quad\quad\quad\quad\quad\quad\quad 0.4\%$

Figure 8.4 Standard cost control calculation.

Figure 8.4 illustrates how total standard cost and total standard cost percentage are calculated. The actual cost figure for the same period is calculated as follows:

> Inventory at bar at beginning of period
> + Value of requisitions filled during period
> − Inventory at bar at the end of the period

The actual cost figure may have to be adjusted for interbar transfers (Figure 8.2).

Differences

With the standard cost control method, the difference between the standard and actual cost percentages should normally be no larger than 0.5 percent. Note that it is 0.4 percent in Figure 8.4. Any difference greater than 0.5 percent should be checked. You would normally expect the actual cost to be higher than the standard cost because the standard cost is based on what the cost should be if no errors are made.

Full-bottle Adjustment

If any bottles were sold as full bottles for less revenue than if those bottles were sold by the individual drink, you must adjust both cost and revenue figures for those full-bottle sales because otherwise comparison of standard and actual figures will not be very meaningful.

Sales Mix Change

Finally, note that with this method, the standard cost percentage for each period will change because during each period the actual quantities sold of each drink are used. Unless these quantities stay the same each period (and it is highly unlikely that they would), each subsequent period's standard cost percentage will be affected by the changed sales mix.

QUANTITY (OUNCE) CONTROL

Another useful bar control method is quantity (ounce) control. This method ignores both cost and sales dollars and uses only quantities used and sold, comparing the quantity of each type of liquor used in ounces according to inventory records with the quantity used in ounces according to sales records.

Consider the following illustration for just one type of liquor: house rum. Suppose (in addition to rum highballs) a bar served four other drinks that contained rum and the following figures show the Rum Quantity and number of Drinks Sold for each of these five drinks during a certain period:

Drink	Rum Quantity	Drinks Sold	Total Rum Sold
Rum highball	1.5 oz.	336	504 oz.
Drink #2	1.25	208	260
Drink #3	1	106	106
Drink #4	1.75	128	224
Drink #5	1.5	56	84
			1,178 oz.

The Total Rum Sold figure is calculated by multiplying (for each of the drinks) the Rum Quantity by the Drinks Sold. As you can see, 1,178 ounces has been sold. Assume that inventory records show that the opening inventory of rum was 4.6 bottles, 46 bottles were issued by requisition, there were no interbar transfers, and the closing inventory was 3.7 bottles. Assuming 750-milliliter (25-ounce) bottles of rum are used, inventory records then show 1,172 ounces used:

$$4.6 + 46.0 - 3.7 = 46.9 \times 25 \text{ oz.} = 1,172 \text{ oz.}$$

The difference between the two figures is 6 ounces. This would normally be quite satisfactory, since part bottles are estimated in tenths and a mistake in estimating a part bottle by one-tenth represents 2.5 ounces in a 25-ounce bottle.

If a spillage amount were permitted in this bar, the inventory usage figures would be adjusted to compensate. For example, if there were a 1-ounce spillage per bottle, the 46.9 bottles used according to inventory would be multiplied by 24 instead of 25 ounces.

Even though the quantity control method has been demonstrated using ounces, it can just as easily be used with metric numbers. Note also that quantity control is not dependent on percentage figures. The cost percentage could go up and down daily, but as long as the ounce (or metric) numbers were in line there would be no need for concern.

Time Problem

The quantity control method calculations illustrated were for only one type of liquor. Some restaurant operators argue that it is too time-consuming to complete an entire inventory control using this method, unless the sales register can provide sales quantities converted to total ounces by brand or type of liquor.

Alternatively, since in the typical bar 80 to 90 percent of all liquor sold is from the basic house brands of the most common liquors (rye, rum, scotch, gin, vodka, and bourbon), it may be possible to use this method only for those six brands because loss or fraud is most likely to occur in the high-selling items.

A suggestion is to control each of these high-selling brands on a rotational basis or to use quantity control in conjunction with either the standard cost method (discussed earlier) or the standard revenue method (to be discussed in the next section) where those methods show a higher than normal variance for any particular period. In other words, you can use the quantity control method to isolate the variance (shown by either of the other two methods) to a particular type of liquor.

STANDARD REVENUE CONTROL

Another method of control is to use standard revenue as the measuring objective. This method is sometimes referred to as the potential revenue (or sales) control method. It is not concerned at all with cost percentages. However, it is probably the most common method used by restaurant bar operators today because most of them do not have a detailed record of every type of drink sold that the standard cost control and quantity (ounce) control methods require.

The standard revenue control method converts the quantity of liquor used (according to inventory records) into standard revenue to be compared with actual revenue from sales. The method assigns a standard sales or revenue value that each type or brand of liquor should produce per bottle used.

Standard Revenue per Bottle

In a simple situation, it is easy to calculate the standard revenue per bottle. For example, if 1-ounce bar drinks are sold, then a 750-milliliter (25-ounce) bottle of house gin should produce 25 drinks (assuming no spillage allowance). If a gin highball sells for $1.80, then standard revenue for house gin is

$$25 \times \$1.80 = \$45.00$$

If metric measures are used, the approach is no different. For example, if gin is purchased in liter (1,000-milliliter) bottles, and if the standard drink calls for 30 milliliters of gin with a selling price of $1.80, the standard revenue for that liter bottle of gin will be

$$\frac{1,000}{30} \times \$1.80 = \$60.00$$

Unfortunately, the contents of a bottle of house gin (and other types of liquor) are seldom dispensed in the same quantities for all drinks served. For example, even though the basic portion of gin in a highball is 1 ounce, it might be served in 1.5-ounce portions in martinis and in different portion sizes in other types of cocktail. To solve this dilemma, you can use a weighted average to calculate the standard revenue per bottle for each type of liquor used.

Weighted Average

To calculate a weighted average, you must first tally up all the various kinds of drinks sold during a test period. Your sales register (particularly if it is an electronic one) should be able to provide this information readily.

The test period should be for at least one week to even out the daily changes in the sales mix. Suppose that your test period showed the following for drinks that contain gin:

Drink	Quantity Sold
Highball	1,600
Martini	600
Drink #3	100
Drink #4	50
Drink #5	80

The next step is to multiply the quantity of each drink sold by the amount of gin it contains:

Drink	Quantity Sold	Gin Quantity	Total Gin
Highball	1,600	1.25 oz.	2,000 oz.
Martini	600	1.75	1,050
Drink #3	100	1	100
Drink #4	50	1.5	75
Drink #5	80	1.25	100
			3,325 oz.

The total amount of gin used is, therefore, 3,325 ounces, and if you are using 750-milliliter (25-ounce) bottles, 133 bottles (3,325 ounces divided by 25 ounces) have been used.

At this point, you must determine the total sales derived during the test period for drinks containing gin. Again, it is possible that your sales register can provide this information. Alternatively, it can be calculated as follows:

Drink	Quantity Sold	Selling Price	Total Sales
Highball	1,600	$2.00	$3,200
Martini	600	2.50	1,500
Drink #3	100	1.75	175
Drink #4	50	1.80	90
Drink #5	80	1.60	128
			$5,093

The final step is to divide the total sales by the number of bottles sold to obtain the standard revenue for each 25-ounce bottle of gin:

$$\frac{\$5,093}{133} = \$38.29$$

If metric measures are being used, the approach is just the same. You would have to make similar calculations for each separate type of liquor carried in inventory. Once the calculations are made, the standard revenue control method is easy to use.

Simply add the inventory at the bar at the beginning of the control period (a week, ten days, a month, depending on your policy) to the quantity of bottles requisitioned from the storeroom during that period and then deduct the inventory at the bar at the end of the period. Figure 8.5 shows how the calculations are made.

Note in this figure that part bottles of liquor are measured in tenths because accuracy in ounces is not necessary. Quantities used of each type of liquor are simply multiplied by their previously calculated standard revenue values, and, finally, total standard revenue is compared with actual revenue.

Differences Allowed

Any difference between total standard revenue and actual revenue (from the sales register) should be no more than 1 percent of standard revenue. In other words, you would expect actual revenue to range from 1 percent below standard to 1 percent above.

In Figure 8.5, 1 percent of standard revenue of $2,502.20 is $25.02 and the calculated difference is only $11.30. Therefore, the difference would be acceptable.

You expect a difference because the standard revenue per bottle calcu-

	Opening Inventory	Added per Requisitions	Total	Closing Inventory	Used	Standard Revenue per Bottle	Total Standard Revenue
House rye	2.6	18.0	20.6	2.9	17.7	$40.20	$ 711.54
House rum	4.1	9.0	13.1	4.2	8.9	41.80	372.02
House gin	0.9	6.0	6.9	1.4	5.5	35.90	197.45

Total standard revenue		$2,502.20
Total actual revenue		2,490.90
Difference		$ 11.30

Figure 8.5 Calculation of total standard revenue.

lations are based on the historic sales mix for each type of liquor used during the test period. It is unlikely that the sales mix will stay the same in all future periods.

Therefore, it might be a good idea to test the sales mix for various types of liquor from time to time so that standard revenue figures per bottle do not drift too far out of line. This is particularly true if your bar is in a seasonal area where customer tastes (and therefore the sales mix) change with changing weather conditions.

Obviously, if recipe portion sizes or drink selling prices are changed, you must recalculate standard revenue per bottle figures.

Shortcut Method

You can use a shortcut standard revenue control method by using requisitioned quantities multiplied by standard revenue per bottle to arrive at total standard revenue.

However, this shortcut has the same disadvantage as does the use of the requisition cost control method outlined earlier in the chapter. That is, it can be inaccurate because it takes no account of part bottles of liquor in inventory at the bar.

Nevertheless, even though this inaccuracy may exist on a daily basis, the part-bottle overages and shortages will tend to even out over time.

Full-Bottle Adjustments

If any full bottles are sold at less than the standard revenue per bottle, you must adjust for this in the total standard revenue calculations. The easiest way is to adjust the total standard revenue figure to bring it into line with actual revenue (including full-bottle sales).

In other words, if standard revenue per bottle of a particular liquor is $35, and a full bottle of that liquor is sold during the period at $20, deduct $15 from total standard revenue so that it can be compared correctly with total actual revenue.

Happy Hours

In bars where it is legal, prices of drinks are reduced during the so-called happy hour. At other times they may be increased to help pay for entertainment provided.

In such cases the standard revenue per bottle calculations must take this into consideration. Another alternative is to separate costs and sales for these special periods, even though that can create a great deal of extra work.

A problem associated with reducing drink prices during certain hours is that earlier sales made at regular prices may not all be recorded by bartenders in the sales register at that time. Sales are held over and recorded as sales made at the reduced prices, and bar employees keep the cash difference between the regular and lower prices.

This requires your supervision. In addition, you should calculate the amount of sales that are made during the happy hour or entertainment period as a percentage of total sales each day and watch for deviations from normal in this percentage.

BANQUET CONTROL

If your restaurant operates a banquet department with its own liquor storage area, you can control that storeroom and bar in the same way as for any other bar by using one or more of the methods described in this chapter.

If your banquet department does not have its own controlled, locked storage room, it must requisition needed beverages for each separate banquet function from the main storeroom or bar, returning unused quantities to that storeroom or bar at the end of the banquet. This is a double interbar transfer, and a specially designed form can be used to control these transfers and calculate the banquet beverage cost.

A form that would serve this end is illustrated in Figure 8.6. This form has space for the signatures of those responsible for both issuing and returning bottles. The Bottle Cost column figures are taken from the related perpetual inventory cards so that Total Cost information can be calculated. The Total Drinks column figures are calculated by multiplying the Bottles Used column figure by the Drinks per Bottle figure, rounded to the nearest whole number. Total Standard Revenue is the product of Total Drinks times Drink Selling Price.

Ticket Sales

The total number of drinks sold can be compared with the total number of tickets sold in a no-host banquet bar situation (a "no host" bar is one where each customer pays for his or her own drinks, as opposed to a hosted bar, where the association, group, or company organizing the function pays the entire bar tab). The total standard sales should also agree with the cash collected from ticket sales.

If tickets are sold for drinks, there can sometimes be a problem created by a bartender's having to sell tickets, handle cash, and possibly even ring up sales. Under pressure this can lead to errors and other problems.

Item	Size	Bottles Issued	Bottles Returned	Bottles Used	Bottle Cost	Total Cost	Drinks per Bottle	Total Drinks	Drink Selling Price	Total Standard Revenue
Room __Banquet__ Function __Contractor's Association__ Date __April 2__										
Bourbon	1 L	12.0	2.1	9.9	$6.00	$59.40	32	316	$1.50	$474.00
Scotch	0.75 L	5.0	2.0	3.0	$7.50	22.50	25	75	2.00	150.00
					Totals	$185.40		718		$841.00

Cost Percent $\dfrac{\$185.40}{\$841.00} \times 100 = 22.0\%$

Bottles issued by __G.A. Jones__   Returned by __R.J. Henton__
Bottles issued to __R.J. Henton__   Returned to __J.B. Cant__

Ticket Information	Ticket price	$1.50	$1.75	$2.00	$2.25				
	Closing number								
	Opening number								
	Tickets used								
	Less: voided								
	Tickets sold								
	Drinks sold								
	Differences								

Figure 8.6 Banquet liquor control form.

To overcome these problems, it may be a good idea to have a separate person (located away from the bar) sell tickets. The bartender simply exchanges tickets for drinks. Tickets can be color coded for differently priced drinks. The ticket seller's labor cost will more than likely be offset by the increased efficiency of the bartender and the reduced possibility of errors and/or bartender dishonesty.

The ticket seller and bartender, however, can still work together for dishonest purposes. For example, the bartender can hand back "used" tickets to the ticket seller so they can be resold and the two employees then split the profits.

To help prevent this, provide the bartender with a locked box with a slot on top into which used tickets must be immediately inserted when exchanged for drinks. Management supervision is also required.

If it is a hosted bar situation, then no ticket or cash handling is involved. In that case the total standard sales figure from Figure 8.6 will be the amount billed to the customer.

Note that in some host bar situations, the host organization is charged for all full bottles used and also for those opened. In other words, there is an agreed charge per bottle (rather than per drink) and the host pays full price for any partly used bottles.

Another variation is for the host to be charged a fixed fee per person per hour, regardless of how many drinks are consumed. You have to estimate the average number of drinks that the typical person will consume per hour. A rule of thumb is that in a "normal" situation, guests will have three drinks each during the first hour, two in the second, and one in the third (or an average of 6 divided by 3 = 2 drinks per hour). Thus, if there were a three-hour reception with 100 guests in attendance and drink selling price is $3.00, the organization will be charged

$$100 \times \$6 \times 3 \text{ hours} = \$1,800$$

regardless of how many drinks are actually consumed.

BEER AND WINE

The comments made up to now concerning bar control methods have been limited to liquor control. Beer and wine can also be controlled using any of the basic methods outlined. However, some additional comments follow.

Beer

For bottled or canned beer, you can use any of the control methods described (requisition control, standard cost control, quantity or ounce control, or standard revenue control).

For keg beer (also known as draft or tap beer), the problem is a little more complicated and offers opportunities for theft because it is often not so easy to control beer as distilled spirits.

The first step is to convert keg containers into total ounces of beer. This total-ounce figure can then be divided by the number of ounces served in your bar's standard beer glass. This will yield the number of servings that should be obtained from a keg. The number of servings can then be multiplied by the selling price of a glass to provide the total standard revenue from a keg.

However, beer kegs (because of their design) do not yield 100 percent of potential revenue because there is always a small amount of beer that cannot be extracted, and problems such as line pressure can cause excessive foam and beer loss at the dispensing tap. For these reasons, you can expect actual cash from a keg to be as much as 5 percent less than standard revenue.

It is important to make a daily (or even shift) calculation of the number of kegs used and compare this figure with revenue. Indeed, in some operations a register reading is taken after each keg is emptied so that the amount of revenue is known on a per-keg basis. Even where two or more different beers are on tap at different prices, control can still be maintained by having a separate sales register, or separate key on the register, for each type of beer. Unfortunately, when beer from the same keg is sold in different-sized glasses at different prices, control is more complicated.

One item in particular that you should monitor is the size or depth of head desired. The larger the head, the smaller the amount of beer in the glass. A dishonest bartender can significantly increase the number of servings per barrel (and make a personal gain as a result) by increasing the size of the head.

Wine

Sale and cost control of full bottles of wine can also be handled in the same way as liquor and canned or bottled beer sale and cost control.

However, one variable to be considered is bottled wine sold by the glass, particularly if your restaurant buys large glass containers (jug wine) and sells it as house wine by the liter, half liter, or glass.

The best way to handle house wine is to use the standard revenue control method, using a weighted average approach to establish the standard revenue for each type or brand of house wine carried.

MIXES AND GARNISHES COST

In most bars, the cost of mixes (carbonated beverages), food (for example, sugar, syrup, and eggs), and garnishes (orange slices, maraschino cherries, and similar items) is included as a cost of the particular drink recipe in which these ingredients are included. In other words, their cost is part of overall beverage or liquor cost.

You may find it useful to determine what percentage of total liquor sales these "other" ingredient costs constitute. This is simple enough to do because the cost of these items purchased, requisitioned, and used can be added up over a period of (let us say) a month and be divided by total liquor sales for that month.

For example, if these other ingredient costs for a typical month were $1,000 and your liquor sales $50,000, then ingredient costs would be

$$\$1,000/\$50,000 \times 100 = 2\% \text{ of liquor sales}$$

If your liquor sales next month were $60,000, ingredient costs that month ought to be

$$2\% \times \$60,000 = \$1,200$$

You should calculate the actual ingredient cost percentages from time to time so that any variations from what is considered "normal" can be detected.

DISPENSING EQUIPMENT

There are many types of automatic and electronic beverage dispensing equipment available for both alcoholic and nonalcoholic beverages. These vary from individual dispensing heads that attach to each bottle and require the bottle to be raised manually for pouring to systems that dispense from stored inverted bottles using gravity feed or pumps. In the latter case, liquids move through flexible plastic tubes to a dispensing head (linked electronically to a sales register) that dispenses a controlled portion size.

With the more expensive models, the dispenser will only operate if a sales check is inserted into the sales register before the appropriate sales keys are depressed. Bottles as large as a half gallon (approximately 1.75 liters) can be stored, attached to the system in a remote storeroom controlled by lock and key. One storage location can even serve several different bars. Sales can be recorded for each separate bar by brand, and even by bartender, on individual counters.

By using larger liquor bottles with dispensing equipment, a cost saving should occur because the cost per ounce is usually lower for the larger sizes. The same savings is not feasible with a manual pouring system because the weight of the glass containers makes it too difficult to pour from them.

Advantages

The following are some of the advantages of liquor dispensing systems:

- Sales control is improved, particularly if a drink cannot be served without going through the system. If this can be achieved, a critical control problem has been overcome. In such a situation, you do not need to worry about bartenders' bringing in their own bottles because the sales will be automatically recorded anyway and your restaurant will be entitled to the revenue! (Also, with a remote storeroom, by management observation you will easily spot unauthorized bottles at the bar). Cash control will thus be far more effective.

- Bartender errors from spillage and over- or underpouring are reduced or eliminated.

- Losses from liquor theft are reduced, particularly if your bar inventory is remote from the bar and only accessible to you or other authorized employees.
- Drink preparation may be faster and fewer bartenders needed.
- Bartender training may be lessened and employee turnover costs thus reduced.
- Less manual dexterity is required by bartenders.
- Back-bar space is freed.
- Accurate inventory information is available, with records of drinks sold by category and inventory constantly updated.
- Draft beer monitoring and pouring can be incorporated into some systems.
- Pricing decisions (for example, exactly when the happy hour begins) are not made by your employees. With many of the new systems, you can change the prices from a control panel in an office remote from the bar.

The more sophisticated and expensive electronic bar control systems provide direct cost savings such as accurate drink measuring, complete draining of all bottles, and labor cost savings. They also provide indirect benefits such as ease of control because each drink dispensed is individually recorded by a remote drink counter, resulting in reduced liquor losses.

You should never assume, however, that equipment can provide absolute control and that other controls and management supervision are no longer required. If your restaurant installs this type of equipment, you might well continue to rely on some of the traditional manual controls outlined earlier in this chapter, using as an aid the inventory information provided by the dispensing equipment drink counters.

Disadvantages

Consider also the disadvantages of automatic dispensing equipment:

- In some cases this equipment can slow drink service.
- Not all drinks can be dispensed through the equipment. Some (such as liqueurs with a high syrup density) may still have to be manually poured.
- The atmosphere of your bar and customer attitude may be against using dispensing equipment; in particular, customers may complain that they can no longer see the bottle from which the product is being poured.

- There will undoubtedly be employee resistance to change at the time the equipment is installed.

- In the event of equipment malfunction, it may be necessary to return to manual dispensing until the equipment is repaired. The cost of repair must also be considered and added to initial equipment costs.

Therefore, you must evaluate both the pros and cons before making the final decision.

Benefits of Information

Modern sales register equipment available to restaurant bars today can provide a great deal of information for rational and effective management decision making and control. In the past few years there have been major advances in the versatility of electronic information-producing equipment combined with a similar reduction in its cost. Your restaurant can benefit from this equipment in a number of ways:

- Numbers of customers and menu (beverage) selections can be translated into order quantities for effective inventory investment. Eventually, it may be possible to link suppliers directly to such systems to bypass some of the paperwork involved in manual ordering systems.

- Continually updated inventory printouts are available because inventory by brand recorded in the machine is automatically reduced as each individual drink sale is recorded. Purchases are added into inventory in the machine at the time of delivery from purchase invoices.

- Storeroom requisitions can be automatically produced on the basis of liquor used at the bar. In other words, automatic requisitioning is available each day (or even shift) to replenish to par stock.

- Drink recipes can be automatically cost-updated if the purchase price of any ingredient changes.

- Statistical information regarding what is and is not selling is available, thus allowing removal of dead stock, or the introduction of special promotions to use up that stock.

The availability of this information should not only be viewed as an asset to you (that is, more data on which to make decisions) but also as the opportunity to free up labor that would otherwise be occupied doing tedious manual work. This freed-up labor can then be put to creative use (improving the ambiance of your bar, creating special new drinks, paying more attention to customers' needs, and so on). Your employees would probably like this since it provides them the time to develop their skills through implementing positive control!

Evaluating Systems

In order to analyze and evaluate installing an automated alcoholic beverage system, you must ask, and obtain answers to, the following questions:

- What is the bar's present liquor cost percentage? What liquor cost saving is the system likely to provide?
- Can most of the drinks sold be routed through the system, or will many of them still have to be hand poured or mixed?
- How are the physical facilities (storage and bar areas) likely to be affected?
- How is employee productivity going to be improved, and will this have any effect on your management productivity and overall labor cost in the bar operation?
- Does the system do more than the bar really needs?
- How reliable is the manufacturer, with particular reference to repairs and service when equipment malfunctions?
- How reliable is the equipment? In other words, what has its performance record been in other restaurants?

This is just a bare-bones list of questions that should prompt others that may be unique to your restaurant's bar operation. You need to analyze your own operation carefully to be perfectly sure that the investment costs can be adequately covered by the benefits.

NINE

Employee Policies

In your restaurant, a major cost needing tight control is labor. Most restaurants have legal requirements that they must conform to with regard to employees, including paying minimum wage levels, providing statutory holidays, using fair employment practices, allowing employees to unionize and bargain collectively, maintaining safety standards, and making pay withholdings such as for income tax and unemployment insurance.

INSTITUTING POLICIES

In addition, you need to institute some sort of employee practices (or personnel policies) as a minimum first step toward controlling your labor cost. The owner of even the smallest restaurant usually has some personnel policies. An owner who simply says, "When I need a new employee, I'll hire the first person I can find who seems capable of doing the job, and I'll pay the minimum hourly rate" has established the following policies:

- When the decision to hire will be made.
- That no systematic advertising of job openings will be done.
- That the person hired must appear capable.
- What the rate of pay will be.

Job Descriptions

In formulating your restaurant's personnel policies, you need to develop job descriptions for each type of job or employee position. A job description states

- What a job entails.
- What routines must be performed.
- When those routines must be performed.

In a small restaurant, the job description may be so simple as specifying that an employee must welcome customers pleasantly and look after their needs.

In a large restaurant, each job has more complexities, and it may be difficult—particularly if several different jobs have to be filled—to remember the many aspects of each. For that reason, job descriptions are best put into writing, and when employees are to be hired you can provide them with a written copy of the job description.

There are no standard job descriptions that fit every restaurant. Although some common elements exist for any particular job type, the descriptions for each individual restaurant must be prepared for that operation.

Job descriptions should not be too detailed, but they should include sufficient information to enable both employee and supervisor to be certain of what duties the job entails. Job descriptions must be kept simple, must be easily understood, and should include the skills (such as an ability to get along with the public) that are required if the employee is to perform well in the job.

Task Procedures

In many small restaurants, positions or jobs require the employee to carry out a variety of different tasks during a shift or work period. Indeed, the smaller the restaurant the wider the variety of tasks is likely to be, since several jobs might be assigned to a single worker. In such cases, exactly how a particular task is to be performed should be detailed step by step. Task procedures should also be written.

Task procedures could, of course, be demonstrated and taught without first being written down, but your new employees will probably feel more comfortable—particularly if they are being shown a number of different sets of procedures that their job entails—if the demonstrated steps can be supported in writing.

EMPLOYEE SELECTION

Once you have defined job skills through job descriptions and task procedures, the next step is to match appropriate employees with positions available.

Finding Applicants

In small restaurants, advertising for employees can be done informally, through family connections or friends of present employees. This is certainly a cost-free method. Some restaurants advertise available positions in local newspapers to encourage as many prospective applicants as possible to apply, although this does cost money.

Sometimes it is useful to use personnel agencies (whose offices are generally found only in large cities) to seek out needed employees. If you provide the personnel agency with job descriptions of the positions that need to be filled, it can use its professional skills to match suitable candidates to your vacancies. This can be an expensive method of hiring, but it does provide a screening service. If you do your own screening, it can be a time-consuming task that involves sifting through applications and then interviewing. You must weigh the time saved by using a personnel agency against the cost of this service.

Application Form

An application form should be used each time a person applies for a job. Even if a position is not open at the time someone asks about a job vacancy, it is a good idea to have the person complete an application form anyway. A few days or weeks from now, you may have a vacancy that the applicant's qualifications could fill.

An application form is useful for summarizing in an orderly fashion basic information about job applicants. The form permits initial screening without having to interview each applicant. A typical application form is illustrated in Figure 9.1.

Interviewing

Interviewing all candidates who have submitted an acceptable application form can take considerable time. You may need to spend an hour with each one (thus the advantage of using a personnel agency to carry out this work). The time spent in interviewing is necessary, however, to ensure that the person who is finally offered the job has the best combination of technical and human skills for your restaurant.

Conduct all interviews in a private area or office. During the interview, you should have the individual's application form available and should be familiar with it so that relevant questions can be posed to the applicant about previous education or experience. You should have a prepared list of questions to ask all applicants, because consistency of evaluation is important.

You should ask questions about the applicant's present job (assuming that he or she has one) and why he or she wishes to leave that job. It may also be desirable to find out what the applicant's career expectations are. In other words, is the applicant too ambitious for the job you have available

Position applied for ———— Date ————————

How did you hear about this possible job opening? ————

Are there any reasons you may be unable to carry out some of the
normal job duties in this position? —————————————

If yes, explain ——————————————————

Name ————————————————————

Address ——————————————————

Town ———— State ——— Code ——— Telephone ———

Social security # —————————

What experience, training or education have you had that would
qualify you for this job? ————————————————

Why are you interested in this job? ——————————

Are you available for work:

Saturdays ——— Nights 6 to 2 ——— Days 10 to 6 ——— Sundays ———

Are you now employed? ——— If yes, where? —————————

References (names of previous employers preferred):

	Name	Company Name/Address/Tel #	Dates employed
1.			
2.			
3.			

Please sign below if you will consent to your present or previous
employer's release of information or discussion of previous performance with us.

Signature of applicant ——————————————

Figure 9.1   Application for employment.

and for the offered wage or salary rate? If technical skills in specific areas
are required, you should ensure that the applicant possesses the necessary
competence in those areas.

Opportunity for Questions

The applicant should have an opportunity to ask questions. You should
provide a job description and should be specific about working hours, rates
of pay, days off, and all other matters related to working conditions. If a
prospective employee is to report to a supervisor, rather than to you, the

applicant and the supervisor should meet. Give the supervisor input into the final selection of the candidate. If the supervisor is to continue to do a good job, there must be compatibility between him or her and any new employee hired.

Taking Notes

During the interview, you should make notes about the applicant and his or her reactions. Written notes can be placed directly on the application form. Alternatively, you could use an interview evaluation form such as that illustrated in Figure 9.2. In summary:

	High 5	4	3	2	Low 1
Date _____ Position _____					
Applicant name _____ Interviewer name _____					
1. General appearance and neatness					
2. Conduct during interview (poise, manners, tact, pleasantness)					
3. Communication skills, ability to explain, self-expression					
4. Apparent desire, motivation, and initiative					
5. Skills and apparent competence for job, previous experience, leadership potential					
6. Overall rating					

References contacted and comments:

1. _____

2. _____

3. _____

Summary of strengths and weaknesses:

_____

_____

_____

Interviewer's comments and recommendation for hiring or not:

_____

_____

_____

Figure 9.2 Interview evaluation form.

- Have a plan or pattern for all interviews.
- Make sure the applicant is at ease.
- Be attentive and interested in what the applicant has to say and do not interrupt.
- Give the applicant sufficient opportunity and time to respond to questions.
- Before closing the interview, invite the applicant to ask questions.
- If notes are not taken during the interview (because this can be distracting to the applicant), all resulting mental notes and impressions should be recorded immediately after the interview.

If an interview is well prepared and handled it can be an excellent screening device, can reinforce the information on the application form, and can reveal points that are not apparent on the application form. Sometimes, a second interview is useful for obtaining an even clearer impression and understanding of an applicant.

Closing the Interview

A good way to end an interview is to advise the applicant how he or she will be informed if selected for the job and approximately when that decision will be communicated.

References

If references are provided on the application form, you should consult them by telephone. If you do not follow them up, there is no purpose in asking for them on the application form. Telephone reference comments are easy to record, and people giving information on the telephone are more likely to be candid than if they are required to provide the reference in the form of a letter.

Information that can be requested of the applicant's previous employers includes the following:

- Job title and tasks performed.
- Dates of employment.
- Reason for leaving.
- Quality of work performed.
- Absenteeism and punctuality record.
- Personal characteristics, strengths, weaknesses, and overall effectiveness.

It may also be worthwhile to ask whether the previous employer would rehire the applicant and determine the reason(s) if the employer would not.

With the information and knowledge gained from employment application forms, interviews, and reference checks, you are in a position to decide which applicant to choose.

Finally, once the selection has been made the application forms of the candidates not selected should be kept. A week or month later a position might be available for which one of the unsuccessful candidates would be very suitable.

EMPLOYEE ORIENTATION

Every person employed should be given an orientation. Many employees are uncomfortable in a new job, and the orientation program serves as an introduction to the job and to your business. In a small restaurant, you should provide the orientation. In a large restaurant, this orientation should be given by the supervisor with whom the employee is to work. The orientation may include information about any or all of the following:

- Your restaurant's history, such as when it was started, who owns it, whether it is part of a chain or franchise, and its objectives.

- A copy of the organization chart (if your restaurant is large enough to need one), showing where the employee fits in and to whom he or she reports.

- A copy of the job description and task procedures.

- Hours of operation.

- When employee shifts are changed (frequency), how much advance notice of a change is given, and who produces these shift schedules.

- Employee vacation entitlement (how it is calculated and who produces vacation schedules) and statutory holidays.

- Employee dress and/or uniform requirements and (if uniforms are required) who maintains them and how frequently they are to be changed.

- Employee appearance and grooming requirements.

- Your policy on employee meals: their cost, when and where they are taken, and whether any items (such as coffee and/or soft drinks) are free.

- Employee conduct expected (promptness, attendance, how and to whom absence or illness should be reported).

- Pay policies such as paydays, deductions made, overtime rates, pay advances, and how work hours are determined (time clocks, and so on).

- Employee benefit entitlements (sick leave, health and/or life insurance, dental plan, and educational assistance).
- Employee training: who does it and how long it lasts.
- Probationary period, if any. (It is a good idea to hire new employees on a probationary basis. The job or the skill level at which the person was hired will determine the appropriate length of the probationary period.)
- Employee evaluation process (how it is handled, who does it, when it is done, and what happens to its results).
- Grounds for dismissal and dismissal procedures.
- Any special rules (such as safety, sanitation, smoking, bonding, or special policies for tipped employees).
- Policy on customer complaints and how they are to be handled by the employee who receives them.
- Introduction to fellow employees.
- For a large restaurant a tour of the facilities to show restricted areas, staff entrance, and location of time clocks, changing rooms, parking areas, and so forth, by you or a delegated employee.
- Opportunity for the new employee to ask questions during the orientation.

This list is only a suggested one, to be adapted for your operation. Many restaurant operators compile orientation facts into a written manual or handbook that the employee is required to study at the start of employment.

EMPLOYEE TRAINING

The orientation is the beginning of an ongoing employee training process. This process includes such matters as employees' learning what your operation's standards are and how they can be met, what level of performance is expected of new employees, and how to adapt to day-to-day situations as they arise. It should not be the employees' responsibility (even though in practice, unfortunately, that is often the case) to train themselves in these matters. The employee needs to be taught through discussion and demonstration, followed by practice. In small restaurants, training is usually done on the job by the owner or manager; in a larger operation, training is handled by the employee's supervisor. Proper training can

- reduce employee stress and absenteeism.
- lower employee turnover.
- limit costs due to careless use of supplies and equipment.
- improve sanitation and safety.
- increase employees' morale, cooperation, interest in the job, job knowledge, productivity, and chances for promotion.

In short, training leads to more satisfied customers and fosters professionalism.

Job Rotation

Job rotation is another useful technique you can use. Employees can be trained at different jobs so that they can be moved from one to another (where a union contract does not prohibit this) as the need arises. Besides giving the employee a variety of challenges, this ensures that employees can help out at different jobs in an emergency, reduces employee boredom, and (eventually) ensures that promoted employees make better supervisors because they have become familiar with all the jobs under their supervision.

EMPLOYEE EVALUATION

The final step in personnel planning is employee evaluation. If your restaurant is very small, evaluation may simply be handled through observation. By personal observation, you should quickly be able to determine whether or not a new employee is able to do a good job after proper training. Incompetent employees may have to be released or, if open positions are available, moved to a job whose demands on their skills are not so great. On the other hand, competent employees should be encouraged to continue to do a good job and should be challenged (with more responsibility) or promoted when possible.

Formal Evaluation

If your restaurant is a large one with many employees, evaluations will be more formal and may be carried out once or twice a year with each employee's supervisor instructed to fill out an evaluation form. In such situations, the employee should be allowed to read the completed evaluation and sign it to indicate acceptance of what it says. A sample evaluation form is illustrated in Figure 9.3.

	Excellent	Good	Average	Below average	Poor
Employee name _____ Position _____ Date employed _____ Date of evaluation _____					
Knowledge of job: Clear understanding of duties related to job and ability to do the job					
Dependability: Conscientious, punctual, reliable					
Courtesy: To guests, fellow employees, and supervisor					
Cooperation: Ability and willingness to work with supervisors and fellow employees					
Work quality: Thoroughness, neatness, accuracy and completeness					
Work quantity: Ability to handle assigned volume under normal pressures and conditions					
Personal qualities: Personality, sociability, integrity, leadership potential					
Appearance: Hygiene and neatness					

Overall performance: Satisfactory ( )   Unsatisfactory ( )

Supervisor's signature _____

Employee's signature _____

Figure 9.3 Employee evaluation form.

In evaluating, your supervisors should judge employees with reference to the whole job. For example, an employee should be evaluated on his or her performance with customers, with other employees, and with the supervisor—not just on one of those three specific relationships.

The evaluation must be carried out objectively, despite the fact that the process itself is subjective. In other words, personal bias for or against an employee should not be allowed to affect the assessment. In some restaurants, the responsibilities included in a job description are the basis for an employee evaluation. Indeed, some assessors believe that the points to be evaluated should match those on the job description.

Even if you do not formalize the evaluation on a document that the employee can see and read, the results of the evaluation, both the good and the bad points, should be discussed with the employee. Communicating with employees about their performance should improve that performance.

Pay Raises

The evaluation process also necessitates your considering pay raises at least once a year (unless these are negotiated with a union). In the absence of a union contract, the following factors influence the size of an employee's wage increase:

- Your restaurant's ability to pay higher wages.
- The demands of each job.
- The pay rate for each job compared to that for a similar job in competitive restaurants.
- The results of each employee's evaluation.
- The general inflation rate.
- The local supply of and demand for employees.

Promotions

Whenever job vacancies arise, it is usually a good idea to seek replacements from within the ranks of your present employees, particularly if this will create a promotion for a deserving employee. Employees who recognize that there are advancement opportunities within your restaurant have an incentive to stay, and they generally perform better.

Although seniority is sometimes the basis for promotion into a vacant position, that type of promotion should only occur if the person promoted has the necessary qualifications and capabilities for the new job, especially if it requires considerable responsibility and authority. Employee evaluation forms can be helpful in making promotion decisions.

Discipline

Your restaurant will likely have employment rules and regulations that employees are to follow. Some of these rules and regulations will be restrictive; others will be for safety reasons; and others still may serve to protect the employees' rights.

You should make sure that employees know and understand these rules during their orientation/training process. In some cases, where rules are broken, employees should simply be reminded of the rule(s). In other cases, disciplinary action may be necessary.

Such action could take the form of a written memo to the employee explaining the measures being taken in response to breaking the rule, identifying the specific incident that prompted the action, detailing any further action that might be taken if the rule is broken again, specifying a time frame after which a review of the situation will occur, and providing a method for the employee to acknowledge receipt of the warning or disciplinary action.

A copy of the memo should remain with the employee, a copy should go to the employee's supervisor (if there is one), and a copy (preferably with the employee's signature on it acknowledging that he or she has been made aware of the situation) should be placed in the employee's file.

Termination

Sometimes, employees must be disciplined by termination of employment. This should only occur as a last resort and only in response to the most critical of situations. Generally, you must show cause for dismissal. Cause can often be documented by the number of disciplinary action memos that have accumulated in the employee's file.

One of the values in having clearly written job descriptions is that they can indicate, at the time the employee is hired, the level of job performance required. If the employee has failed to meet that required level, and this fact can be supported by memos in the employee's file, then cause for termination can be documented.

If it is necessary to terminate an employee, the actual firing should be done in private on a one-to-one basis by the employee's supervisor or, in a small restaurant, by the owner or manager. The employee should be given reason(s) for termination. A good way to terminate the process is to emphasize the employee's strong points and perhaps suggest alternative employment opportunities for that person's future.

EMPLOYEE RECORDS

Your restaurant should maintain a record for each of its present employees. The record might simply be a file containing each employee's application form, a notation on each form of the employee's current wage or salary, and attached to it any other information that needs to be recorded (such as disciplinary warnings).

Alternatively, a separate employee record card or file should be started as each new employee is hired. Such a card is shown in Figure 9.4. You can use this card to record the date on which the employee was hired, the position filled, and the initial rate of pay. Subsequent changes in the status of the employee can be recorded as they occur, with the date of the change. Changes in status includes such information as a move to another job within the operation, a change in wage or salary, and the date when employment was terminated; each change recorded should be accompanied by the reason for the change, summarized in the Comment column.

Employee record cards or files are useful for providing up-to-date information about current employees and for preserving information about former employees who are being reemployed or where references are being checked by other prospective employers. Also placed in each employee's file should be the evaluation form (Figure 9.3) if a formal evaluation process is used. Any other correspondence or notes about the employee should also be placed in the employee file. In this way all relevant information about each employee is maintained in a single centralized location.

It is a good idea to arrange employee files or cards in alphabetical order. The records for current employees should be kept together, and new files should be inserted as new employees are hired. As employees leave, their records should be removed from the current employee group and placed, again in alphabetical order, with the files of all other former employees.

| Employee name _____ Date employed _____ |
| Initial position _____ |
| Starting wage/salary _____ |

Date	Change status to	New wage/salary	Comments

Figure 9.4   Employee record card.

As a general rule, you should keep the files of past employees for a minimum of two years and a maximum of five. When files are no longer needed, all the information in them should be destroyed.

Because employee files contain confidential information, access to them should be restricted to you or (in a large restaurant) a responsible person who is authorized to keep the employee records up-to-date.

EMPLOYEE TURNOVER

Because of the high cost of employee turnover you should try to reduce turnover in order to cut this cost. Turnover is the loss and replacement of an employee. One way to reduce turnover, particularly during a new employee's first few weeks on the job, is to observe the following four guidelines:

- Be honest about the job. Make sure that applicants understand both its good and its bad aspects.
- Make sure that applicants are not overqualified for the job. Overqualified individuals are likely to become unhappy and leave because they are not challenged.
- Monitor new employees' performance from the first day and let each new employee have early feedback of preliminary assessment.
- Watch for signs of trouble such as absenteeism or drinking on the job. If problems are evident, deal with the issue quickly to see whether the problem can be resolved to everyone's satisfaction.

Turnover Cost

Turnovers may be voluntary or involuntary. A voluntary turnover occurs when an employee leaves by choice. An involuntary turnover occurs when an employee has to be replaced because he or she is not suited for the job or for some other reason.

Both direct and indirect costs are associated with each turnover. Direct costs include such items as advertising for, recruiting, selecting, orienting, and training new employees. Indirect costs are more difficult to measure but are nevertheless there. For example, one cost is the low morale of other employees when good employees leave. This can also be translated into reduced customer satisfaction, compounded by the fact that the new employees may not initially provide the same quality of service. Double staffing, or overtime, may also be required while new employees are being trained. Also, an employee (knowing he or she is going to be leaving) might tend to reduce his or her level of service, adding to customer dissatisfaction and shifting the burden to other staff. Again, this affects staff morale.

Although turnover costs are difficult to calculate accurately, it has been estimated that they are as high as $500 per turnover. Because many restaurants have turnover rates as high as 200 or 300 percent a year, total turnover cost can be quite high. In a restaurant with 30 employees, a 200 percent turnover means that sixty job separations occurred during the year. If each turnover costs $500, total annual turnover cost would be

$$60 \times \$500 = \$30,000$$

Turnover Rate

One way to monitor this cost is to calculate the monthly turnover rate. The equation for this is

$$\frac{\text{Number of separations during month}}{\text{Number of employees on payroll}} \times 100$$

Suppose your restaurant has thirty employees and six separations occur during a month. The turnover rate would be

$$\frac{6}{30} \times 100 = 20\%$$

Annual turnover rates can be calculated in a similar way using annual figures.

```
Date___April 10___        Department _____Coffee shop_____

Employee name _____Darlene Robertson_____

Date employed  _____April 6_____

Length of employment _____4 days_____

Employee's reason for leaving ____States she was not made aware__
of shift hours

Supervisor's comment ____Was advised of shift hours when____
employed but was unable to handle job pressure

Action taken  _____None_____

Would supervisor reemploy? ___No_____

Supervisor's signature _____
```

Figure 9.5 Exit interview form.

DEPARTMENTS	VOLUNTARY					INVOLUNTARY				SERVICE				NUMBER OF SEPARATIONS		
	1.	2.	3.	4.		5.	6.	7.		a.	b.	c.				
	Personal	Opportunity	Dissatisfied	Unknown	TOTAL	Performance	Conduct	Staff reduction	TOTAL	Less than 30 days	1–12 months	Over 1 year	TOTAL	Average number on payroll	This month	Year-to-date
Front Office																
Reservation																
Sales																
Service																
Housekeeping																
Telephone																

Figure 9.6   Labor turnover analysis form.

Because of the high cost of employee turnover, your restaurant can profit by trying to reduce the turnover rate. Some turnovers are uncontrollable (for example, death, disability, or retirement). The remaining turnovers are controllable to a greater or lesser degree. One way to reduce the turnover rate is to try to determine the causes for turnovers and then attempt to correct the underlying problems. An exit interview form is useful for gathering information. If an employee leaves without notice and with no opportunity for an exit interview, some relevant information may be obtainable from fellow employees. A word of caution: the reason employees give for leaving and the real reason may not be the same; you must therefore try to determine the real reason. An exit interview form is illustrated in Figure 9.5, and a turnover analysis form appears in Figure 9.6.

TEN

Labor Cost Control

LABOR COST RATIOS

Because the restaurant industry is so diverse, it is impossible to be specific in establishing guidelines within which the labor cost as a percentage of sales should fall for any particular operation. (This also applies, of course, to food and beverage cost percentages discussed in earlier chapters.) For example, the labor cost for most restaurants will generally be between 25 percent and 35 percent of total sales. However, it could well be lower than 25 percent in some restaurants and higher than 35 percent in others.

Causes of Differences in Labor Cost

Many factors can cause these differences in labor cost from one restaurant to another. Some of these are:

Layout. Your restaurant's layout may dictate more or fewer employees on duty at any time than for similar restaurants. An efficiently planned restaurant layout will reduce the number of employees required. The age of the property can also be a factor. Older restaurants are usually less efficient by today's standards and also frequently require more labor for certain jobs.

Location. A well-located restaurant usually enjoys a higher level of business (and thus a reduced labor cost percentage) than a similar restaurant less well located. For example, if you operate a restaurant on a major highway it will, all other factors being equal, enjoy a higher sales level on average than a competitive restaurant located close by but not on a major highway. Similarly, a restaurant catering to the business-luncheon trade and located in the center of the business district will probably have a higher seat turnover, and thus higher revenue and lower labor cost percentage, than a similar restaurant located on the fringe of the business area.

Market Demands. The particular clientele that your restaurant caters to can be affected by the demands of the market and thus change the labor cost ratio. For example, a restaurant catering to the middle-income-bracket customer might find its sales dropping drastically and its labor cost percentage increasing as a proportion of revenue in recessionary times or when unseasonal weather continues for a long period. Weather can also affect certain types of operation on a daily basis. For example, a drive-in restaurant catering primarily to ice-cream-related menu items can have a high fluctuation in daily sales, and thus labor cost percentage, on cold, wet days.

Unions.   Restaurants whose employees are covered by a union contract generally have a higher labor cost relative to sales than establishments whose employees are not under union contract. Unions generally obtain higher levels of pay and more fringe benefits (which are a part of total labor cost) for their members.

Use of Equipment.   If you can use and afford certain items of restaurant equipment, you may be able to reduce the number of employees and thus their labor cost. More automated dishwashing machines, electronic liquor-dispensing systems, and computerized sales controls systems are all improvements that generally mean that fewer employees are required.

Menus.   Menu items offered can also affect your labor cost. The menu is often dictated by the type of market your restaurant is catering to, but the number of individual items offered, the amount of kitchen preparation time required, the style of service needed for certain menu items, and the availability and use of prepared or convenience foods are typical of the factors that can affect the labor cost.

Consider, for example, convenience foods. If you design your menu to make use primarily of prebutchered and preportioned meats, you will not need an employee on site to do the butchering. Your meat purchase prices will probably be higher (because the supplier is now doing the butchering), but your labor cost as a percentage of sales will decline, and you will probably find your combined food and labor cost percentage has also been reduced. The reason for this is that convenience foods have a labor cost "shelf" life. In other words, a butcher employed on site would normally be paid a full day's pay regardless of the volume of business. That wage cost is an expense for that day, even if the butcher has little or nothing to do. Convenience foods, on the other hand, with a built-in labor cost, do not become an expense until the product is actually sold. Deferring the labor cost expense in this way is a form of labor cost reduction.

PROBLEM OF PRODUCTIVITY

One of the key words in measuring employee performance, and in labor cost control, is productivity. Traditionally, it is thought that, for many reasons, the productivity of employees in the restaurant industry, which is measured in different ways, has been very low compared with productivity in many other industries. Whether comparisons with other industries (such as manufacturing) are fair is open to question. Some of the reasons why low productivity has prevailed and can be improved are discussed.

Fluctuating Sales Volume

The peaks and valleys of demand for the products and services offered by the typical restaurant, combined with an insensitivity of much of the labor cost to fluctuating and frequently unpredictable demand, can mean that at certain times you can do nothing about the productivity (or lack of it) of some employees. In other words, the industry generally has a high fixed labor cost, so that minor changes in volume of sales can have a major effect on labor cost ratios and net income. Figure 10.1 illustrates this. On a normal day, labor cost is 40 percent of revenue. On a good day, it drops to 37 percent; on a poor day, it jumps to 45 percent. The reason for these swings is that, even if you could adjust the variable portion of labor to revenue, the fixed portion cannot be changed.

Limited Ability to Produce for Inventory

Manufacturing industries that are subject to cyclical demand can continue to produce during low-demand periods and hold the goods in inventory until demand again increases. Productivity is stabilized and labor cost per unit of production can be held constant. This is not true of a restaurant. Since the industry is primarily a service one, it is impossible to store the

	Normal Day		Poor Day		Good Day	
Revenue	$1,000	100%	$800	100%	$1,200	100%
Food cost	400	40	320	40	480	40
Gross profit	$ 600	60%	$480	60%	$ 720	60%
Labor cost:						
Fixed	$200		$200		$200	
Variable 20% × Revenue	200	400	40	160	360	45	240	440	37
Income before other expenses	$ 200	20%	$120	15%	$ 280	23%

Figure 10.1 Effect of volume on labor cost.

labor cost. The only opportunity you may have to do this is to have food-production employees produce meals that can be frozen during low-demand periods. Alternatively, as mentioned earlier in this chapter, by using more convenience foods, the labor cost provided by suppliers and included in the price of the product can be stored. But a waiter's labor cost cannot be inventoried.

Lack of Labor-Saving Equipment

Since the industry is highly labor-intensive because of its service nature, it is difficult for you to replace employees with machines. Customers expect personal service. Where equipment can be introduced to reduce labor cost, then you should seriously consider this. For example, the use of certain types of beverage-dispensing equipment in a bar may mean that fewer bartenders are required.

Poor Facilities Layout

Poor layout is probably more common in older properties. For example, many older restaurant kitchens were designed when extensive menus were more common. Today's more limited menus save in some areas but may also mean that fewer kitchen employees now spend more time moving from one area to another, thus decreasing their productive time. However, many new restaurants are still designed without enough consideration given to employee movement (and thus employee productivity).

Poor Management and Supervision

One of your most important tasks in the improvement of productivity and the reduction of labor cost is to hire and train the right kind of supervisors (department heads or managers). These managers must in turn be competent at training their employees to be efficient. Such managers should be hired on the basis of their administrative skills combined with technical skills — not just their technical skills. A good technical employee may not be a good administrator. A superior waitress may make a poor dining room supervisor. The manager's or supervisor's skills should include such abilities as selecting good employees, training employees to be more productive, enforcing standards, motivating employees, preparing staffing schedules, maintaining employee morale (to reduce employee turnover), and implementing procedures to control both labor and other costs. A poor manager or supervisor will fail to extract the full potential from employees and thus will add to overall labor costs.

Part-time Employees

Part-time employees are often viewed as a solution to reducing high labor costs. However, these employees can create problems if their use is not carefully planned and implemented. Properly determining what is known as the "employee mix" between full- and part-time employees requires experience and judgment.

One of the problems is the hidden cost of a part-time employee. Although the total cost per day for a part-time person is obviously less than that for a full-time employee, you will need more individual employees than if only full-time employees were used. This entails a higher training cost for the extra people. There is also likely to be a higher turnover cost, which in turn increases the training cost for replacement employees. Other hidden costs relate to the potential unreliability of part-time employees. For example, since they may not have the same commitment to your restaurant that full-time employees have and since they may have full-time jobs elsewhere, absenteeism can occur because the full-time job takes precedence. That full-time job may even be a commitment as a home-maker! If the part-timers are students, their schoolwork (or even school vacations) can take precedence.

Part-time employees, however, can be an asset to your restaurant. For example, if your dining room has only a single turnover of seats at lunch, and two turnovers at dinner time, the full complement of employees required for the four-hour evening meal period cannot be gainfully sched-uled (and thus given a full eight hours work for the day) for the four-hour luncheon period. A sensible solution to this problem would be to hire the extra dinnertime employees needed from among applicants who only want to work part-time in the evening.

Fast-food restaurants, which frequently have several peaks and valleys of volume during a day, often hire students (who are only seeking part-time work) to work in their operations, scheduling most of them to work during the peak-volume periods. One of the advantages that fast-food operations have is that they can use mainly part-time employees, each of whom is given only a limited number of hours of work per week. All of these part-timers are on call, as required. Because of their large pool of potential employees, these establishments can overcome the absenteeism problem. When employees prove themselves to be reliable, they can be given more hours of work and preferred shifts as a reward. Employees who are not reliable are simply dropped from the pool.

Overtime

Overtime pay is sometimes inevitable, for example, in an emergency when service must be continued beyond normal hours because of an unanticipated demand or when there is no time for you to call in part-time people to cope with an unexpected demand situation. Overtime work is often seen as a cause of higher labor cost, but it can be used strategically as a tool to reduce labor cost.

For example, if you need an extra employee for two hours of work but, if called in, that employee must legally or by union agreement be paid for a minimum of four hours, it would be more profitable (less costly) to pay a full-time employee who has already worked a full shift to perform the extra two hours at time-and-a-half pay, which in this case amounts to the equivalent of three hours. The net saving is thus one hour of labor cost. It is also likely that the full-time employee is more skilled and better trained than the part-time employee who is called in only when the perceived need to avoid overtime arises. Overtime becomes an unnecessary cost when it is the result of poor planning.

Incentive Schemes

Some restaurants have successfully introduced incentive schemes to increase productivity. These include such practices as paying bonuses for low absenteeism and/or a good record of punctuality and giving extra pay for high productivity (for example, serving more customers than your restaurant's standard, although, in such cases, you must consider the possible reduction in quality of service provided to customers).

Increasing Demand

Mention was made earlier in this chapter about the high fixed labor cost of most restaurants. Rather than concentrate solely on a reduction of labor cost to conform to anticipated demand, an alternative might be to increase the demand during the slack periods. This is a matter of analyzing your market and establishing sales strategies that will increase demand. An optimum situation, though it may be difficult to achieve in practice, would be to have your restaurant always operating at peak demand. In this way, productivity of all employees could be maximized.

LABOR COST PERCENTAGE

In earlier chapters, both food cost percentage and beverage cost percentage were discussed as measures of the effectiveness of the food and beverage cost control systems. In both cases, it was emphasized that there may be difficulties in relying solely on the percentage as a basis for evaluating actual operating results. The main problem is that you can have a high cost percentage yielding a high gross profit or, alternatively, a low percentage yielding a low gross profit.

There may also be risks in relying on payroll labor cost percentage as a measure of labor cost control because labor cost percentage depends on five variables, some of which cannot be controlled:

1. The number of customers served. This number is normally unpredictable, other than in the case of banquet guests, when a guaranteed number has been contracted for.

2. The average check. This is relatively predictable, on the basis of past performance.

3. The number of employees called in on duty. This can usually be predicted and controlled on the basis of volume forecasts.

4. The hours worked by employees who are not on a fixed salary. This is a known factor (other than when unforeseen emergencies such as those requiring overtime hours arise).

5. The hourly wage rate. This is normally a known and predictable figure.

All of these variables are continually shifting with respect to each other. Some of them (such as the number of guests) shift randomly from day to day; others (such as wage rate increases) are relatively constant but shift over time. Therefore, you should only use labor cost as a percentage of sales as a planning and operating guideline. It should not be used as a real measure of payroll cost and employee productivity.

For example, labor cost percentage can decrease if your menu prices are increased while productivity goes down (for example, as fewer guests are served). This problem is not even apparent when you use labor cost percentage as a measure of labor cost control.

An analysis of labor cost that relies entirely on labor cost percentage has an additional pitfall. This problem, which is illustrated in Figure 10.1, relates to the fixed nature of a certain proportion of labor cost. This characteristic differentiates labor cost from food and beverage cost, which, almost without exception, are proportionate to sales (that is, they go up and down as sales go up and down). The effect of this fixed element may be hidden over time, when labor cost peaks and valleys offset each other and tend to smooth out what might otherwise be a volatile cost percentage.

If you exclude fixed salaries from labor cost before it is calculated as a percentage of sales, however, the measure may have some validity, particularly if fixed salaries are low in comparison to variable wages and if your restaurant can quickly adapt variable wages to fluctuating sales volume.

On the other hand, labor cost based on a standard of employee productivity predetermined on the basis of forecast volume of business overcomes the cost percentage problems. The remainder of this chapter discusses how to establish employee productivity standards and how to use them in labor cost planning and control.

LABOR PRODUCTIVITY STANDARDS

A preliminary step to the preparation of labor productivity standards is to ensure that your restaurant's quality standards are well understood. For example, the productivity of a waiter or waitress measured in number of customers served in a normal shift can be easily increased by reducing the time spent on each customer or having customers wait longer before being served. This is not a good idea if it reduces your quality standards and results in customer complaints.

Jobs in the restaurant industry can generally be categorized into three broad types: fixed cost employees, semifixed cost employees, and variable cost employees.

Fixed Cost Employees

Fixed cost employees, sometimes referred to as nonproductive employees, are those employees whose positions are not dependent on volume of sales unless there is a major change in this volume. These employees generally receive a monthly or annual salary, regardless of number of hours actually worked. As long as analysis of each position in this category shows that the employee is needed, no productivity standard is normally established.

Although fixed cost employee positions, as mentioned, are not generally affected by sales, employees in these positions can sometimes be used in slack times to assume jobs, either part- or full-time, that would otherwise be carried out by employees in the semifixed or variable categories. Although this does not affect the labor cost of fixed employees, it does reduce overall labor cost.

Semifixed Cost Employees

The production-related group of semifixed cost employees are those whose positions are dependent to some extent on the volume of sales. This dependence could be on a daily basis, or, alternatively, the employee might work each day but the hours of work (subject to a minimum guaranteed number of hours) might fluctuate daily according to sales volume. In order to have cost flexibility, these positions would normally have an hourly pay rate attached to them.

This category would include employees such as hostesses, cashiers, and food preparation employees. For each of these various positions, productivity standards should be established.

Variable Cost Employees

The employees in the variable cost group are entirely dependent on customer demand, both as to number of employees required each day and as to number of hours to be worked by each employee. Note that if your employees are covered by a union contract, these employees might still have to be paid for a minimum number of hours (for example, four) if called in any particular day. This category would include certain types of food-preparation employees, waiters, and waitresses. The establishment of productivity standards is most critical for this group of employees, particularly if your restaurant's volume fluctuates widely on a daily basis or even by meal period.

Establishing Productivity Standards

Although you could establish productivity standards based on past performance, there is no guarantee that past results were appropriate. For example, on the basis of historical records, the number of guests to be served by each waiter or waitress might be established at thirty during each four-hour meal period. How can you be sure thirty is the most productive number?

Observation of employees on the job is helpful in determining the best number of customers that the average, reasonably good waiter or waitress can cope with, keeping your quality standards in mind. The number will vary from one restaurant to another because of such matters as the layout of the business (for example, proximity of the kitchen food pickup area to the dining room), type of menu, whether or not alcoholic beverages are served and how far from the bar pickup area the dining area is, and type of clientele. (In some restaurants, the standards may be written into the union contract and thus are not subject to unilateral change by either party.)

After each type of position has been appropriately studied and all necessary factors considered, final standards should be established in discussion with the employees' department head if your restaurant has supervisors for each department.

Each standard consists of a number of customers or sales dollars that an employee is expected to "produce" within a certain period. Periods for food-preparation and bar personnel are usually for a normal shift. For restaurant serving employees, the period is a meal period. For example, a food waiter may be expected to serve twenty customers during the four-hour lunch period in the dining room.

In strictly beverage outlets (bars and lounges), the production standard is generally a monetary unit, for both bartenders and serving personnel. The reason is that the normal customer in an eating area has a meal, with or without drinks, and the time he sits there and his average spending fall within a relatively narrow range. This may not be true in a cocktail bar, where one customer may occupy a seat and have five $3 drinks. His average check would be $15. Alternatively, five different customers may occupy that seat in turn and each have a single $3 drink. The average check for each is $3. Thus, the number of customers served in a lounge is a less realistic standard than sales dollars.

Once standards have been established, you should review them from time to time and revise them if necessary. For example, the introduction of a new piece of equipment or a redesign of your restaurant could change the affected employees' productivity.

Staffing Guides

After standards are established, you must develop staffing guides department by department. These staffing guides indicate the number of employees required on duty for various levels of business volume. These staffing guides can be compiled in terms of monthly volume, but they are probably more useful if prepared on a weekly or even a daily volume basis in situations where staff levels can be adjusted daily in accordance with anticipated volume.

In developing the guides, you must consider both minimum and maximum volume levels. The minimum level identifies the minimum number of employees necessary to maintain a smooth operation. The maximum level is the point beyond which no additional staffing is allowed. For example, in a banquet, it would be useless to staff beyond the level required to handle the largest number of guests that could be seated at any one time. Figure 10.2 shows a partial weekly staffing guide for a coffee shop.

Just as productivity standards must be revised as conditions warrant, so, too, should your staffing guides. Remember, however, that staffing guides are an aid in labor cost analysis, not a substitute for it. You should use them for such purposes as discussing schedules with the responsible department heads; they should not be taken as a rigid guide for absolute implementation. Properly handled, they can provide a useful basis for negotiation with the relevant department heads when staffing schedule revisions are required.

Volume per week in covers	Category A Hostess Hours per week	Category B Waitress Hours per week	Category C Bus help Hours per week	Total Hours per week
Up to 1,260	120	224	112	456 min.
1,261–1,485	120	240	112	472
1,486–1,710	120	320	112	512
5,311–5,535	160	960	240	1,360 max.

Figure 10.2   Coffee shop staffing guide.

Forecasting

The next step in labor cost control is forecasting work-load units (covers served, dollars of revenue) for each department. These forecasts (budgets) are developed from records of past events adjusted for current factors. Although for budgeting purposes many restaurants forecast in months, for staffing these budgeted figures should be broken down on a weekly basis prior to each week of actual operations. In this way, the figures can be adjusted to reflect current conditions and recent trends that can affect your volume of business.

A sample restaurant volume forecast is illustrated in Figure 10.3. Even though these illustrated forecasts cover weekly periods, your figures should be revised daily if possible, and the related staffing guides should then be used for staff scheduling.

Period				June 9–15				
Department	Sunday 9	Monday 10	Tuesday 11	Wednesday 12	Thursday 13	Friday 14	Saturday 15	Totals
Coffee Shop								
Breakfast	150	210	285	280	290	260	190	1,665
Lunch	200	280	300	310	310	330	250	1,980
Dinner	115	180	195	195	210	210	110	1,215
Dining Room								
Lunch	—	180	200	225	180	175	225	1,185
Dinner	350	175	175	210	210	240	275	1,635

Figure 10.3   Restaurant volume forecast.

An alternative to scheduling on the basis of customer counts is to forecast dollars of sales and then to schedule labor on that basis. For example, if the standard is $20 of sales for each labor hour expended, and if sales are forecast at $1,000, then $1,000 divided by $20 = 50 hours of labor should be scheduled. The disadvantage of this method is that it is sales-based rather than customer-count-based. Nevertheless, you could use it in a beverage operation where the guest count is less meaningful than dollars of sales.

Staff Scheduling

There are two basic types of staff schedules: stacked or shift schedules and staggered schedules. Stacked (or shift) schedules would be used for fixed and/or semifixed cost employees who would normally work a full shift regardless of volume of business. For all other employees, staggered schedules must be used.

Even though your staffing guides indicate the number of employees or work-hours that are to be used for each level of sales, they do not indicate when those employees are to work. Generally, an analysis of number of customers served or dollars of revenue earned during each hour must be made. This analysis will indicate the low-, medium-, and high-volume periods. You should schedule employees so that the maximum number are on duty during high-volume periods and the minimum during low-volume periods, thus staggering the hours when employees are working.

A staggered schedule might appear as shown in Figure 10.4. This type of schedule reduces idle time, provides for overlap of employees, recognizes variations during the day in level of sales, and can lead to reduction or elimination of overtime costs. In most cases, you would prepare schedules for each department in advance, week by week, and would show, each

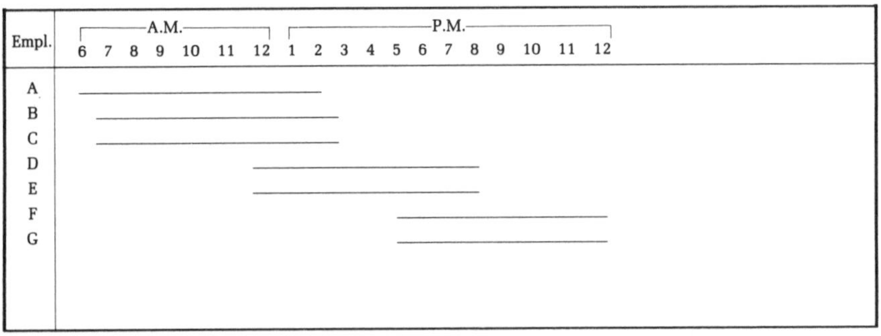

Figure 10.4 Staggered schedule.

Dining Room			Week Commencing	April 8			
Employee	Sunday	Monday	Tuesday	Wednesday	Thursday	Friday	Saturday
C. Jones	9-5	9-5	9-5	9-5	9-5	off	off
J. Hathaway	off	off	8-4	8-4	8-4	8-4	8-4
S. Heil	7-3	7-3	7-3	7-3	7-3	off	off
P. Mintz	12-8	12-8	12-8	off	off	12-8	12-8
A. Smith	7-3	7-3	off	off	7-3	7-3	7-3
C. Cody	10-5	10-5	10-5	10-5	off	off	8-4

Figure 10.5 Employee schedule.

day for each employee, the scheduled times of arrival and departure. These times would be subject to daily review prior to each workday for adjustment (where necessary) to a changed forecast. Days off would also appear on the schedule. A completed individual employee schedule is illustrated in Figure 10.5.

Once staff schedules have been completed, it may be useful to cost them out, calculating the cost percentage to see whether it meets your restaurant's overall labor cost percentage goal (if it has one). If the cost percentage does not meet this goal, rescheduling must be done where feasible within the established standards. Sometimes rescheduling is not feasible, because of the way the peaks and valleys of sales occur. If the overscheduling is permanent, a new labor cost percentage goal will probably be required.

Labor Cost Analysis

Since you can carry out volume forecasting and labor scheduling on a daily basis, an analysis of actual labor cost with forecast or budgeted cost can also be made daily. This daily analysis is much easier than daily food or beverage analysis because, with labor cost, you do not have to contend with the problem of inventories.

The analysis compares the actual work-hours or work-days used and to be paid for with the forecast work-hours or work-days for that day. In a large restaurant, the comparison can even be made by meal period. If your restaurant is a small one where daily variations are to be expected, the comparison might then be made on a weekly, biweekly, or monthly basis. In a small restaurant, it might well be that overstaffing and understaffing on individual days will even out and only minor variances will occur overall.

However, because the objective of labor cost analysis is to discover all variances, an analysis should preferably be made daily. In this way, you can determine the causes of all variances and the entire process of forecasting and thus controlling labor cost can be made more effective. Generally, variances can be caused by one or more of the following:

- Manpower guidelines that are inappropriate.
- Forecasts that are not accurate.
- Poor scheduling and excessive overtime.
- Volume fluctuations that were unpredictable.

When making comparisons between forecast and actual hours, and when this comparison is made on a man-days basis, then the hours of part-time employees must be converted to equivalent man-days. If the standard man-day for a full-time employee were eight hours, then equivalent man-days would be calculated by dividing total part-time hours for all such employees by 8. The actual hours figures would be taken from payroll records (time cards or sign-in/sign-out sheets).

Comparisons between forecast and actual figures can also be made on a dollar basis. This requires converting hours forecast and hours actually worked to dollars. In the case of hourly paid employees, hours are simply multiplied by the related hourly rate of pay. In the case of salaried employees, the daily rate will vary, depending on the number of days in a month. For example, an employee paid $1,500 a month is assumed to be responsible for his department even on days off and will have a daily rate of $50 during a thirty-day month and $48.39 during a thirty-one-day month.

If desired, the labor cost analysis could include labor cost percentage figures. This simply involves dividing each department's labor cost dollars by its sales and then multiplying by 100. But again do not rely too much on the percentage figures for analytical purposes. A sample daily labor cost analysis form is illustrated in Figure 10.6.

OTHER MEASUREMENT METHODS

To conclude this chapter, three other methods of measuring labor costs are discussed.

Sales per Man-hour by Department or Subdepartment Compared to a Standard

For example, if your sales were $1,000 and fifty hours of labor were expended to generate those sales, sales per man-hour would be $1,000 divided by 50 = $20. This $20 could then be compared to whatever the

	Number of employees today		Labor cost today		Labor cost to date		Labor cost variance	
					Date	April 11		
Department	Budget	Actual	Budget	Actual	Budget	Actual	Today	To date
Food Dining room	13	14	$ 456	$ 487	$1,368	$1,399	$ + 31	$ + 31
Coffee shop	7	6	245	217	735	707	– 28	– 28
Banquet	11	11	440	440	1,674	1,674		

Figure 10.6 Labor cost summary and analysis.

standard is for this situation. With this measure, it is important to watch trends over time. The main disadvantage of this method is that sales depend on relatively unpredictable guest counts and even on the sales mix (what menu items will customers consume?). If you change your prices, the standard must also then be changed.

A further problem with this method relates to deciding what payroll hours to use. For example, should you use only variable wage employee hours, or only fixed (that is salaried) hours, or both? For a salaried employee, what is the number of standard hours per day: eight, ten, or some other number? In using this measure, it is, therefore, best to analyze labor in departments where salaried hours can be excluded. This tool is most useful as a short-run measure of productivity in areas such as the dining room or cocktail lounge where dollars of sales per server hour worked can easily be calculated.

Dollar Labor Cost per Guest Served

For example, if 500 guests are served in your dining room and the labor cost to serve those guests is $400, the labor cost per guest served is $400 divided by 500 = $0.80. This measure is useful as long as wage rates are not changed. A wage rate increase, however, will increase the labor cost per guest unless it is compensated for by reducing the number of hours worked and paid for. It is feasible to improve the ratio (that is, to decrease labor cost per guest) if the number of hours worked can be decreased to more than compensate for a wage rate increase. Even with an increasing labor cost per guest, however, this ratio can hide a productivity improvement. Consider the following situation:

$$100 \text{ hours worked} \times \$4 \text{ per hour} = \$400 \text{ cost}$$

If 400 guests are served, labor cost per guest is

$$\$400/400 = \$1.00$$

Suppose that there is a 15 percent wage increase and a 10 percent reduction in hours worked, with no change in the number of guests served. The result would be the following change in cost:

$$90 \text{ hours worked} \times \$4.60 \text{ per hour} = \$414 \text{ cost}$$

If 400 guests are served labor cost per guest is

$$\$414/400 = \$1.035$$

In the preceding example, the wage increase (despite a reduction in hours worked) has caused an increase in the labor cost per guest served from $1.00 to $1.035. Nevertheless, there has been an increase in productivity, as will become apparent when we look at the next method.

Guest Count per Man-hour

On the basis of the figures from the preceding example, the guest count per man-hour in the first situation is

$$400 \text{ guests}/100 \text{ hours worked} = 4 \text{ guests per man-hour}$$

And in the second situation, the ratio comes out as

$$400 \text{ guests}/90 \text{ hours worked} = 4.4 \text{ guests per man-hour}$$

This shows that there has been an increase in productivity. However, the productivity increase is not high enough to compensate for the increase in hourly wage from $4.00 to $4.60, as shown by the labor cost per guest figure calculated earlier.

Nevertheless, the guest count per man-hour has the advantage of being unaffected by wage and price changes, and for this reason it may be the best measure of productivity over time, if properly interpreted. It also recognizes that sales result from guests, not from reduction of the number of employees or their wage rates. Hence, if more guests can be served with no increase in hours paid or rates of pay, there will automatically be a productivity gain.

This type of labor analysis is not applicable in all departments or situations. For example, in a banquet the number of guests served per hour of labor may be far less significant than the banquet guests' spending. If you can sell a banquet for $11, rather than for $10 (a 10 percent sales increase), this may be much more important than raising the guests-served productivity 10 percent (from 4 to 4.4 per employee hour worked).

A similar situation prevails in a cocktail lounge, where average check could be $5 or $15 per guest without any change in hours worked or paid for, or in total revenue. For example, during an hour each of three customers can occupy the same seat for twenty minutes, each spending $5. Average check is $5, and total revenue is $15. It has taken one hour of labor to serve three guests. Alternatively, one customer could occupy the same seat for the entire hour and spend $15. Average check is $15, and so too is total revenue, but in this case one hour of labor has been expended to serve only one guest. To compare guest counts per hour worked in this type of situation is quite meaningless, since the same total revenue and the same amount of labor are involved despite the big differences in average check and in the labor cost per guest served.

ELEVEN

Pricing

The way in which you establish prices for food and beverage products in your restaurant is going to dictate, to a degree, whether you will achieve your financial goals. If your prices are too high you may drive away customers who do not believe they are obtaining value for money. If your prices are too low, you will not be maximizing your sales potential. In either event, your profits will be lower than they should be.

PRICING METHODS

A number of different methods, each with its pros and cons, are used by restaurant operators to establish prices.

Intuitive Method

The intuitive method requires no real knowledge of the business (costs, profits, prices, competition, the market). The operator just assumes that the prices established are the right ones. This method has no advantages. Its main disadvantage is that the prices charged are unrelated to profits.

Rule-of-thumb Method

Rule-of-thumb methods (such as that a restaurant should price its menu items at 2.5 times food cost to achieve a 40 percent cost of sales) may have had validity at one time but should not be relied on in today's highly competitive environment because they pay no attention to the marketplace (competition, offering value for money, and so forth).

Trial-and-error Method

With the trial-and-error method, prices are changed up and down to see what effect they have on sales and profits. When profit is apparently maximized, prices are established at that level. However, this method ignores the fact that there are many other factors (such as general economic conditions and the competition) that affect sales and profits apart from prices, and what appears to be the optimum pricing level may later be affected by these other factors. This method can also be confusing to customers during the price testing period.

Price-cutting Method

Price-cutting occurs when prices are reduced below those of the competition. This can be a risky method if it ignores costs, because if variable costs are higher than prices then profits will be eroded. Some restaurant operators set their food menu prices below costs on the risky assumption they will more than make up the losses by profits on alcoholic beverage sales. To use this method demand must be elastic. In other words, the reduction in prices must be more than compensated by selling additional products. If the extra business gained is simply taken away from your competitors, then the competitors will be forced also to reduce their prices and a price war may result.

High-Price Method

Another method is to deliberately charge more than competitors and to use product differentiation, emphasizing such factors as quality that many customers equate with price. If this strategy is not used carefully, however, it can encourage customers to move elsewhere when they realize that high price and high quality are not synonymous.

Competitive Method

Competitive pricing means matching prices to those of the competition and then differentiating in such areas as location, atmosphere, and other nonprice factors. When there is one dominant restaurant in the market that generally takes the lead in establishing prices, with its close competitors matching increases and decreases, this method is then referred to as the follow-the-leader method. Competitive pricing tends to ensure there is no price-cutting and resulting reduction in profits. In other words, there is market price stability. This may be a useful method in the short run. However, if competitive pricing is used without knowledge of the differences that exist (in such matters as product and costs) between one restaurant and another, then this method can be risky.

Markup Method

The markup method uses the restaurant's traditional food cost percentage (as it appears on past income statements) and applies it to determine the price of any new menu items offered. For example, if traditionally the restaurant has been operating at a 40 percent food cost, then any new menu items offered will be priced so that they also result in a 40 percent food cost. The major problem with this method is that it assumes that 40 percent is the correct food cost percentage for the restaurant to achieve its desired profit.

USING THE RIGHT METHOD

Many of the pricing methods briefly reviewed are commonly used because restaurant operators understand them and they are generally easy to implement. Unfortunately, if your restaurant is not operating as efficiently as it should, these methods simply tend to perpetuate the situation and sales and profit will not be maximized. Restaurant owners or managers who use these methods are not fully in control of their operations and are probably failing to use their income statements and other financial accounting information to guide them in improving their operating results.

Pricing is a marketing tool that you can effectively use to improve profitability. The dilemma is often a matter of finding the balance between prices and profits. In other words, prices should only be established after considering the effect they have on profits. For example, you can lower your prices to attract more customers, but if those prices are reduced to the point that they do not cover the costs of serving those extra customers, profits will decline rather than increase.

Long-run or Strategic Pricing

Over the long run price is determined in the marketplace as a result of supply and demand. When prices are established to compete in that marketplace, they must be set with your restaurant's overall long-term financial objectives in mind. A typical objective could be any one of the following: to maximize sales revenue, to maximize return on owners' investment, to maximize profitability, to maximize business growth (in a new restaurant), or to maintain or increase share of market (for an established restaurant). A clearly thought out pricing strategy will stem from the objective or objectives of your business, as well as recognize that these objectives may change over the long run.

TACTICAL PRICING

As well as a long-run pricing strategy, you also need short-run or tactical pricing policies to take advantage of situations that arise from day to day. The following are some of these situations:

- Reacting to short-run changes in price made by competitors.
- Adjusting prices because of a new competitor.
- Knowing what discount to offer to accept group business while still making a profit in a banquet or similar situation.
- Knowing how much to increase prices to compensate for an increase in costs.
- Knowing how much price increases can be justified to compensate for renovations made to premises.
- Adjusting prices to reach a new market segment.
- Knowing how to discount prices in the off-season to attract business.
- Offering special promotional prices.

In order to use tactical pricing effectively, you must keep four factors in mind: elasticity of demand, cost structure, competition, and product differentiation.

Elasticity of Demand

Elasticity of demand is related to the responsiveness of demand for a product when prices are changed. When there is a large change in demand resulting from a small change in prices, this is referred to as elastic demand. When there is a small change in demand following a large change in prices, this is referred to as inelastic demand.

Perhaps the easiest way to test whether demand is elastic or inelastic in your restaurant is to note what happens to total sales when prices are changed. If demand is elastic, a decline in price will result in an increase in total sales because, even though a lower price is being received per meal, enough additional meals are now being sold to more than compensate for a lower price.

An Example.   For example, assume that your restaurant's average check is $10.00 and that an average of 1,000 customers per week is served. Total sales per week are $10,000. If the average check is reduced by 5 percent to $9.50, and average weekly customer count goes up 10 percent to 1,100, total sales will now be 1,100 × $9.50 or $10,450, which is $450 more than before. Demand is elastic. A generalization is that if demand is elastic, a change in price will cause total sales to change in the opposite direction.

If demand is inelastic, a price decline will cause total sales to fall. The small increase in sales that occurs will not be sufficient to offset the decline in average check. Again, you can generalize and say that if demand is inelastic a change in price will cause total sales to change in the same direction. In other words, when demand is inelastic, a price change will have little or no effect on the number of meals sold, but it will affect total sales. If your menu prices are increased, total sales will increase, and if prices are decreased, total sales will decrease. Therefore, when demand is inelastic, there is little value in cutting menu prices because your sales and net profit will decline.

Availability of Substitutes.   One of the factors that influences elasticity of demand is the availability of substitutes. Generally, restaurants that charge the highest prices are able to do so because there is little substitution possible. An elite restaurant with little competition can charge higher menu prices because its customers expect to pay higher prices, can afford to do so, and generally would not move to a lower-priced, less luxurious restaurant if menu prices were increased. Demand is inelastic.

On the other hand, a restaurant that is one of many in a particular neighborhood catering to the tourist family trade that wants budget-priced meals would probably lose considerable business if it raised its menu prices out of line with its competitors. Its trade is very elastic. Its price-conscious customers will simply take their business to another restaurant. That is to say, one restaurant can easily be substituted for another. Alternatively, a high-average-check restaurant will probably find less customer resistance to an increase in menu prices. You can then say that, in general, the lower the income of a restaurant's customers, the more elastic is their demand, and vice versa.

Customers' Habits.   Closely related to income levels are the habits of a restaurant's customers. The more habitual the customers are, the less likely they are to resist some upward change in prices because customers tend to have "brand" loyalties to restaurants just as they have to other products they buy. Nevertheless, if your restaurant needs to count on repeat business you must be very conscious of the effect that price changes may have on that loyalty. For example, loyalty and demand for a product (or a particular restaurant) tend to be more elastic the longer the period under consideration. Even though customers are creatures of habit and do develop loyalties, those habits and loyalties can change over time.

You must, therefore, be aware of the elasticity of demand of the market in which you operate and the loyalty of your customers. In other words, you must have a market-oriented approach to pricing. This market orientation is particularly important in short-run decision making, such as in promoting special food and beverage prices during slow periods. These reduced prices are particularly appropriate where demand is highly elastic.

Cost Structure

The specific cost structure of your restaurant is also a major factor influencing pricing decisions. Cost structure in this context means the breakdown of costs into fixed and variable. Fixed costs are those that normally do not change in the short run, such as a manager's salary or insurance premiums. Variable costs (such as food cost) are those that increase or decrease, depending on sales volume.

If your restaurant has high fixed costs relative to variable costs, the less stable your profits are likely to be as volume of sales increases or decreases. In such a situation, having the right prices for the market becomes increasingly important. In the short run, any price in excess of the variable costs will produce a contribution to fixed costs and profit, and the lower the variable costs the wider is the range of possible prices.

Note that this concept of variable or marginal costing is valid only in the short run. Over the long run prices must be established so that all fixed and variable costs are covered in order to produce a long-run net profit.

The Competition

Your restaurant's competitive situation is also critical in pricing. Very few restaurants are in a monopolistic situation (although some are, such as a restaurant operation that has the only concession at an airport).

Where there is a monopolistic or near-monopolistic situation, you have greater flexibility in determining prices and may, indeed, tend to charge more than is reasonably fair. In these situations, however, the customer still has the freedom to buy or not buy a meal or drink. Also, in most monopolistic free-enterprise situations where high prices prevail, other new restaurant entrepreneurs are soon attracted to offer competition.

Most restaurants, however, are in a purely competitive situation where the demand for the menu products of any one is highly sensitive to the prices charged. In such situations, there is little to choose, from a price point of view, from one restaurant to the next. Prices, therefore, tend to be highly competitive. Where there is close competition, competitive pricing will often prevail without thought to other considerations. Unfortunately, an operator practicing competitive pricing may fail to recognize that his particular restaurant is superior in some ways to his competitors' and could command a higher price without reducing demand.

Product Differentiation

In a highly competitive situation, an astute restaurant operator will not copy competitors' prices but rather look at the strengths and weaknesses of his own situation as well as those of his competitors. In analyzing strengths and weaknesses, you should try to differentiate your restaurant and your products from your competitors' and emphasize your uniquenesses.

The restaurants that are most successful in differentiating have more freedom in establishing their prices. This differentiation can be in such matters as ambiance and atmosphere, decor, location, and view. Indeed, with differentiation psychological pricing may be practiced. With psychological pricing the prices are established according to what the customer expects to pay for the unique products offered. The greater the differentiation, the higher your prices can be. For example, this situation prevails in fashionable restaurants where a particular market niche has been created and a monopolistic or near-monopolistic situation may prevail.

Pricing Summary

In summary then, there is no one method of establishing prices for all restaurants. Each restaurant will have somewhat different long-run pricing strategies related to its overall objectives and will adopt appropriate short-run pricing tactics depending on its market situation.

A LOGICAL APPROACH TO PRICING

In the discussion so far, the role of profit in establishing prices has been generally ignored. Because there is a relationship between prices charged and total sales, prices must affect your restaurant's ability to cover all costs and provide a profit that yields an acceptable return on your investment.

A useful approach in pricing, therefore, might be to start with the profit that is required, calculate fixed and variable costs, and determine what sales are required and what prices are to be charged in order to achieve the desired profit.

This approach assumes that profit is a cost of doing business, as indeed it is. If a bank lends money at a particular interest rate to your restaurant, the interest cost is considered to be an expense for your business. The bank is an investor. You, as owner, are also an investor. You, too, expect interest on your investment of money and/or time, except that your "interest" is called profit. Therefore, profit is just another type of cost. This concept can be useful in calculating what your menu prices ought to be to yield the desired profit.

Let us consider the following situation about Chuck's Charbroiler, a restaurant with 100 seats that wishes to determine what its average check (average customer spending) needs to be next year. Chuck's fixed costs, including the profit desired, are $165,000, and his variable costs are 80 percent of sales. If variable costs are 80 percent of sales, then fixed costs must be 20 percent of sales (because total sales are given the value of 100 percent). Therefore, total sales next year to give the desired profit can be calculated as follows:

$$\text{If } 20\% \text{ of sales} = \$165,000$$

$$\text{Then } 100\% = \$165,000/20\% = \$825,000$$

We can verify this by preparing a traditional income statement as follows:

Sales	$825,000
Variable costs 80% × $825,000 =	660,000
Fixed costs 20% × $825,000	= $165,000

Average Check

Now that we know that Chuck needs $825,000 in annual sales in order to have the desired profit, we can have a look at this $825,000 in relation to the individual restaurant customer.

For example, what must Chuck's average check (average customer spending) be, assuming the restaurant is open six days a week (or 6 × 52 = 312 days a year) and each seat turns over or is occupied, on average, twice a day. The equation is

$$\text{Average check} = \frac{\text{Total annual sales}}{\text{Seats} \times \text{Daily turnover} \times \text{Days open in year}}$$

$$= \frac{\$825,000}{100 \times 2 \times 312}$$

$$= \frac{\$825,000}{62,400} = \$13.22$$

If Chuck thought that, by giving faster service, the turnover rate could be increased to 2.5, the average check could be allowed to drop to $10.58 from $13.22, calculated as follows:

$$\text{Average check} = \frac{\$825,000}{100 \times 2.5 \times 312}$$

$$= \frac{\$825,000}{78,000} = \$10.58$$

Note that the figure of $10.58 does not tell Chuck what every item on the menu must be priced at, only what the average customer should spend. Some will spend more, some less. Nevertheless, it gives him some idea of what the pricing structure of the menu should be with a balance of prices, some of which will be higher than the average, some lower.

The average check also tells him, as the year progresses, whether he will achieve the profit required. If he sees that the actual average spending per customer is less than required and no other items have changed (seat turnover rate, operating and other costs) then Chuck knows something must be done if he is not to have a shortfall in profit. Turnover rate must be improved, selling prices might have to be increased, costs must be decreased, or a combination of these variables might be required.

Average Check by Meal Period

The average check discussed so far for Chuck's Charbroiler is the average for all meals combined. But because most restaurants have an average check that differs by meal period (breakfast is usually the lowest, dinner the highest, and lunch somewhere in between), it would be desirable to calculate what the average check needs to be by meal period rather than by day.

To do this, Chuck needs to know what percentage of sales are derived from each meal period and what the seat turnover is for each meal period. Let us assume Chuck's restaurant is open for both lunch and dinner and that 40 percent of total sales are from lunch trade, the other 60 percent from dinner business. Seat turnovers are 1.25 for lunch and 0.75 at dinner. The equation to calculate meal period average check is

$$\frac{\text{Meal period percentage of total sales} \times \text{Total sales}}{\text{Seats} \times \text{Meal period turnover} \times \text{Days open}}$$

Therefore, average lunch check will be

$$\frac{40\% \times \$825,000}{100 \times 1.25 \times 312}$$

$$= \frac{\$330,000}{39,000} = \$8.46$$

and the average dinner check will be

$$\frac{60\% \times \$825,000}{100 \times .75 \times 312}$$

$$= \frac{\$495,000}{23,400} = \$21.15$$

We can verify the accuracy of these average check calculations as follows:

Lunch:

100 seats × 1.25 turns × $8.46 average × 312 days = $329,940

Dinner:

100 seats × 0.75 turns × $21.15 average × 312 days = 494,910
Total sales $824,850

The original sales total calculated earlier was $825,000. The difference is caused by rounding Chuck's meal period average checks to the nearest cent.

Even though the illustration is for two meal periods, the same approach can be used if there are three meal periods. Also, if your restaurant is open more days for some meal periods than others (for example, five days a week for lunch and six evenings a week for dinner), the same basic equation can still be used. The days-open number will change, depending on the meal period for which the average check is being calculated.

PRICING MENU ITEMS

One of the common approaches to menu pricing is to calculate, given the recipes and specific ingredient purchase costs, the standard cost (what the cost should be) for each different menu item. This cost is then multiplied by a factor obtained by dividing the overall food cost percentage desired into 100 to get the selling price.

For example, let us assume that your restaurant wished to have an average food cost of 40 percent: 100 divided by 40 = 2.5, which is the multiplication factor. To illustrate its use, let us suppose a menu item has been costed out to $4.00. Then $4.00 × 2.5 would give the selling price of $10.00. However, it may not be practical to apply this multiplication factor across the board for all menu items.

When developing menu selling prices, you must keep in mind what market you are selling to (what the customers will bear and what they expect to pay for certain menu items) and what competitive restaurants are charging for the same items. It becomes a bit of a juggling act, with some items having a higher markup, some a lower. In other words, some will have more than a 40 percent food cost; some will have less than 40 percent. Also, as discussed and illustrated in Chapter 6, the individual food cost percentage of a menu item is less important than its gross profit (selling price less food cost).

Sales Mix

What people choose from a variety of menu selections is known as the sales mix. In menu pricing it is a good idea to keep the likely sales mix in mind because the average check, and ultimately profit, can be influenced by a change in the sales mix. To illustrate this refer to the following, which shows a sales mix for a fast-food restaurant with an average check of $4.66.

Menu Item	Quantity Sold	Selling Price	Total Sales
1	25	$3.00	$ 75.00
2	75	4.00	300.00
3	50	5.00	250.00
4	60	5.00	300.00
5	40	6.00	240.00
Totals	250		$1,165.00

$$\text{Average check } \frac{\$1,165.00}{250} = \$4.66$$

Assume that, by promotion or other means, the sales mix is changed, and twenty-five people no longer select menu item two. Five switch to menu item one, and the other twenty choose menu item four. The new sales mix is shown next with a new higher average check of $4.72.

Menu Item	Quantity Sold	Selling Price	Total Sales
1	30	$3.00	$ 90.00
2	50	4.00	200.00
3	50	5.00	250.00
4	80	5.00	400.00
5	40	6.00	240.00
Totals	250		$1,180.00

$$\text{Average check } \frac{\$1,180}{250} = \$4.72$$

The higher average check would normally result in a higher gross profit and net profit, in addition to higher sales.

Seat Turnover

Note also that seat turnover can be a further consideration in pricing. The higher each seat is turned over, or is occupied, each meal period, the lower the average check can be to achieve the same desired profit. The reverse is also true. In other words, if seat turnover declines, then average check must be higher to achieve the same desired profit.

Summary

Therefore, menu pricing can be a complex task because

- Different menu items must be offered with different prices and different markups.
- Gross profit dollars vary from menu item to menu item.
- Food cost percentage by itself may not be a meaningful guide to determining selling prices.
- The sales mix must be kept in mind.
- Seat turnover must be considered.

Beverage Pricing

Even though in this chapter the discussion has centered around food menu pricing, exactly the same principles can be applied to beverage pricing. However, the process can be simplified. Many restaurant operators price their drinks in categories: all drinks in a certain category have the same selling price. For most restaurants, the following are the major categories:

Highballs—well brands
Highballs—call brands
Cocktails—well brands
Cocktails—call brands
Brandies and liqueurs
Frozen and ice-cream drinks
Specialty drinks
Beer—regular
Beer—premium
Wine

Integrated Pricing

In pricing food and alcoholic beverages, you should also keep integrated pricing in mind. This simply means that products should not be priced independently of each other, particularly if the beverage operation is closely integrated with the food operation: that is, the customers eating in your dining area are the customers who provide most of the business for your beverage operation. In such cases, both food and beverage prices should complement each other to achieve your profit objectives. Generally, in such a situation, the more food you sell, the higher will beverage sales be (a concept known as derived demand), and vice versa. To ensure that integrated pricing prevails, you (as owner) should not delegate the pricing of products to others (such as your dining room and/or bar manager) because they are unlikely to have the same overall view of the operation you have.

TWELVE

Income Statement Analysis

COMPARATIVE STATEMENTS

A periodic income statement is useful for presenting information about your restaurant's operations and monitoring the progress of the business, particularly if financial statements are produced on a monthly basis.

The income statement is more meaningful, however, if it is compared with the statement for the previous period. When the current period's income statement is placed alongside the previous period's, changes that have occurred between the two periods can be seen. Making a straight side-by-side comparison between the two sets of figures, however, is not easy because the extent of changes is not always obvious. Therefore, to aid in making the comparison it is useful to use comparative analysis (also known as horizontal analysis) so that you have additional information calculated and added to the two statements.

Additional Information

For example, refer to the two income statements illustrated in Table 12.1, showing Ethel's Eatery's operating results for each of the years 0001 and 0002. Alongside the income statements are two additional columns: one showing the difference in dollars for each item and the other expressing this dollar difference as a percentage increase or decrease over the previous year.

These two extra columns are helpful to Ethel in pinpointing large changes that have occurred, either in dollars or in percentages from one year to the next. The percentage change figures are calculated by dividing the dollar change figure by the base figure in year 0001 and multiplying by 100. For example, food sales have gone up almost 2.0 percent, calculated as follows:

$$\frac{\$11,700}{\$589,500} \times 100 = 1.98\%$$

TABLE 12.1
Comparative Income Statement Analysis

	Year ending Dec. 31, 0001		Year ending Dec. 31, 0002		Change from year 0001 to year 0002	
					Dollars	Percentage
Sales						
Food	$589,500		$601,200		+ $11,700	+ 2.0%
Beverage	262,100	$851,600	267,900	$869,100	+ 5,800	+ 2.2 + 2.1%
Cost of Sales						
Food	$235,400		$242,900		+ $ 7,500	+ 3.2%
Beverage	87,000	322,400	98,300	341,200	+ 11,300	+13.0 + 5.8
Gross Profit						
Food	$354,100		$358,300		+ $ 4,200	+ 1.2%
Beverage	175,100	$529,200	169,600	$527,900	− 5,500	+ 0.3 − 2.5%
Expenses						
Salaries and wages	$277,400		$304,500		+ $27,100	+ 9.8%
Employee benefits	34,500		37,800		+ 3,300	+ 9.6
Operating supplies	37,200		38,000		+ 800	+ 0.2
Marketing	7,500		8,400		+ 900	+12.0
Utilities	10,200		12,100		+ 1,900	+18.6
Administration	6,500		7,200		+ 700	+10.8
Maintenance	2,900	376,200	4,000	412,000	+ 1,100	+37.9 + 35,800
Profit (before rent, depreciation, and income tax)		$153,000		$115,900	− $37,100	− 24.2%

The other percentage change figures are calculated in the same way. As Ethel can see, beverage sales have increased by 2.2 percent and total sales by 2.1 percent.

Even with the total sales increase, however, profit (before rent, depreciation, and income tax) has declined $37,100, or 24.2 percent. This is a drastic change. With sales up, all other factors being equal, profit should also be up, not down.

All other factors are, obviously, not equal, because analysis of costs shows that the majority of them have increased at a greater rate than the sales increase. To select only one as an example, the salaries and wages expense has increased by $27,100 over the year, or 9.8 percent. Why is this so? Was there a wage increase? Has Ethel's operation become less efficient in staffing? Was a one-time bonus paid to employees? Ethel needs to analyze each expense to account for large changes such as that for the salaries and wage expense. In this particular illustration, assuming the increased costs were inevitable, perhaps they have not yet been adjusted for by Ethel in menu selling prices.

Absolute versus Relative Changes

In comparative analysis you should distinguish between absolute and relative changes. Absolute changes show the dollar change from one period to the next. The relative change is that absolute change expressed as a percentage. For example, the wage cost in Table 12.1 shows an absolute change of $27,100, which in relative terms is a change of 9.8 percent.

An absolute change may sometimes appear large (for example, $10,000) but when compared to its base figure (for example, $1,000,000) represent a relative change of only 1 percent. By the same token, a relative change may seem high (for example 50 percent) but when compared to its base figure be quite small in absolute terms (for example, a $50 base figure that increases to $75). In terms of the total income statement this $25 change (even though it shows a relative increase of 50 percent) is insignificant. Therefore, when analyzing comparative income statements, both the absolute and the relative change should be looked at; only those that exceed both acceptable norms would be of concern.

For example, a particular restaurant may establish absolute changes of concern at $10,000 and relative changes at 5 percent, and only those changes that exceeded both $10,000 and 5 percent will be investigated. The following changes will not be investigated:

- Above $10,000 but below 5 percent.
- Above 5 percent but below $10,000.
- Below $10,000 and below 5 percent.

COMMON-SIZE STATEMENTS

Another type of income statement analysis is known as vertical or common-size analysis. Common size simply means that all income statement dollars are converted to a percentage basis. Total sales are given the value of 100 percent, and all other items (except cost of sales and gross profit figures) are expressed as ratios of that 100 percent. Table 12.2 illustrates Ethel's two income statements from Table 12.1 converted to a common-size basis.

Note how food cost for year 0001 is converted to a percentage of sales by dividing it by food sales and multiplying by 100 as follows:

$$\frac{\$235,400}{\$589,500} \times 100 = 27.6\%$$

Food gross profit also uses food sales as the denominator:

$$\frac{\$354,100}{\$589,500} \times 100 = 41.6\%$$

Beverage cost and beverage gross profit calculations both use beverage sales as the denominator. Thus, beverage cost for year 0001 is

$$\frac{\$\ 87,000}{\$262,100} \times 100 = 10.2\%$$

and beverage gross profit is

$$\frac{\$175,100}{\$262,100} \times 100 = 20.6\%$$

For all other items (total cost of sales, total gross profit, and expenses), total sales of $851,600 in year 0001 are used as the denominator. For example, total cost of sales in year 0001 is

$$\frac{\$322,400}{\$851,600} \times 100 = 37.8\%$$

Total gross profit is

$$\frac{\$529,200}{\$851,600} \times 100 = 62.2\%$$

Salaries and wages are

TABLE 12.2

Common-Size Income Statement Analysis

	Year ending Dec. 31, 0001		Year ending Dec. 31, 0002	
Sales				
Food	$589,500	69.2%	$601,200	69.2%
Beverage	262,100	30.8	267,900	30.8
	$851,600	100.0%	$869,100	100.0%
Cost of Sales				
Food	$235,400	27.6%	$242,900	28.0%
Beverage	87,000	10.2	98,300	11.3
	322,400	37.8	341,200	39.3
Gross Profit				
Food	$354,100	41.6%	$358,300	41.2%
Beverage	175,100	20.6	169,600	19.5
	$529,200	62.2%	$527,900	60.7%
Expenses				
Salaries and wages	$277,400	32.6%	$304,500	35.0%
Employee benefits	34,500	4.0	37,800	4.3
Operating supplies	37,200	4.4	38,000	4.4
Marketing	7,500	0.9	8,400	1.0
Utilities	10,200	1.2	12,100	1.4
Administration	6,500	0.8	7,200	0.8
Maintenance	2,900	0.3	4,000	0.5
	376,200	44.2	412,000	47.4
Profit	$153,000	18.0%	$115,900	13.3%
(before rent, depreciation, and income tax)				

$$\frac{\$277{,}400}{\$851{,}600} \times 100 = 32.6\%$$

Profit before occupation costs (rent, depreciation, and income tax) is

$$\frac{\$153{,}000}{\$851{,}600} \times 100 = 18.0\%$$

Figures for year 0002 are calculated in a similar way.

Comparative, Common-size Income Statements

Even though an individual periodic common-size income statement can be of some value, it is of more value if two or more successive income statements are compared to each other on a common-size basis as illustrated in Table 12.2. In this way, changes from one period to the next are more apparent.

The reason for converting dollar amounts to percentages for purposes of comparison is that it makes comparison a lot easier.

For example, refer to Table 12.2 and note that Ethel's Eatery's profit (before occupation costs) was $153,000 in year 0001 and $115,900 in year 0002. These figures tell us that, in absolute terms, the profit has declined (despite a sales increase)—but how much is the profit relative to sales in each of the two years? This is not easy to tell by looking only at the dollar figures. But by converting the net profit to a percentage of sales, Ethel can see that it has declined from 18.0 percent of sales in year 0001 to only 13.3 percent of sales in year 0002. That is to say, out of each dollar of sales in year 0001 there was 18 cents profit, and in year 0002 this had declined to 13.3 cents. In other words, in year 0001, Ethel had a larger proportion of sales represented by profit, and a declining ratio of profit to sales is not normally a desirable trend.

Causes of Changes.   What is the reason for this trend? One cause that is obvious is that food and beverage cost of sales has increased from 37.8 to 39.3 percent of sales. What is the reason? Have increased purchase costs not been passed on in higher selling prices or was Ethel in year 0002 less effective in controlling this cost? That is, is there a problem in the food and beverage cost control systems?

Another obvious problem area is in salaries and wages that have increased from 32.6 to 35.0 percent of sales. This 2.4 percent increase translates into almost $21,000 (2.4 percent of sales of $869,100). In other words, if salaries and wages had remained at 32.6 percent of sales in year 0002 (rather than increasing to 35.0), profit would have been almost

$21,000 higher. Although there are minor increases, relative to sales, in other expenses, none is very serious compared to labor cost.

AVERAGE CHECK, COST, AND PROFIT PER GUEST

Table 12.3 illustrates another way of analyzing Ethel's income statements by calculating average revenue (more commonly known as average check or average cover), average cost, and average profit on a per guest basis.

The average check is calculated by dividing the revenue in a sales area by the number of guests served. For example, in the food area in year 0001, Ethel's average food check is

$$\frac{\$589,500}{50,802} = \$11.60$$

and the average beverage check is

$$\frac{\$262,100}{50,802} = \$5.16$$

All other items (cost of sales, gross profit, expenses, and profit before rent, depreciation, and income taxes) are calculated by dividing the item by 50,802 (the number of guests). For example, salaries and wages cost per guest in year 0001 is

$$\frac{\$277,400}{50,802} = \$5.46$$

and average profit is

$$\frac{\$153,000}{50,802} = \$3.01$$

By comparing the figures from year 0001 to 0002, Ethel notices that the total average check has declined from $16.76 to $16.58. This is caused by a decline in average guest spending in both food and beverages. Has the menu been changed? Has the sales mix changed? Are customers just spending less?

Combined with a declining average check, cost of sales per guest has increased from $6.34 to $6.51. As a result of a declining average check and an increasing cost of sales, gross profit per guest is down $0.35 (from $10.42 to $10.07).

TABLE 12.3

Sales, Cost, and Profit Per Guest Analysis

	Year ending Dec. 31, 0001		Year ending Dec. 31, 0002		Guests: 50,802 Year ending Dec. 31, 0001		Guest: 52,411 Year ending Dec. 31, 0002	
Sales								
Food	$589,500		$601,200		$11.60		$11.47	
Beverage	262,100	$851,600	267,900	$869,100	5.16	$16.76	5.11	$16.58
Cost of Sales								
Food	$235,400		$242,900		$ 4.63		$ 4.63	
Beverage	87,000	322,400	98,300	341,200	1.71	6.34	1.88	6.51
Gross Profit								
Food	$354,100		$358,300		$ 6.97		$ 6.84	
Beverage	175,100	$529,200	169,600	$527,900	3.45	$10.42	3.23	$10.07
Expenses								
Salaries and wages	$277,400		$304,500		$ 5.46		$ 5.81	
Employee benefits	34,500		37,800		0.68		0.72	
Operating supplies	37,200		38,000		0.73		0.72	
Marketing	7,500		8,400		0.15		0.16	
Utilities	10,200		12,100		0.20		0.23	
Administration	6,500		7,200		0.13		0.14	
Maintenance	2,900	376,200	4,000	412,000	0.06	7.41	0.08	7.86
Profit (before rent, depreciation, and income tax)		$153,000		$115,900		$ 3.01		$ 2.21

Further, expenses per guest have increased by $0.45 (from $7.41 to $7.86) per guest, primarily because of the salaries and wage cost per guest, which has increased by $0.35 (from $5.46 to $5.81).

Finally, as a result of all these changes, profit per guest has declined by $0.80 (from $3.01 to $2.21).

SELECTION OF ANALYSIS METHOD

Note that, even though three different methods of income statement analysis have been demonstrated so far in this chapter, you would not in practice use all of them. Each is useful, and each shows basically where problem areas are. Therefore, you must select whichever one you think is most appropriate in your operation and shows the situation most clearly to you.

OPERATING RATIOS

A number of operating ratios are also useful in analyzing your restaurant's sales.

Food and Beverage Sales Ratios

The food sales ratio is calculated by dividing the food sales by the combined sales of food and beverage; the beverage sales ratio is calculated by dividing beverage sales by combined sales of food and beverage. For example, assume your food sales for a period were $150,000 and beverage sales for that same period were $50,000: total sales are thus $200,000. The food sales ratio is

$$\$150,000/\$200,000 \times 100 = 75.0\%$$

and the beverage sales ratio is

$$\$50,000/\$200,000 \times 100 = 25.0\%$$

Note that, when these two ratios are added together, they should always total 100 percent:

$$75\% + 25\% = 100\%$$

Normally, it is preferable to have a high beverage sales ratio relative to the food sales ratio. In other words, in our particular case it would be more profitable to have the food ratio 70 percent (rather than 75 percent) and the beverage ratio 30 percent (rather than 25 percent). The reason is that the food cost as a percentage of food sales is usually higher than the beverage cost percentage is as a percentage of beverage sales. In other words, beverage sales are more profitable than food sales.

With reference to Table 12.2, you can see that Ethel's food and beverage sales ratios have been calculated and that there has been absolutely no change in them from year 0001 to year 0002. In each year food is 69.2 percent and beverage is 30.8 percent of total sales.

Average Sales per Seat

Another way to analyze sales is to calculate the sales per seat. Suppose that Ethel's Eatery has 200 seats. With reference to Table 12.1, total sales per seat in year 0001 are

$$\$851,600/200 = \$42,580$$

and for the year 0002 total sales per seat are

$$\$869,100/200 = \$43,455$$

In this particular sales analysis, it was assumed that beverage sales were generated from customers consuming alcoholic beverages while dining, and therefore total (combined food and beverage) sales per seat were calculated. If desired, and to provide more information, average sales per seat could be broken down separately into food and beverages.

If the restaurant is separated from the beverage area, which has its own seats where customers can drink and/or eat if they wish, then each department should be treated as a separate entity and the average sales per seat in the beverage area should not be mixed in with average sales per seat of the dining area.

Obviously, over time it is desirable for this trend to show an increasing average sales per seat because higher sales per seat generally translate into higher net profit.

Other Sales Ratios

Three other major sales ratios (percentages) are food cost, beverage cost, and labor cost. These have been fully discussed in earlier chapters.

Seat Turnover Ratios

The seat turnover ratio is obtained by dividing the number of customers in your restaurant during a period of time (meal period, day, week, or month) by the number of seats in your restaurant.

One way to combat declining average customer spending is to increase seat turnover. It can also be useful for certain types of decision making. Let us take a look at a situation of a 200-seat restaurant with the following daily seat turnovers:

	Customers	Seat Turnover
Sunday	200	1.0
Monday	250	1.25
Tuesday	350	1.75
Wednesday	350	1.75
Thursday	450	2.25
Friday	550	2.75
Saturday	650	3.25
Total	2,800	2.00

With reference to the figures, the Sunday turnover is calculated as follows:

$$\frac{200}{200} = 1.0$$

and the Monday turnover is

$$\frac{250}{200} = 1.25$$

Turnovers for the remaining days are calculated in a similar way. The average seat turnover for the week is calculated as follows:

$$\frac{2,800}{7 \times 200} = 2.0$$

But this average hides some important information that calculating turnover by day of the week discloses. Daily analysis shows how the customers are distributed during the week, with the number (and the seat turnover) increasing toward the end of the week. This can be of value in employee scheduling and also in advertising, that is, advertising to bring in more customers early in the week to increase the turnover during the low-ratio days of Sunday and Monday.

If your restaurant has more than one department, the seat turnover ratio should be kept separate for each profit center. Seat turnovers vary substantially by type of restaurant. A fast-food operation generally has a relatively high turnover, and a high-priced table service gourmet restaurant a relatively low turnover.

COMPARISON WITH BUDGET

One other way in which to make income statement comparisons is to compare actual results with budgeted figures. This subject will be covered in more depth in Chapter 16.

TREND RESULTS

To date, we have limited our analysis of the income statement to only two periods. However, limiting an analysis to only two periods (weeks, months, or years) can be misleading if anything unusual has distorted the results for either of the two periods. Looking at results over a greater number of periods can often be useful. For example, consider trend figures for Buffy's Buffet for six successive months:

Month	Sales	Change in Sales	Percentage Change
1	$25,000		
2	30,000	+$5,000	+20%
3	33,000	+ 3,000	+10
4	35,000	+ 2,000	+ 6
5	36,000	+ 1,000	+ 3
6	36,000	0	0

In the preceding figures the change in sales dollar amounts for each period is calculated by subtracting from each period's sales the sales of the preceding period. For example, in period 3,

$$\$33,000 - \$30,000 = \$3,000 \text{ change in sales}$$

The percentage change figures are calculated by dividing each period's change in sales amount by the sales of the previous period and multiplying by 100. For example, in period 3

$$\frac{\$3,000}{\$30,000} \times 100 = 10\%$$

Over a long enough period, trend results show the direction in which your restaurant is going. In Buffy's case, the trend results indicate that, although business has been increasing over the past few months, it now seems to have leveled off. Has Buffy's Buffet reached its maximum potential in sales? Trend information such as this is useful in forecasting or budgeting (as we shall see in Chapter 16).

Index Trends

An index trend is a method of looking at trends by first converting the dollar amounts to an index. For example, the following sales and wages cost dollars have each been converted to an index trend:

Period	Sales	Wage Cost	Sales Index	Wage Cost Index
1	$25,000	$ 7,500	100	100
2	30,000	9,200	120	123
3	33,000	10,300	132	137
4	35,000	10,800	140	144
5	36,000	11,100	144	148
6	36,000	11,200	144	149

An index is calculated by assigning a value of 100 (or 100 percent) in period one (the base period) for each item being tabulated. The index figure for each succeeding period is calculated by dividing the dollar amount for that period by the base period dollar amount and multiplying by 100. For example, in period 2 (with reference to the previous discussion) the sales index is

$$\frac{\$30,000}{\$25,000} \times 100 = 120$$

In period 4 the wage cost index is

$$\frac{\$10,800}{\$ 7,500} \times 100 = 144$$

The completed index trend results in this particular case show us that the wage cost has been increasing faster than sales. Expressed another way, sales are up 44 percent (144 − 100) and wage cost is up 49 percent (149 − 100). This is normally an undesirable trend needing investigation and possible correction.

Adjusting for Inflation

When comparing operating results, and in particular when analyzing trend figures, you must be aware of the effect changing dollar values have on the results. One hundred pounds of potatoes purchased for your restaurant a few years ago weighed exactly the same as 100 pounds of potatoes today, but the amount of money required to buy that quantity today is probably quite different from the amount needed a few years ago. And this is true of all expenses. Prices change over time. Therefore, when you compare income and expense items over a period of time, you must consider the implications of inflation.

Consider a small restaurant with the following sales in two successive years:

Year 1	$200,000
Year 2	$210,000

This is a $10,000, or 5 percent, increase in sales from year one to year two. But if the restaurant's menu prices have been increased in year two by 10 percent over those of year one because of inflation, then the year two sales should have been at least $220,000 just to stay even with year one sales.

In other words, when comparing sales for successive periods in inflationary times you are comparing unequal values. Last year's dollar does not have the same value as this year's. What $1.00 would buy last year may now cost $1.15, or even more. Is there a method that will allow you to convert previous period's dollars into current period dollars so trends can be analyzed more meaningfully? The answer is yes: the use of index numbers.

Selecting an Appropriate Index

The Consumer Price Index is probably one of the most commonly used and widely understood indexes available. But many other indexes are produced by the government and other organizations. By selecting an appropriate index, conversion of previous period's dollars into current year dollar values is simple. Consider the following, showing trend results for sales of Denise's Diner for the past five years.

Year	Sales	Change in Sales	Percentage Change
1	$420,000	0	0
2	450,000	$30,000	7.1%
3	465,000	15,000	3.3
4	485,000	20,000	4.3
5	510,000	25,000	5.2

The trend shows increasing sales each year, generally a favorable trend. But is it reasonable to compare $420,000 of sales in year one with $510,000 of sales in year two? By selecting an appropriate index (such as the Consumer Price Index) and adjusting all sales to comparable year five dollar values, a more realistic picture of Denise's sales may emerge. Denise must also use an index that is based on the same period for which she wishes to adjust her sales (or expenses). Assume the index numbers were as follows:

Year	Index Number
1	100
2	107
3	113
4	122
5	135

The equation for converting past period's (historic) dollars to current (real) dollars is

$$\text{Historic dollars} \times \frac{\text{Index number for current period}}{\text{Index number for historic period}} = \text{Current dollars}$$

The following shows Denise's sales dollar information converted by the index numbers to express the five-year sales in terms of current dollars:

Year	Index	Historic Sales		Conversion Equation		Current Dollars
1	100	$420,000	×	135/100	=	$567,000
2	107	450,000	×	135/107	=	568,000
3	113	465,000	×	135/113	=	556,000
4	122	485,000	×	135/122	=	537,000
5	135	510,000	×	135/135	=	510,000

As you can see, the resulting picture is quite different from the unadjusted historic figures. In fact, Denise's annual sales have generally declined from year one to year five, and this would not normally be a desirable trend.

THIRTEEN

Ratio Analysis

In the previous chapter we had a look at some of the ways in which income statement information can be presented and analyzed. In this chapter we will have a look at a balance sheet, in conjunction with some income statement information, to do ratio analysis. To do this we will use the information from Figure 13.1 (balance sheet) and Figure 13.2 (income statement) for Charley's Charbroiler, a restaurant that owns its own land and building.

DEFINING RATIOS

In its simplest terms, a ratio is a comparison of two figures. A comparison can be expressed in several ways. For example, you have already seen one type of ratio comparison in the previous chapter, where common-size income statements were compared using percentages. A percentage is a ratio. You will see other types of ratios in this chapter. An important point in using ratios is that when two numbers are converted to a ratio, the relationship between them must be realistic and meaningful. For example, food cost can be compared to food sales and produce realistic and meaningful information. However, if food cost is compared to management salaries, this is not a realistic analysis.

Current Ratio

The current ratio is one of the most commonly used ratios to measure a restaurant's liquidity or its ability to meet its short-term debts (current liabilities) without difficulty. The equation for this ratio is

$$\frac{\text{Current assets}}{\text{Current liabilities}}$$

or, using figures from Charley's balance sheet,

$$\frac{\$92,200}{\$68,400} = 1.35$$

CHARLEY'S CHARBROILER
BALANCE SHEET AS OF DECEMBER 31, 19X1

ASSETS

Current Assets

Cash	$ 25,400	
Accounts receivable	15,200	
Marketable securities	32,000	
Inventory	14,700	
Prepaid expense	4,900	$ 92,200

Fixed Assets

Land	$ 60,500	
Building	882,400	
Furniture and equipment	227,900	
China, glass, silver, linen	18,300	
	$1,189,100	
Less: Accumulated depreciation	(422,000)	767,100
Total Assets		$859,300

LIABILITIES AND OWNERS' EQUITY

Current Liabilities

Accounts payable	$ 16,500	
Accrued expenses	4,200	
Income taxes payable	20,900	
Credit balances	800	
Current portion of mortgage	26,000	$ 68,400

Long-term Liability

Mortgage payable		486,800
Total Liabilities		$555,200

OWNERS' EQUITY

Common shares	$ 200,000	
Retained earnings	104,100	304,100
Total Liabilities and Owners' Equity		$859,300

Figure 13.1   Balance sheet.

The ratio shows that for every $1.00 of short-term debt (current liabilities) Charley has $1.35 of current assets. In general business, a rule of thumb is that there should be $2.00 or more of current assets for each $1.00 of current liabilities.

However, most restaurants can operate without difficulty with a cur-

CHARLEY'S CHARBROILER INCOME STATEMENT FOR YEAR ENDING DECEMBER 31, 19X1		
Food Sales **Food Cost of Sales**		$1,175,200 419,400
Gross Profit		$ 755,800
Operating Expenses Payroll and related expense Operating supplies Administration and general Marketing Maintenance and repairs Energy Property taxes Insurance Interest Depreciation	$319,200 101,400 57,900 20,700 15,400 25,100 28,800 13,100 51,900 41,900	 675,400
Profit before tax **Income tax**		$ 80,400 40,200
Net profit		$ 40,200

Figure 13.2   Income statement.

rent ratio of much less than 2 to 1. One reason for this is that a current ratio of 2 to 1 is typical of manufacturing businesses that must normally carry large inventories as part of their current assets because it takes weeks, or sometimes months, to have inventory delivered once it is ordered. In comparison, most restaurants carry relatively small inventories because they can purchase most of what they need from day to day. Indeed, for most restaurants a current ratio of 2 to 1 would show an inefficient use of its current assets if that high ratio were due to carrying too much inventory. Money tied up in inventory is money that is not earning interest it could earn if it were left in the bank.

For your restaurant, you must determine what the most effective current ratio is in order to have a current ratio position that neither creates short-term liquidity problems (too low a ratio) nor sacrifices profitability for safety (too high a ratio). If the ratio is too high, you have too much money tied up in working capital (current assets less current liabilities) that is not earning a profit. With the current ratio, as with most ratios, its trend is important.

Conditions of short-term loans from banks often require that this ratio be at or above a certain level at each balance sheet date. If it drops below this required level, the bank may have the right to call in (terminate) the loan. In such circumstances, the ratio should be assessed immediately before your balance sheet date to ensure that it is at a safe level.

Quick Ratio

Because total current assets includes some assets that are not very liquid, bankers and other lenders frequently like to calculate the quick (or acid test) ratio. The quick ratio has as its numerator only cash, accounts receivable, and marketable securities:

$$\frac{\text{Cash} + \text{Receivables} + \text{Marketable securities}}{\text{Current liabilities}}$$

In Charley's case this is

$$\frac{\$25,400 + \$15,200 + \$32,000}{\$68,400}$$

$$= \frac{\$72,600}{\$68,400} = 1.06$$

Under normal circumstances, lenders like to see this ratio at 1 to 1 or higher. In Charley's case it is 1.06 to 1, or about what is normally considered an acceptable level. However, note again that this is a restaurant, and the "normal" ratio of 1 to 1 is more applicable to manufacturing and similar companies, and restaurants can often effectively operate with a quick ratio of less than 1 to 1.

Accounts Receivable Ratios

Many restaurants that have extensive credit sales run into financial and cash flow difficulties because they lose control over their accounts receivable. There are several useful ratios for assessing your receivables.

Accounts Receivable to Charge Sales.   The ratio of accounts receivable to charge sales is usually expressed as a percentage. This percentage indicates the accounts receivable that are uncollected and is calculated as follows:

$$\frac{\text{Accounts receivable}}{\text{Charge sales for year}}$$

For Charley, assuming that out of total annual sales $320,000 was for charge sales, the figures are

$$\frac{\$\ 15,200}{\$320,000} = 0.05 \text{ percent}$$

This is a very small percentage of sales. Technically, in this ratio charge sales should be separated from cash sales so that only the charge sales figure is used in the denominator as was demonstrated for Charley. However, for many restaurants it is not practical to keep a separate record of these two types of sale.

Although the trend of this ratio is of some value, some other accounts receivable ratios are often more useful because they provide additional information.

Accounts Receivable Turnover.   The accounts receivable turnover is calculated as follows:

$$\frac{\text{Charge sales for year}}{\text{Accounts receivable}}$$

For Charley, this is

$$\frac{\$320,000}{\$\ 15,200} = 21 \text{ times}$$

In a typical restaurant that allows a thirty day limit for payment of accounts and that is successful in collecting its accounts within this time limit, an annual turnover of 12 would be acceptable. In Charley's case, he is well within that limit. If the turnover is higher than 12 this is good; if it is much lower, this is normally not considered good.

Day's Sales in Receivables.   Another way of assessing the receivables situation is to calculate the day's sales outstanding in receivables. This requires two steps. First you must calculate the average daily charge sales:

$$\frac{\text{Charge sales for year}}{365}$$

The figure 365 is used as the denominator because Charley's restaurant is open seven days a week all year round. If your restaurant were closed on Sundays, then the denominator would be 313 (365 less 52). In Charley's case, the figures are

$$\frac{\$320,000}{365} = \$877 \text{ average daily charge sales}$$

The next step is to calculate the average number of days that the accounts receivable figure represents. The equation for this is

$$\frac{\text{Accounts receivable}}{\text{Average daily charge sales}}$$

For Charley, this is

$$\frac{\$15,200}{\$877} = 17.3 \text{ days}$$

Again, this figure for Charley shows that his average accounts receivable are being collected in about 17 days. This is very acceptable if 30 days is the normal credit limit.

Aging of Accounts.   One other method of evaluating accounts receivable is to age the accounts. This technique will be demonstrated in Chapter 17.

When your accounts receivable results indicate that the turnover rate or number of days outstanding is over the desirable limit of, let us say, thirty calendar days, you need to ask and answer the following questions:

- Can you continue to carry these overdue accounts without impairing your cash position?
- Is a thirty day limit normal for your type of restaurant?
- Have you been unwise in extending more than thirty days' credit to some customers?
- Can anything be done to encourage more prompt payment of outstanding accounts?
- Would an interest charge on overdue accounts speed up collections?
- Has the bad debt loss amount increased because some customers do not pay within the normal thirty day limit?

Inventory Turnover

Another useful balance sheet ratio is inventory turnover. A full discussion of this ratio is deferred until Chapter 17.

Total Liabilities to Total Equity Ratio

Total assets in a restaurant can be financed by either liabilities (debt) or equity (shares and retained earnings in an incorporated company, and total capital in a proprietorship or partnership). The total liabilities to total equity ratio (commonly called the debt to equity ratio) illustrates the relationship between these two forms of financing. It is calculated as follows:

$$\frac{\text{Total liabilities}}{\text{Total owners'equity}}$$

In Charley's case, the figures are

$$\frac{\$555,200}{\$304,100} = 1.83$$

This ratio tells us that for each $1.00 that Charley has invested, the creditors (or lenders) have invested $1.83. The higher the creditors' ratio, or debt to equity ratio, the higher is the risk to the creditor or lender. In such circumstances, if a restaurant needed additional money to expand its operations it might find it difficult to borrow the funds.

The contradiction is that, although your creditors prefer not to have the debt to equity ratio too high, you will often find it more profitable to have it as high as possible. A high debt to equity ratio is known as having high leverage. Using leverage, or trading on the equity, will be discussed later in this chapter.

Number of Times Interest Earned

Another measure that creditors sometimes use to measure the safety of their investment is the number of times interest is earned during a year. The equation for this is

$$\frac{\text{Profit before interest and income tax}}{\text{Interest expense}}$$

or, for Charley's,

$$\frac{\$132,300}{\$\ 51,900} = 2.55 \text{ times}$$

Note that, in this equation, interest of $51,900 is added back to the profit before tax of $80,400 (to arrive at the total of $132,300). Generally an investor or creditor considers the investment safe if interest is earned two or more times a year because profit before interest could decline significantly without reducing the risk to creditors.

Net Profit to Sales Ratio

The net profit to sales ratio (also known as the profit margin) is one of the more common measures of the profitability of a restaurant. The equation is

$$\frac{\text{Net profit}}{\text{Sales}} \times 100$$

For Charley, the figures are

$$\frac{\$40,200}{\$1,175,200} \times 100 = 3.4\%$$

This means that, out of each $1.00 of sales, Charley has only 3.4 cents net profit. The net profit to sales ratio of many restaurants falls in the range of 3 to 7 percent (however, there are exceptions to this guideline). In absolute terms, the profit margin percentage may not be very meaningful, because it does not necessarily fully represent the profitability of the business. Consider the following two cases:

	Restaurant A	Restaurant B
Sales	$100,000	$100,000
Net profit	5,000	10,000
Net profit to sales ratio	5%	10%

With the same sales it seems that Restaurant B is better. It is making twice as much net profit, in absolute terms, as Restaurant A ($10,000 to $5,000). This doubling of net profit is supported by the net profit to sales ratio (10 percent to 5 percent). If these were two similar restaurants, or two branches of the same restaurant chain, these figures would indicate the relative effectiveness of the management of each in controlling costs and generating a satisfactory level of profit. However, in order to determine the true profitability of a restaurant you need to relate the net profit to the owners' investment by calculating the return on the owners' equity.

Return on Owners' Equity

The equation for return on owners' equity is

$$\frac{\text{Net profit}}{\text{Owners' equity}} \times 100$$

In Charley's case this is

$$\frac{\$40,200}{\$304,100} \times 100 = 13.2\%$$

This ratio shows the effectiveness of the use of owners' funds (or equity). How high should the ratio be? This is a matter of individual opinion. If you could put money either into the bank at a 10 percent interest rate or into a restaurant investment at only 8 percent (with more risk involved), the bank might appear to be the better of the two choices. Many people feel that 15 percent (after tax) is a reasonable return for the owner of a restaurant (with all its risks) to expect.

If we return now to the Restaurant A and Restaurant B situation discussed earlier, assume that the investment in A were $40,000 and in B $80,000. The return on investment of each would be

$$\text{Restaurant A } \frac{\$5,000}{\$40,000} \times 100 = 12.5\%$$

$$\text{Restaurant B } \frac{\$10,000}{\$80,000} \times 100 = 12.5\%$$

As you can see, despite the wide difference in net profit and net profit to sales ratio (calculated earlier), there is no difference between the two restaurants as far as profitability is concerned. They are both equally good, each yielding a 12.5 percent return on owners' equity. You could, therefore, conclude that it makes sense first to determine the return on owners' equity that is desired, then to establish what profit to sales ratio (profit margin) is required.

For example, suppose that the amount of money desired next year to provide an adequate return on owners' equity in your restaurant is $20,000 and that estimated sales next year are $400,000. The required profit as a percentage of sales is

$$\frac{\$20,000}{\$400,000} \times 100 = 5\%$$

By taking this approach you will know what level of sales you have to achieve to have an adequate return on owner equity. Obviously, if anticipated sales do not reach $400,000, then the profit to sales ratio will be less than 5 percent and the profit less than $20,000.

It is unfortunate that most restaurant operators do not know what their sales level has to be or relate their required profit to their owner equity in advance. They just wait until the results are out without any advance profit planning.

RATIO COMPARISONS

A ratio by itself has little value. For example, a restaurant's profit margin of 4 percent may appear good, but it can only be fully judged after you compare it with some standard, such as what is normal in the restaurant industry for that type of restaurant. It is only when compared with some base figure, or standard, that ratios take on any meaning. One of those standards is, of course, an industry average for that type of restaurant, but that standard of comparison is generally the least valuable of all, because it generally includes all restaurants of that type and those restaurants may be spread over a very broad territory where different operating conditions prevail in different locations. As a result, there may not be a single restaurant that is just like the "average" restaurant.

Another basis of comparison might be a comparable figure from a direct competitor. However, how do you find out your competitor's ratios? Also, if your figure differs from your competitor's, which one is better? There may be many reasons to explain why particular ratios differ between competitors.

A better method is to compare a ratio with those of previous periods. How does it compare with the same ratio last month or the same month last year? What is the trend of the ratio? Is that trend good or bad, and how do you know whether it is good or bad? One of the problems with comparing ratios with those of prior periods is that restaurants operate in a dynamic environment and comparing current ratios with previous ratios may be comparing apples and oranges.

The best comparison of all is to judge any ratio against a standard determined for your own restaurant. This standard can consider both internal and external factors about your operation. Internal factors may include such matters as your fixed and variable costs, operating policies, changes in operating methods, and similar matters. External factors can include such matters as the general economic environment and what the competition is doing. Often these standards can be determined by establishing operating plans (including ratio standards) in an annual budget. Budgets can consider not only the past and the present but also expectations about the future. Because of the importance of budgeting for any restaurant, this topic is covered in some depth in Chapter 16.

Ratio Limitations

You should be aware of some of the limitations of ratios:

- Many of the ratio guidelines or rules of thumb given in this (and in previous) chapters have assumed ownership of all assets. If assets (particularly land, building, and furniture and equipment) are leased rather than owned, then comparison with industry guidelines or with competitors' figures can be quite meaningless.

- Even though there are many ratios available, it is not a good idea to try to use all of them all the time. Selectivity is important. You should use only those that are of benefit in evaluating the results of your restaurant in relation to its objectives (that is, its plan or budget).

- Ratios should not be an end in themselves. For example, a restaurant's objective may be to have the lowest food cost percentage in town. But to achieve this, menu prices may have to be raised so high and portion sizes so reduced that customers stay away and the restaurant does not survive.

- Financial ratios are generally produced from historical accounting information. As a result, some accounting numbers reflect historic costs rather than present values. An example is a building's cost recorded on the balance sheet at its original purchase price and offset by accumulated depreciation to produce net book value. A ratio based on total assets may show a result that is more than acceptable but if based on the current replacement cost of those assets would produce a much more realistic ratio that could then be compared with alternative investments.

- Ratios are only of value when two related numbers are compared. For example, the current ratio compares current assets with current liabilities. This is a meaningful comparison. On the other hand, if current assets are compared to owner equity this has little value because there is no direct relationship between the two numbers.

- Finally, ratios solve no problems. Analysis of ratios shows only that problems may exist. Only your interpretation of the problem and subsequent action can solve it. For example, the trend of the accounts receivable ratio may show that the time that it is taking to collect the average accounts receivable is becoming longer. That is all the ratio shows. Only management analysis of this problem to discover the causes can correct this deteriorating situation.

INCREASING PROFIT LEVELS

There are, of course, limits to the amount of profit that a restaurant can achieve without expanding its premises or starting another restaurant. For example,

- Space and time limitations constrain the number of customers who can be served at any meal period.
- Competition controls to a great extent the prices of menu items.
- Quality of food served cannot be reduced (in order to save on purchase costs) or service reduced (to save on labor cost) without losing business from customers who will not accept this reduced quality.

Nevertheless, you can increase profit in two basic ways: increasing sales and/or decreasing expenses given your restaurant's limitations or constraints. Generally, to increase profit it is easier to decrease expenses than to increase sales. The reason is that to increase sales, part of each extra sales dollar has to be spent on certain costs (variable costs) that increase with sales.

For example, to sell more food, part of that sales dollar has to be spent to purchase more food and to pay more labor to prepare and serve it. This is true even though many of your restaurant's costs may be fixed (do not change with a change in sales). Examples of fixed costs are management salary, rent, and interest on borrowed money.

On the other hand, if expenses can be reduced by more effective operating procedures, each dollar of expense saved adds directly to profit. Consider the following situation for Vicky's, a restaurant whose average monthly sales are $30,000.

Sales		$30,000
Expenses		
Variable (60% of sales)	$18,000	
Fixed	9,000	27,000
Profit		$ 3,000

Suppose that Vicky could increase sales by 10 percent, or $3,000 per month. The new income statement would be

Sales		$33,000
Expenses		
Variable (60% of sales)	$19,800	
Fixed	9,000	28,800
Profit		$ 4,200

In this latter case, the sales increase of $3,000 contributes an additional $1,200 to profit because 60 percent of the sales increase (or $1,800) has to be paid out for additional variable costs. The fixed costs, of course, do not change.

As an alternative to increasing profit by $1,200, Vicky may be able to reduce a fixed expense by the same amount with a lot less effort than is required to increase sales by $3,000. If this does occur, the following will result:

Sales		$30,000
Expenses		
Variable (60% of sales)	$18,000	
Fixed	7,800	25,800
Profit		$ 4,200

In other words, profit is increased by the full amount of the expense saving. Obviously, if Vicky's sales can be increased and combined with an expense saving, an even better situation will result.

FINANCIAL LEVERAGE

Earlier in this chapter the concept of financial leverage, or trading on the equity, was introduced. To illustrate this, consider the case of a new building that two partners (Stew and Brew) are considering leasing for restaurant purposes. Their investment will be $250,000 (for equipment and working capital).

Stew and Brew have the cash available, but they are considering not using all their own money. Instead, they wish to compare their relative return on equity on the basis of using either all their own money (100 percent equity financing) or using 50 percent equity and borrowing the other 50 percent (debt financing) at a 10 percent interest rate.

Regardless of which financing method they use, sales will be the same, as will all operating costs. With either choice, they will have $50,000 profit before interest and taxes.

There is no interest expense under 100 percent equity financing. With debt financing, interest will have to be paid. However, interest expense is tax-deductible.

Assuming a tax rate of 50 percent on taxable profit, Table 13.1 shows the comparative operating results and the return on the partners' equity (ROE) for each of the two options.

In this situation, not only do Stew and Brew make a better ROE under a 50/50 debt/equity ratio (15 percent ROE versus 10 percent) but they still have $125,000 cash that they can invest in a second venture.

TABLE 13.1

Effect of Leverage on ROE

	Option A	Option B
Investment required	$250,000	$250,000
Equity financing	$250,000	$125,000
Debt financing	0	$125,000 @ 10%
Income before interest and income tax	$ 50,000	$ 50,000
Interest expense	0	(12,500)
Income before income tax	$ 50,000	$ 37,500
Income tax (50%)	(25,000)	(18,750)
Net income	$ 25,000	$ 18,750
Return on equity	$\dfrac{\$ 25,000}{\$250,000} \times 100$	$\dfrac{\$ 18,750}{\$125,000} \times 100$
	=10%	=15%

You could, therefore, ask, if a 50/50 debt to equity ratio is more profitable than 100 percent equity financing, would not an 80/20 debt to equity ratio be even more profitable? In other words, what would be the ROE if Stew and Brew used only $50,000 of their own money and borrowed the remaining $200,000 at 10 percent? Table 13.2 shows the result of this more highly levered situation.

Under this third option, the return on initial investment has now increased to 30 percent, and Stew and Brew still have $200,000 cash, enough for four more similar business ventures.

TABLE 13.2

Effect of High Leverage on ROE

	Option C
Investment required	$250,000
Equity financing	$ 50,000
Debt financing	$200,000 @ 10%
Income before interest and income tax	$ 50,000
Interest expense	(20,000)
Income before income tax	$ 30,000
Income tax (50%)	(15,000)
Net income	$ 15,000
Return on equity	$\dfrac{\$15,000}{\$50,000} \times 100 = 30\%$

Advantages of Leverage

The advantages of leverage are obvious: the higher the debt to equity ratio, the higher will be the ROE. However, this only holds true if profit (before interest) as a percentage of debt is greater than the interest rate to be paid on the debt. For example, if the debt interest rate is 10 percent, the profit before interest must be more than 10 percent of the money borrowed (the debt) for leverage to be profitable.

With high debt (high leverage) there is a risk. If profit declines, the more highly leveraged the business is, the sooner it will be in financial difficulty. In 50/50 financing in Table 13.1 (relatively low leverage), profit before interest and income tax could decline from $50,000 to $12,500 before net profit would be zero. In Table 13.2 (relatively high leverage) profit before interest and income tax could decline from $50,000 to only $20,000.

FOURTEEN

Cost Management

TYPES OF COST

Most of the cash from restaurant sales goes toward expenses: as much as 95 cents or more of each sales dollar may be used to pay for them. Therefore, expense or cost management is important. In order to manage costs, you must understand that there are many different types. If you can recognize the type of cost you are dealing with, then you can make better decisions about it. Some of the more common types of cost are defined in the following sections.

Discretionary Cost

A discretionary cost is one that may, or may not, be incurred at the discretion of a particular person, usually the restaurant owner or manager. Nonemergency maintenance is an example. Your restaurant's exterior could be painted this year, or the painting could be postponed until next year. In either case, sales should not be affected. As the owner, you can use your own discretion, thus it is a discretionary cost.

Relevant Cost

A relevant cost is one that makes a difference to a decision. For example, a restaurant is considering replacing its sales register with a new one. The relevant costs would be the price of the new machine (less any trade-in on the old one), the cost of training employees on the new equipment, and maintenance and stationery supply costs for the new machine.

Sunk Cost

A sunk cost is a cost already incurred and about which nothing can be done because it cannot affect any future decisions. For example, if the restaurant in the preceding paragraph had spent $250 for a consultant to study the relative merits of different sales registers available, the $250 is a sunk cost. It cannot make any difference to the decision.

Standard Cost

A standard cost is what the cost should be for a given volume or level of sales. For example, for each eight-hour shift in your restaurant's bar, a cocktail server might be expected to handle $480 in sales, or an average of $60 an hour. If the wage rate for the employee is $5 per hour, the standard labor cost is $5 for each $60 of sales.

Fixed Cost

Fixed costs are those that, over the short run (a year or less), do not change or vary with volume. Examples of these would be your restaurant manager's salary, insurance expense, and interest on a bank loan. Over the long run all these costs can change. but in the short run they are normally fixed.

Variable Cost

A variable cost is one that varies with sales. Very few costs are truly variable, except food cost and beverage cost.

Mixed Costs

Many costs do not fit into either the fixed or variable category. Most have an element of fixed expense and an element of variable—and the variable element is not always variable directly to sales. Examples of these mixed costs include labor, maintenance, and energy costs. In order to make useful decisions, you must break down these mixed costs into their fixed and variable elements.

BREAKING DOWN MIXED COSTS

A number of different methods can be used to break down mixed costs into their fixed and variable elements. Two will be illustrated:

Maximum/minimum method

Multipoint graph method

Maximum/minimum Method

To demonstrate the two methods of breakdown of a mixed cost, consider Patti's Pantry, a restaurant that has an annual salary and wage (labor) cost of $120,000. Since the cost of labor is closely related to the number of customers the restaurant serves, Patti needs a month-by-month breakdown of the sales for each month and the related wage cost for each month. (This information could be broken down by week, but there should be sufficient accuracy for all practical purposes with a monthly analysis.) The sales and labor cost monthly breakdown is as follows:

	Sales	Labor
January (minimum)	$ 5,000	$ 7,200
February	9,000	8,000
March	14,000	9,000
April	13,000	10,700
May	13,000	12,300
June	15,000	12,000
July	21,000	13,000
August (maximum)	21,000	13,200
September	15,000	11,900
October	10,000	7,600
November	10,000	7,600
December	7,000	7,500
Totals	$153,000	$120,000

Note that the month of January has the word *minimum* alongside it. In January, sales and wage cost were at their lowest for the year. In contrast, August was the maximum month.

Three Steps.   There are three steps in the maximum/minimum method:

Step 1: Deduct the minimum from the maximum figures for both wages and sales:

	Sales	Labor
August (maximum)	$21,000	$13,200
January (minimum)	5,000	7,200
	$16,000	$ 6,000

Step 2: Divide the wage difference by the sales difference to get the variable cost per dollar of sales:

$$\frac{\$\ 6,000}{\$16,000} = \$0.375 \text{ variable cost per dollar of sales}$$

Step 3: Use the answer to step 2 to calculate the fixed cost element:

August total wages	$13,200
Less variable costs $21,000 × $0.375	7,875
Fixed wage cost	$ 5,325

Note that in Step 3 we used the maximum month (August) to calculate Patti's fixed cost. We could equally well have used January (the minimum month) with no change in the result:

Step 3: January total wages	$7,200
Less variable costs $5,000 × $0.375	1,875
Fixed wage cost	$5,325

Patti's fixed labor cost is $5,325 a month, or

$12 \times \$5,325 = \$63,900$ a year (or $64,000 to the nearest thousand)

We can now break down Patti's total annual labor cost into its fixed and variable elements:

Total annual wages	$120,000
Fixed cost	64,000
Variable cost	$ 56,000

Using a Two-point Graph. The calculation of the monthly fixed cost figure has been illustrated arithmetically. The maximum/minimum figures could have been plotted equally well on a graph, as illustrated in Figure 14.1.

In this illustration, the maximum figure is first plotted (the upper right-hand point) and then the minimum figure is plotted (the lower left-hand point) and the two points are joined by a solid line. The solid line is then continued by a dotted line down and to the left, and the fixed cost is where the dotted line intersects the vertical axis. If the graph is accurately drawn, the same monthly fixed wage cost figure of approximately $5,300 calculated arithmetically earlier is derived.

The maximum/minimum method is quick and simple. It uses only two sets of figures. Unfortunately, either one or both of these sets of figures may not be typical of the relationship between sales and labor costs for the

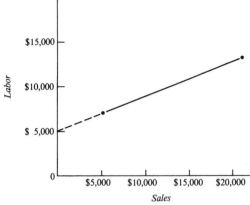

Figure 14.1   Maximum/minimum graph.

year (for example, a one-time wage bonus may have been paid during one of the months selected), thus distorting the figures. As long as you are aware of them, these distortions can be eliminated by adjusting the raw figures.

Another way to improve the maximum/minimum method and remove possible distortions in individual monthly figures is to plot the cost and sales figures for each of the twelve months (or however many periods there are involved) on a multipoint graph.

Multipoint Graph Method

Figure 14.2 illustrates a multipoint graph for Patti's sales and labor cost for each of the twelve months. Sales and costs were taken from the figures listed earlier. The graph illustrated is for two variables (sales and labor). In this case labor is given the name *dependent variable* and is plotted on the vertical axis. Labor is dependent on sales: it varies with sales. Sales, therefore, is the independent variable. The independent variable is plotted on the horizontal axis.

Note that, in drawing this graph, the point where the vertical and horizontal axes meet should be given a reading of zero. The figures along each axis should then be plotted to scale from zero.

After plotting each of the twelve points, Patti has what is known as a scatter graph: a series of point scattered around a line that has been drawn through them. A straight line must be drawn.

There is no limit to how many straight lines could be drawn through the points. The line Patti wants is the one that, to her eye, seems to fit best. Each restaurant operator performing this exercise would probably view the

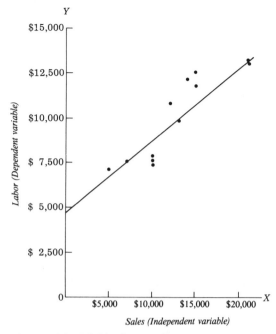

Figure 14.2 Multipoint graph.

line in a slightly different position, but most people with a reasonably good eye would come up with a line that is close enough for all practical purposes.

The line should be drawn so that it is continued to the left until it intersects the vertical axis (the dependent variable). The intersect point reading is the fixed cost (wages in this case). Note that, in Figure 14.2, the fixed cost reading is $5,000 (approximately). This is Patti's monthly cost. Converted to an annual cost it is

$$\$5,000 \times 12 = \$60,000$$

The total annual wage cost would then be broken down as follows:

Total wages	$120,000
Less fixed	60,000
Variable	$ 60,000

Difference in Methods

With the maximum/minimum method, Patti's total annual fixed cost is $64,000. With the multipoint graph method it is $60,000, a difference of

$4,000. This difference is due primarily to the fact that with the maximum/minimum method there is a higher risk of inaccuracy because only two of the twelve months are used and, as was mentioned earlier, these two months may not be typical of the entire year. For this reason, the multipoint graph is generally more accurate.

Other Mixed Costs

This chapter has attempted to show how one type of mixed cost can be broken down into its fixed and variable elements using two different methods. Once a method has been selected, you should apply it to each of the mixed costs that you have so that each one can be broken down into its two elements.

Alternatively, a simpler (but perhaps less accurate) method is to add all mixed costs together before separating them in total into their fixed and variable elements. This method has the advantage of considerably reducing the number of calculations that you have to make. As a result, it may give a less accurate breakdown of the fixed and variable costs. Nevertheless, the figures arrived at can probably still be used for most decisions.

Let us look at some of the ways in which a breakdown of costs into their fixed and variable elements helps in decision making.

CAN WE SELL BELOW COST?

The obvious answer to the question, Can we sell below cost? is, Not unless you want to go broke. But before you can intelligently answer that question, you should first ask, Which cost? If the answer is, Below total cost but above variable cost, then, yes, indeed, you can sell below total cost under certain circumstances.

Consider the situation of Cathy's Catering Company, which rents its premises for $80,000 a year and has other fixed costs (including management salaries, insurance, and furniture and equipment depreciation) of $66,000 a year. This is a total fixed cost of $146,000, or

$$\frac{\$146,000}{365} = \$400 \text{ a day}$$

Cathy's banquet room can only handle one function a day and operates at a variable cost (food, wages for food preparation and service staff, and supplies) of 60 percent of sales. Cathy has been approached by an organization that wishes to have a lunch for only sixty people at a price of $10.00 per person. Normally, Cathy would not handle a group as small as this, but on this occasion she does not see any likelihood of having the hall used by any other organization. If Cathy handles the function, the income statement for that day will be

Sales 60 × $10.00	$600
Variable costs 60% × $600	(360)
Fixed costs	(400)
Net loss	($160)

The net loss does not look good, but what is the loss if Cathy does not accept this function? It will be $400, because the fixed costs for that day will still have to be met. But, by selling below total cost of $760 ($400 fixed and $360 variable), Cathy's loss is less than it would otherwise be.

In the short run, as long as sales are greater than variable costs, it pays to accept business because the excess of sales over variable costs will contribute to (help pay for) the fixed costs that are there in any case. We can arrange Cathy's income statement to illustrate this concept of contribution margin as follows:

Sales	$600
Variable costs	(360)
Contribution margin	$240
Fixed costs	(400)
Net loss	($160)

SHOULD WE CLOSE IN THE OFF-SEASON?

One of the uses of a breakdown of fixed and variable costs is to answer the question of whether or not to close in the off-season. Consider the case of Rosa's Restaurant, which has the following annual income statement:

Sales	$150,000
Expenses	130,000
Net profit	$ 20,000

Rosa decided to make an analysis of her sales and costs by month and found that for ten months she was making money and for two months had a loss. The following summarizes her findings:

	10 months	2 months	Total
Revenue	$135,000	$15,000	$150,000
Variable costs	$ 25,000	$ 1,000	$ 26,000
Fixed costs	80,000	24,000	104,000
Total costs	$105,000	$25,000	$130,000
Net income	$ 30,000	($10,000)	$ 20,000

Rosa's analysis seems to indicate that she should close to eliminate the $10,000 loss during the two-month loss period. But if she does, the fixed costs for the two months ($24,000) will have to be paid out of the ten months' profits, and $30,000 (ten months' net profit) less the two months' fixed costs of $24,000 will reduce her annual net profit to $6,000 from its present $20,000. If she does not want a reduction in annual net profit, she should not close.

There may be other factors in such a situation that Rosa needs to consider and that would reinforce the decision to stay open. For example, there could be sizable additional closedown and start-up costs that would have to be included in the calculation of the cost of closing.

Also, would key employees return after an extended vacation? Is there a large enough pool of skilled labor available and willing to work on a seasonal basis only? Would there be recurring training time (and costs) at the start of each new season? These are some of the types of questions that would have to be answered before any final decision to close was made.

WHICH BUSINESS TO BUY?

Just as a business owner/manager has to make choices between alternatives on a day-to-day basis, so too does an entrepreneur going into the restaurant business or expanding an existing restaurant frequently have to choose between alternatives. Let us look at one such situation, again involving fixed and variable costs.

Ernie Entrepreneur has an opportunity to take over one of two similar existing restaurants: Dan's Diner or Claudia's Cafe. The two restaurants are close to each other in location, have the same type of clientele and size of operation, and the same asking price. Each is presently making $1,000,000 a year in sales, and each has a net profit of $100,000 a year. With only this information, it is difficult for Ernie to make a decision as to which would be the more profitable investment. But a cost analysis as shown in Table 14.1 illustrates there are differences between the two restaurants.

Structure of Costs

Although the sales and net profit are the same for each restaurant, the structure of their costs is different, and this will affect the decision about which one could be more profitable.

Ernie is optimistic about the future. He feels that, without any change in fixed costs, he can increase annual sales in either business by 10 percent. What effect will this have on the net profit of Dan's versus Claudia's? The net profit for each of the two restaurants will not increase by the same amount. Dan's variable cost is 50 percent. This means that, out of each dollar of additional sales, it will have variable expenses of $0.50 and a net profit of $0.50 (fixed costs do not change). Claudia's has variable costs of 30 percent (or $0.30 out of each sales dollar), leaving a net profit of $0.70 from each additional sales dollar (again, fixed costs do not change).

Assuming a 10 percent increase in sales and no new fixed costs, the income statements of the two restaurants have been recalculated in Table 14.2. Note that Dan's net profit has gone up by $50,000 (to $150,000), but Claudia's has gone up by $70,000 (to $170,000). In this situation, Claudia's would be the better investment.

High Operating Leverage

A business that has high fixed costs relative to variable costs is said to have high operating leverage. Compared to Dan, Claudia has high operating leverage. From a profit point of view, Claudia will do better in times of rising sales than will Dan with low operating leverage (low fixed costs relative to variable costs). A business with low fixed costs, however, will be

TABLE 14.1

Statements Showing Differences in Cost Structure

	Dan's Diner		Claudia's Cafe	
Revenue	$1,000,000	100.0%	$1,000,000	100.0%
Variable costs	$ 500,000	50.0%	$ 300,000	30.0%
Fixed costs	400,000	40.0%	600,000	60.0%
Total costs	$ 900,000	90.0%	$ 900,000	90.0%
Net income	$ 100,000	10.0%	$ 100,000	10.0%

TABLE 14.2

Effect of Increased Revenue on Costs and Net Income

	Dan's Diner		Claudia's Cafe	
Revenue	$1,100,000	100.0%	$1,100,000	100.0%
Variable costs	$ 550,000	50.0%	$ 330,000	30.0%
Fixed costs	400,000	36.4%	600,000	54.5%
Total costs	$ 950,000	86.4%	$ 930,000	84.5%
Net income	$ 150,000	13.6%	$ 170,000	15.5%

better off when sales start to decline. Table 14.3 illustrates the new situation for Dan's Diner and Claudia's Cafe given the assumption that each is going to have a decline in sales of 10 percent from the present $1,000,000 level and that there will be no change in fixed costs.

Table 14.3 shows that with declining sales, Dan's net profit will be higher than Claudia's. In fact, if sales decline far enough Claudia will be in financial difficulty long before Dan. If the break-even point were calculated (the break-even point is that level of sales at which there will be neither a profit nor a loss), Dan's sales could go down to $800,000, and Claudia would be in difficulty at $857,000. This is illustrated in Table 14.4.

You could determine the break-even level of sales by trial and error (although this would be rather tedious). However, there is a formula available for quick calculation of this level. The formula, and a more in-depth discussion of fixed and variable costs and how an awareness of them can be of great value in many types of decision, will be covered in Chapter 15.

TABLE 14.3

Effect of Decreased Revenue on Costs and Net Income

	Dan's Diner		Claudia's Cafe	
Revenue	$ 900,000	100.0%	$ 900,000	100.0%
Variable costs	$ 450,000	50.0%	$ 270,000	30.0%
Fixed costs	400,000	44.4%	600,000	66.7%
Total costs	$ 850,000	94.4%	$ 870,000	96.7%
Net income	$ 50,000	5.6%	$ 30,000	3.3%

TABLE 14.4

Dependence of Break-even Revenue Level on Cost Structure

	Dan's Diner		Claudia's Cafe	
Revenue	$ 800,000	100.0%	$ 857,000	100.0%
Variable costs	$ 400,000	50.0%	$ 257,000	30.0%
Fixed costs	400,000	50.0%	600,000	70.0%
Total costs	$ 800,000	100.0%	$ 857,000	100.0%
Net income	0	0	0	0

PAYING A FIXED OR A VARIABLE LEASE

Another situation where fixed and variable cost knowledge can be very useful is in comparing the lease with a fixed cost to a lease based on a variable percent of sales. For example, consider the case of Stella's Steakhouse, a restaurant that has an opportunity to pay a fixed rent for its premises of $5,000 a month ($60,000 a year) or a variable rent of 6 percent of its revenue. What Stella needs to determine first is the break-even point of sales at which the fixed rental payment for a year would be identical to the variable rent. The equation for calculating this is

$$\text{Annual break-even revenue} = \frac{\text{Fixed annual lease cost}}{\text{Variable lease percentage}}$$

Inserting the figures we can determine Stella's sales level as follows:

$$\frac{\$60,000}{6\%} = \$1,000,000$$

In other words, at $1,000,000 of sales, it would make no difference whether Stella paid a fixed rent of $60,000 or a variable rent of 6 percent of sales. At this level of sales she would be indifferent. For this reason, the break-even revenue point is sometimes referred to as the indifference point.

If Stella expected sales to exceed $1,000,000, she would select a fixed rental arrangement. If sales were expected to be below $1,000,000, then she would be better off selecting the percentage of sales arrangement.

FIFTEEN

Using Break-even Analysis

QUESTIONS BREAK-EVEN ANALYSIS CAN ANSWER

A great many questions can be asked by the owner of a restaurant, such as the following:

- At what level of sales will I start losing money; that is, what is my break-even sales level?
- What will my net profit be at a certain level of sales?
- What is the extra sales revenue I need to cover the cost of additional advertising and still give me the profit I want?
- By how much must sales be increased to cover the cost of a wage increase and still give the profit to sales ratio I want?

These and many other questions cannot be easily answered from the traditional income statement. However, if you break down your operating costs into their fixed and variable elements as demonstrated in Chapter 14, you can then use this information in a technique known as break-even analysis. However, before you use break-even analysis, you must clearly understand its assumptions and limitations.

Assumptions and Limitations

The following are the assumptions and limitations of break-even analysis:

- It assumes that the costs associated with the present level of sales can be fairly accurately broken down into their fixed and variable elements (see Chapter 14).
- It assumes that fixed costs will remain fixed during the period affected by the decision being made.

- It assumes that variable costs vary directly with sales during the period affected by the decision being made.
- It is limited to situations where economic and other conditions are assumed to be relatively stable. In highly inflationary times, for example, when it is difficult to predict sale and/or cost prices more than a few weeks ahead, it would be risky to use break-even analysis for decisions that affect the distant future.
- Finally, break-even analysis is only a guide to decision making. The break-even approach might indicate a certain decision, but other factors (such as employee or customer relations) may dictate a decision that contradicts the break-even analysis.

Contribution Margin Concept

In this chapter we shall use the following annual income statement information for Resta's Restaurant:

Income Statement

Sales		$306,000
Variable costs	$113,000	
Fixed costs	181,000	294,000
Profit		$ 12,000

In break-even analysis, the income statement is sometimes presented in the form of a contribution statement:

Contribution Statement

Sales	$306,000
Variable costs	113,000
Contribution to fixed costs	$193,000
Fixed costs	181,000
Profit	$ 12,000

The contribution to the fixed cost figure (in Resta's case $193,000) is commonly referred to as the contribution margin and is simply sales less variable expenses. Note that presenting the fixed and variable costs in the form of a contribution statement does not change the profit figure.

From the preceding information we can calculate Resta's variable cost as a percentage of sales:

$$\frac{\$113,000}{\$306,000} \times 100 = 37\%$$

Therefore, because total sales are given the value of 100 percent, the contribution margin percentage is

$$100\% - 37\% = 63\% \text{ or } 0.63$$

Alternatively, contribution margin percentage can be calculated directly by dividing the contribution margin by the sales:

$$\frac{\$193,000}{\$306,000} \times 100 = 63\% \text{ or } 0.63$$

Break-even Equation

The easiest way to use break-even analysis is to use the following equation:

$$\text{Sales level} = \frac{\text{Fixed costs} + \text{Profit desired}}{\text{Contribution margin}}$$

USING THE BREAK-EVEN EQUATION

Let us use the equation to answer some questions for Resta.

At What Sales Level Will I Break Even?

Suppose we want to know the level of sales at which Resta will make neither a profit nor a loss, that is, the break-even point. The solution is

$$\text{Sales level} = \frac{\$181,000 + 0}{0.63}$$
$$= \$287,302, \text{ rounded to } \$287,000$$

(It makes sense to round figures when using the equation because the breakdown of fixed and variable costs may not be accurate in the first place and, in the situation just illustrated, an answer to the closest $1,000 would normally be quite acceptable.)

At What Sales Level Will I Make a Desired Profit?

Suppose Resta wanted to know the sales level required to provide her with a profit of $39,000 (rather than the present profit of $12,000). She can use the same equation for the answer, substituting $39,000 for the profit desired:

$$\text{Sales level} = \frac{\$181,000 + \$39,000}{0.63}$$

$$= \frac{\$220,000}{0.63}$$

$$= \$349,206, \text{ rounded to } \$349,000$$

How Much Must Sales Increase to Cover a New Fixed Cost?

Normally, if fixed costs increase and no change is made in selling prices, you would expect profits to decline by the amount of the additional fixed cost. You could then ask, By how much must sales be increased to compensate for a fixed cost increase and not have a reduction in profit?

A simple answer would be that sales have to go up by the same amount as the fixed cost increase. But this is not correct, because to increase sales (with no increase in selling prices) you have to sell more food and beverages, and if you sell more, your variable costs (such as the cost of food and beverages) are going to increase.

By trial and error you could arrive at a solution, but the break-even equation will quickly answer this kind of question. You simply add the new fixed cost to the old fixed cost and add the profit desired to the numerator of the equation and divide, as before, by the contribution margin. For example, suppose Resta wished to spend $5,000 more on advertising a year, how much more in sales must she have (assuming no menu price changes) to maintain her present profit level of $12,000?

$$\text{Sales level} = \frac{\$181,000 + \$5,000 + \$12,000}{0.63}$$

$$= \frac{\$198,000}{0.63}$$

$$= \$314,286, \text{ rounded to } \$314,000$$

Resta can easily prove the correctness of the result (as she can with any solution to a problem using the break-even equation) as follows:

Sales		$314,000
Variable costs		
37% × $314,000 =	$116,000	
Fixed costs	186,000	302,000
Profit		$ 12,000

The solution tells us that Resta's sales must be $314,000, an increase of $8,000 over the present sales level of $306,000, to pay for the $5,000 advertising cost.

What Additional Sales Do I Need to Cover a Change in Variable Expenses?

You saw in the preceding section how a change in fixed costs can be easily handled in the equation. How do we handle a change in variable costs? A change in the variable costs will change the contribution margin percentage. Therefore, the contribution margin must be recalculated by first calculating the new variable cost percentage.

You will recall that Resta's present variable cost of 37 percent was calculated by dividing total variable costs by total sales and multiplying by 100. Let us assume an increase in wages that will increase the variable costs as a percentage of sales from 37 percent to 39 percent is to be put into effect. The new contribution margin percentage will, therefore, be

$$100\% - 39\% = 61\% \text{ or } 0.61$$

and Resta can now use 0.61 as the denominator in the equation.

What About Multiple Changes in the Variables?

So far, we have considered making only one change at a time. Multiple changes can be handled without difficulty. For example, assume that the $5,000 is to be spent on advertising, that the employees will be given the wage increase (changing the contribution margin to 0.61), and that the profit is to be increased from $12,000 to $20,000. What will Resta's new sales level have to be? The answer is

$$\frac{\$181,000 + \$5,000 + \$20,000}{0.61}$$
$$= \frac{\$206,000}{0.61}$$
$$= \$337,705 \text{ or } \$338,000$$

and to prove this

Sales		$338,000
Variable costs		
39% × $338,000	$132,000	
Fixed costs	186,000	318,000
Profit		$ 20,000

How Can I Convert the Sales Level Directly into Units?

In the equation used so far the denominator has been

100% − Variable costs as a percentage of sales

If we use the break-even equation and express the contribution margin in percentages (as we have been doing), then our sales level will be expressed in sales dollars. If we use the equation and express the contribution margin in dollars, we shall have a sales level expressed in units (meals to be served). Let us test this.

If Resta's average guest check is $20.00 and the variable costs total $7.79 per customer served, the contribution margin is $12.21. Assuming fixed costs are $186,000 (including the $5,000 additional for advertising) and that $20,000 profit is desired:

$$\text{Sales level (in meals)} = \frac{\$186,000 + \$20,000}{\$20.00 - \$7.79}$$
$$= \frac{\$206,000}{\$12.21}$$
$$= \underline{16,871} \text{ meals}$$

The reason Resta may prefer the solution in meals (customers to be served) is that this type of information can be useful in such matters as knowing how many customers need to be served daily and/or by meal period and in calculating required seat turnovers by day or by meal period.

What about the Problem of Joint Costs?

In the problems handled to date, the fixed costs have been identified with a single department or operation. What happens in the case of joint costs, for example, for a restaurant that has a food department and a separate beverage department? Some of the costs involved will be joint costs shared by the entire operation. In such a case, as long as the variable costs can be identified for each department, break-even analysis can still be useful.

Let us consider the restaurant situation in Table 15.1 for Sam's Snackery. Because each of the two departments has a different percentage of variable costs, and therefore a different percentage of contribution margin, a given sales (revenue) increase for one department will affect profit differently than the same sales (revenue) increase in the other. Consider a $15,000 sales increase in each of Sam's two departments in Table 15.1. Assuming no fixed-cost change, the effect on profit will be as follows:

TABLE 15.1

Operation With Joint Fixed Costs

	Food Department		Beverage Department	
Revenue	$150,000	100%	$50,000	100%
Variable costs	75,000	50%	20,000	40%
Contribution margin	$ 75,000	50%	$30,000	60%
Total contribution margin		$105,000($75,000 + $30,000)		
Fixed costs		85,000		
Profit (income)		$ 20,000		

	Food Department	Beverage Department
Revenue increase	$15,000	$15,000
Variable costs	7,500 (50%)	6,000 (40%)
Increase in profit	$ 7,500	$ 9,000

In other words, a $15,000 increase in food sales provides an additional $7,500 profit, and a $15,000 increase in beverage sales provides an additional $9,000 profit. The problem of which department the additional sales are to be derived from if a revenue increase is desired is one of sales mix.

Suppose Sam wanted a $5,000 increase in profits, with no change in the fixed costs or in the variable cost percentages. Under these circumstances, there are three ways for Sam to obtain the extra profit: an increase in food revenue only, an increase in beverage revenue only, and (what is more likely to happen in practice) a combined increase in food and beverage revenue.

Increase in Food Revenue Only. In the case of increasing food revenue only, the solution is arrived at with the following break-even equation:

$$\text{Additional food revenue} = \frac{\text{Additional profit required}}{\text{Food contribution margin}}$$
$$= \frac{\$5,000}{0.5}$$
$$= \$10,000$$

Increase in Beverage Revenue Only. For beverage revenue, the approach is exactly the same as for a food revenue increase only, except that we substitute the beverage contribution margin for the food contribution margin.

$$\text{Additional beverage revenue} = \frac{\$5,000}{0.6}$$
$$= \underline{\$8,333}$$

Combined Increase in Food and Beverage Revenue.   What about the most likely situation, where increases in both food and beverage sales occur at the same time? Since food revenue increases have a different effect on profits than beverage revenue increases, to calculate how much Sam needs in combined total revenue, he has to specify the anticipated ratio of food revenue to total revenue and the ratio of beverage revenue to total revenue. Let us suppose that any revenue increases will be in the ratio of 75 percent food and 25 percent beverage. The equation for solving this type of sales mix problem is

Combined additional revenue required =

$$\frac{\text{Additional profit required}}{\begin{array}{l}\text{(Food revenue to total revenue} \quad \text{(Beverage revenue to total revenue} \\ \text{percentage} \times \text{Food contribution} + \text{percentage} \times \text{Beverage contribution} \\ \text{margin)} \qquad\qquad\qquad\qquad \text{margin)}\end{array}}$$

Substituting the figures, we have

$$= \frac{\$5,000}{(75\% \times 0.5) + (25\% \times 0.6)}$$
$$= \frac{\$5,000}{37.5\% + 15\%}$$
$$= \frac{\$5,000}{52.5\%}$$
$$= \underline{\$9,524}$$

Note that the 52.5 percent contribution margin in Sam's calculations is a weighted figure. It is weighted by the sales mix. Sam can easily check the accuracy of the answer obtained.

	Food	**Beverage**
Revenue	75% × $9,524 = $7,143	25% × $9,524 = $2,381
Variable costs	50% × $7,143 = 3,572	40% × $2,381 = 952
Contribution margin	$3,571	$1,429

Combined additional contribution margin is $3,571 + $1,429 = $5,000, which is equivalent to the additional profit desired (because fixed costs do not change).

Compound Changes. Compound changes can be made with no difficulty. With reference to Table 15.1, let us ask the following question: What would the total revenue level have to be if Sam wanted a profit of $25,000, if fixed costs increased to $87,000, and if the revenue ratio changed to 70 percent for food and 30 percent for beverage? There is no change in the contribution margin percentages. The solution is

$$\text{Total revenue} = \frac{\$87,000 + \$25,000}{(70\% \times 0.5) + (30\% \times 0.6)}$$
$$= \frac{\$112,000}{(35\% + 18\%)}$$
$$= \frac{\$112,000}{53\%}$$
$$= \$211,320 \text{ or } \underline{\$211,300}$$

To confirm whether this is the correct answer, Sam can prepare a new income statement for the restaurant as in Table 15.2.

What about a New Investment?

The break-even equation has been used in this chapter to illustrate how historical information from accounting records can be used to make decisions about the future. But break-even analysis is equally useful when there is no past accounting information to help you. For example, in a proposed new restaurant or expansion of an existing one, you simply make intelli-

TABLE 15.2
Income Statement Proving Correctness of Calculations

	Food Department	Beverage Department
Revenue	70% × $211,300 = $147,900	30% × $211,300 = $63,400
Variable costs	50% × $147,900 = 73,950	40% × $ 63,400 = 25,350
Contribution margin	$ 73,950	$38,050
Total contribution margin	$112,000 ($73,950 + $38,050)	
Fixed costs	87,000	
Profit	$ 25,000	

gent estimates of what the fixed and variable costs are likely to be and then project potential profits from those figures.

INCOME TAX AND BREAK-EVEN

To this point in the discussion of break-even analysis the effect of income taxes has been ignored. Obviously, at the break-even level of sales there are no tax implications because there is no profit. Also, with a proprietorship or partnership the organization pays no income taxes. Any profits are deemed to be paid out to the owner(s), who then pay income tax at personal tax rates.

An incorporated company that has a taxable net income must, however, consider the tax implications when using break-even analysis for decisions. Unfortunately, income tax is neither a fixed cost nor a variable cost dependent on sales. Taxes vary with income before tax and thus require special treatment in break-even analysis. This requires adjusting the break-even equation, substituting the term *profit desired* with *profit before tax.*

Consider the figures used earlier in this chapter, where Resta's profit desired was $39,000 and the sales required to achieve this were calculated to be $394,000. Assume now that Resta's Restaurant is in a 45 percent tax bracket. What sales are required to achieve a $39,000 *after-tax* profit? The $39,000 can be converted to a before-tax figure as follows:

$$\text{Profit before tax} = \frac{\text{After-tax profit}}{1 - \text{Tax rate}}$$

and substituting our figures:

$$= \frac{\$39,000}{1 - 0.45}$$
$$= \frac{\$39,000}{0.55}$$
$$= \$70,909 \text{ (rounded to } \$71,000)$$

This can be proved:

Before-tax profit	$71,000
Income tax 45%	32,000
After-tax profit	$39,000

Thus, if Resta, with fixed costs of $181,000 and a contribution margin of 0.63, wanted a before-tax profit of $71,000, the sales would have to be

$$\frac{\$181,000 + \$71,000}{0.63} = \frac{\$252,000}{0.63} = \$400,000$$

This can be proved as follows:

Sales		$400,000
Variable costs 37% × $400,000 = $148,000		
Fixed costs	181,000	329,000
Profit before tax		$ 71,000

SIXTEEN

Budgeting

CONTROL PROCEDURES

In order to control any aspect of your restaurant (such as its food cost, beverage cost, or labor cost) you must follow these five steps:

1. Establish what you expect the restaurant's performance standards (for example, the food cost percentage) to be.

2. Through your accounting system, collect the information that will allow you to measure actual results against the desired standard.

3. Compare the actual result with the standard, for example, actual food cost with standard food cost.

4. Take corrective action, if necessary, to help ensure that during the next period the actual result is more in line with the performance standard desired. For example, if the actual food cost is too high in comparison with the performance standard, then steps must be taken to reduce the actual food cost by finding out where the problem lies and correcting it. This may require an investigative process and consideration of alternative operating procedures along with the impact those alternative procedures will have on actual results.

5. At the end of the next review period, evaluate the result of any corrective action taken to see whether it was appropriate.

Planning Process

A common control technique that considers all aspects of your restaurant's operation (rather than, for example, food cost in isolation) is budgeting. Budgeting is a planning process, and your budget is a profit plan. In order to be successful and to make meaningful decisions about the future, you must look ahead. One way to look ahead is to prepare budget forecasts. A forecast may be very simple. It may be no more than estimating tomorrow's business in your restaurant so that sufficient employees can be notified today that they are required to work tomorrow, and for how many hours. On the other hand, a forecast of cash flow for a proposed new restaurant may be calculated for as far as five or more years ahead.

Purposes of Budgeting

The main purposes of budgeting are to provide the following information:

- Organized estimates of such factors as future sales, expenses, labor requirements, and fixture and equipment needs, broken down by time period.
- A coordinated long-term and short-term management policy, expressed primarily in an accounting format.
- A method of control so that actual results can be evaluated against budget plans and adjustments, if necessary, can be made. In other words, the standard of performance planned for in the budget can be measured against actual results.

Advantages of Budgeting

Although there are some obvious disadvantages to budgeting, such as the time and cost involved and the difficulty in predicting the future, most successful restaurant operators agree that the advantages far outweigh the disadvantages. Some of these advantages are as follows:

- Involving key employees in the business in budget preparation encourages motivation and improves communication. These key employees can then better identify with your restaurant's plans and objectives.
- Those involved in budget preparation are required to consider alternative courses of action (for example, what if the sales forecast does not reach the budgeted level?).
- Since operating budgets outline in advance the sales to be achieved and the costs involved in achieving those sales, at the end of each budget period actual results can be compared with the budget. In other words, you have a predetermined standard against which actual results can be evaluated.
- Budgeting forces those involved to look ahead. This does not mean that what happened in the past is not important for budget preparation. However, budgets are aimed at the future and require you to consider possibilities such as price changes, increasing labor and other costs, and what the competition is doing.
- Budgeting requires those involved to consider both internal and

external factors. Internal factors include such matters as seating capacity, seat turnover, and menu prices. External factors include competition, local economic environment, and general trend of inflation.

PREPARING THE BUDGET

Budgets can be either long-term or short-term. Long-term budgets are sometimes referred to as strategic budgets and are for periods of more than one year and up to five years ahead. These budgets concern matters such as restaurant expansion, creation of a new market, and financing. From long-term plans evolve policies concerning the day-to-day operations of your restaurant, and thus the short-term budgets.

Short-term budgets may be for a day, a week, a quarter, a year, or for any period less than a year. Short-term budgets involve using your restaurant's resources to meet the objectives of the long-term plans.

Although there are several different types of long-term and short-term budget, this chapter deals only with the short-term operating budget (income statement) for periods up to one year ahead. The operating budget is concerned with projections of sales and expenses, that is, items that affect the income statement.

Who Prepares the Budget?

In a small restaurant, the owner prepares the budget. The owner may have a plan about where he wants to go and operate from day to day to achieve his objective, or come as close to it as possible. For a formal budget, the help of an accountant may be useful in putting figures onto paper and refining them until the budget seems realistic.

In a large restaurant, a number of individuals (department heads) may be involved in budget preparation. These department heads may well, in turn, discuss the budget figures with employees within their own departments.

Short-term operating budgets are generally prepared annually, with monthly projections. Each month, budgets for the remaining months of the year should be revised to adjust for any changed circumstances.

BUDGETED INCOME STATEMENT

The first step in preparation of the budgeted income statement is to establish attainable sales goals or objectives.

Establishing Attainable Sales Goals or Objectives

In setting goals, the most desired situation must be realistic. In other words, if there are any factors that limit your sales to a certain maximum level, these factors must not be ignored. An obvious example is that a restaurant cannot fill more than 100 percent of its seats at any one time. If a restaurant is operating at 100 percent of capacity, sales can only be increased in the short run by menu price increases. But because few restaurants operate at 100 percent year-round, it would be unwise (desirable as it might be) to use 100 percent as the budgeted capacity on an annual basis.

Another limiting factor may be a lack of skilled labor or skilled supervisory personnel. Well-trained employees or employees who can be trained are often not available. Similarly, supervisory personnel who can train others cannot always be found.

Your management policy can also be a limiting consideration. For example, your restaurant manager may suggest that catering to bus tour groups would help increase sales. But if you feel that such groups would be too disruptive to the regular clientele, then this market for increasing sales is not available.

Another limiting factor may be in the area of increasing costs. You may find you are restricted in your ability to pass on increasing costs by way of higher menu prices.

Finally, customer demand and competition must be kept in mind when budgeting. In the short run there is usually only so much business to go around. Increasing the size of the restaurant or adding to the number of menu items offered does not, by itself, increase the demand for food. It takes time for demand to catch up with supply, and new restaurants (or additions to existing restaurants) usually operate at a lower level of sales than desired until demand increases with time.

Preparing Income Statements

The starting point in the income statement budget is an estimate of your sales keeping the limiting factors in mind. Trend analysis of past performance (discussed in Chapter 12) is useful in this process. Even though budgeted income statements are generally prepared for one year ahead, each annual budget should be broken down into 12 monthly budgets so that comparison with actual results can be made each month. If you compare budget and actual figures only on a yearly basis, any required corrective action may already be eleven months too late.

So how exactly do you set about preparing a sales forecast for a restaurant? If you are already in business, you look first at past actual sales and trends.

To forecast your sales, it is preferable to know how many meals you normally sell during each period of each day, week, and month. The number of meals during each daily meal period is the starting point. Note the effect of any special events in your area (such as sports events, conventions, and holidays) as well as weather and seasonal changes and the effect they have had on your sales.

Electronic sales registers can often be programmed to provide these sales data if you first define what you want from the register. Remember, however, to try not to program the production of too much data to the point that you are overwhelmed with useless information or information too complex to simplify or put into understandable terms.

External Factors. In making your sales forecast you may also need to consider the following external factors:

- Population changes
- Political events
- Strikes
- Inflation and similar economic factors
- Consumer earnings
- Food fads
- Competition

Internal Factors. Also, there may be internal factors that you should consider, such as the following:

- Additional advertising and promotion
- Changes in policies (such as accepting credit cards)
- Food quality changes
- Service quality changes
- Price changes
- Possible inventory restrictions
- Working capital problems
- Labor problems

Of course, it is impossible to build all of these factors into precise forecasts of your sales, but this list should alert you to the many factors that you must consider so that you use the most critical or likely ones to refine your sales budget.

An Example.   For instance, suppose your restaurant's sales for the past three years for the month of January were as follows:

Year 1   3,000 meals × $10.00 average check = $30,000
Year 2   3,510 meals × $10.00 average check =   35,100
Year 3   3,600 meals × $10.33 average check =   37,188

It is now December in year three and you are finalizing your budget for year four, commencing with January. The increase in sales for year two over year one was about 17 percent ($5,100 divided by $30,000). The year three increase over year two was approximately 6 percent ($2,088 divided by $35,100). These increases were caused almost entirely by increases in demand for meals, although average check was up slightly in year three.

Your menu prices have not changed in the past three years. No expansion of your sales premises will occur in year four. Because a new competitive restaurant is opening close by, you do not anticipate your sales to increase in January of year four, but neither do you expect to lose any of your current customers. Because of economic trends, you are forced to meet rising costs by increasing menu prices by 10 percent commencing in January of year four. The budgeted sales for January of year four would, therefore, be

$$\$37,188 + (10\% \times \$37,188) = \$40,907$$

The same type of reasoning would be applied for each of the other eleven months of year four.

Deduct Expenses.   Once forecast sales have been calculated, operating expenses that generally depend on sales (that is, your variable costs) can be calculated and deducted.

Historic accounting records generally show that these variable costs vary within narrow limits as a percentage of sales. The appropriate percentage of expense to sales can, therefore, be applied to the budgeted sales in order to calculate the dollar amount of the expense. For example, if food cost varies between 24.5 and 25.5 percent of sales (an average of 25 percent) and sales are expected to be $40,907 for that period, budgeted food cost would be

$$25\% \times \$40,907 = \$10,227$$

There is a risk with this approach, however, in that it may be perpetuating a situation where the percentage applied is higher than it really should be unless an analysis has been carried out to determine that it is the right one.

Similar calculations would be made for all other variable expenses. As you can now see, a breakdown of costs into their fixed and variable elements as discussed in Chapter 14 can be very useful in budgeting. Once variable expenses have been calculated and deducted from sales, your fixed expenses can then be deducted to complete the income statement.

Usually, fixed expenses are estimated on an annual basis (unlike sales and variable expenses, which are generally calculated monthly). The simplest method of allocating these fixed expenses by month is to show one-twelfth of the annual expense as a monthly cost.

Note that, in budgeting, some fixed expenses vary at your discretion. For example, you may decide that a special allocation will be added to the advertising budget during the coming year or that a particular item of expensive maintenance can be deferred for a year.

Compare Budget with Actual Results

Comparing actual results with those planned or budgeted is probably the most important and advantageous step in the budgeting process. Comparing actual with budget results allows you to ask questions such as the following: Actual sales for April were $30,000 instead of the budgeted $33,000. Was the $3,000 difference caused by a reduction in number of customers? If so, is there an explanation (for example, are higher prices keeping customers away, or did a competitive restaurant open nearby)?

These are just some examples of the questions that can be asked (and for which you should seek answers) in analyzing differences between budgeted and actual performance. The budget is, then, a monitor of the actual performance of your restaurant. It allows you to

- Compare your actual performance with budget plans
- Analyze your restaurant and track causes of variances
- Act to solve problems

Variances.   Obviously, your budget and actual performance will not correspond exactly for any month. There are bound to be variances. The question is, When are those variances significant? It is up to you to set limits on allowable variances in both dollars and percentages.

Percentage variances are calculated by dividing the dollar variance by the budgeted figure for that item. For example, if the budgeted figure were $100, and the variance $10, the percentage variance would be

$$\frac{\$10}{\$100} \times 100 = 10\%$$

It is unlikely that any revenue or controllable expense item will not have a variance because, even with comprehensive information available during the budgeting process, budgeted figures are still estimates. The variances to be analyzed are those that show significant differences from budgeted amounts. What is important in this significance test is the amount of the variance in both dollar and percentage terms, and not just in one of them. If only one of them is used it may not provide information that the other does provide.

For example, dollar differences alone ignore the base or budgeted figure, and the dollar difference may not be significant when compared to the base figure. To illustrate, if the dollar difference in revenue is $5,000 (which seems significant) and the budgeted revenue is $5,000,000 the percentage variance is

$$\frac{\$5,000}{\$5,000,000} \times 100 = 0.001\%$$

which is quite insignificant. In other words, if the actual amount can be this close to the budget in percentage terms, this is remarkably effective budgeting. But this is not disclosed if only the dollar difference is considered.

Similarly, considering the percentage difference alone may also not be useful. For example, if a particular expense for this same property were budgeted at $500, and the actual expense were $550, the variance of $50 would represent 10 percent of the budget figure. Ten percent seems to be a large variance but is insignificant when the dollar figure is also considered. In other words, a variance of $50 is insignificant in a business with revenue of $5,000,000 and would not be worth anybody's time to investigate.

What is significant as a dollar and percentage variance depends entirely on the type and size of establishment. You need to establish in advance the variances allowed in both dollar figures and percentages for each revenue and expense item. At the end of each budget period, only those variances that exceed what is allowed in both dollar and percentage terms will be further analyzed and investigated.

Take Any Corrective Action Required

The next step in the budget process requires you to take corrective action (if necessary) because of unacceptable variances between budgeted and actual figures.

The cause of a variance could be the result of an unanticipated circumstance (for example, weather, a sudden change in economic conditions, a fire on the premises). On the other hand, a difference could be caused by the fact that your prices were not increased sufficiently to compensate for an inflationary rate of cost increases or that your sales forecast was not sufficiently adjusted to compensate for the opening of a new competitive restaurant nearby.

Whatever the cause of variance, the problem should be corrected if possible so that future budgets can more realistically predict planned operations.

Improve Budget Effectiveness

The final step in the budgeting process is to try continually to improve the budgeting process. The information provided from past budgets, and particularly that provided from analyzing variances between actual and budgeted figures, will be helpful. By improving accuracy in your budgeting, you improve the effectiveness of your restaurant's operation.

BUDGETING IN A NEW BUSINESS

Owners of new restaurants will find it more difficult to budget in their early years because they have no internal historic information to serve as a base for forecasts. If a feasibility study (business plan) has been prepared prior to opening, it could serve as a base for budgeting. Alternatively, forecasts must be based on a combination of known facts and industry or market averages for that type and size of restaurant.

Some of the sources of information for a new restaurant might be the following:

- Chamber of commerce or board of trade
- City or municipal hall
- Local (federal or state/provincial) government offices
- Local restaurant association
- Trade publications
- Restaurants in the neighborhood where you plan to locate
- Local trade suppliers to restaurants

Once you have contacted as many likely sources as possible to obtain information about possible sales levels and cost information, you can then prepare your budgeted income statement.

Meal Sales

For example, a proposed restaurant could use the following equation for calculating its breakfast sales:

$$\begin{array}{ccccc} \text{Number} & \text{Seat} & \text{Average} & \text{Days} & \text{Breakfast} \\ \text{of} & \times \text{ turnover} & \times \text{ check} & \times \text{ open in} & = \text{ total} \\ \text{seats} & \text{rate} & & \text{month} & \text{monthly} \\ & & & & \text{sales} \end{array}$$

This same equation could be used for the luncheon period, for the dinner period, and even separately for coffee breaks. Meal periods should be separated because seat turnover rates and average check figures can vary considerably from period to period. The figures in the equation for number of seats and days open in the month are known facts. The seat turnover rates and average check figures can be obtained by reference to published information or observation of competitive restaurants. Once monthly sales figures have been calculated for each meal period, they can be added together to give total sales.

Beverage Sales

Beverage figures are a little more difficult to calculate. There are some industry guidelines in that a coffee shop serving beer and wine generates alcoholic beverage revenue approximating 5 to 15 percent of food sales. In a dining room the alcoholic beverage revenue (beer, wine, and liquor) approximates 25 to 30 percent of food sales. For example, a dining room with $100,000 a month of food sales could expect about $25,000 to $30,000 of total liquor sales.

As for beverage figures in a cocktail lounge, there is no simple equation. An average check figure (such as average spending figure per customer) can be misleading. For example, one customer can occupy a seat and spend $3 on five drinks; average spending for that customer is $15. On the other hand, five different customers can occupy the same seat and each spend $3 over the same period of time, average spending $3. Therefore, the equation used for calculating food sales may be difficult to apply in a bar setting. One alternative is to use the current industry average sales per seat per year in a cocktail bar.

$$\begin{array}{ccc} \text{Average annual} & \text{Number} & \text{Total} \\ \text{sales} & \times \text{ of} & = \text{ annual} \\ \text{per seat} & \text{seats} & \text{sales} \end{array}$$

To convert to a monthly basis for budget purposes, this figure can then be divided by twelve and added to the already calculated beverage sales by month generated from the food operation.

Deduct Expenses

Although these equations do not cover all possible approaches they should give you some idea of the methods that can be used when budgeting sales for a new operation. Once sales have been forecast, estimated variable expenses can then be deducted applying industry average percentage figures for each expense to the calculated budgeted revenue. Finally, estimated fixed expenses can be deducted.

Using Equations in an Ongoing Operation

Note that the equations illustrated in this section are not limited to a new operation. They can also be used in an existing restaurant. For example, instead of applying an estimated percentage of sales increase to last year's figure to obtain the current year's budget, it may be better to break down last year's sales figure into its various equation elements and adjust each of them individually (where necessary) to develop the new budget amount.

For example, suppose last year your food sales were $100,212 in June. In June this year you expect a 5 percent increase; therefore, budgeted sales will be

$$\$100,212 \times (5\% \times \$100,212) = \$105,222$$

A more comprehensive approach would be to analyze last year's figure in the following way:

Number of seats		Seat turnover rate		Average check		Days open in month		Total monthly sales
80	×	3.5	×	$11.93	×	30	=	$100,212

You can then apply the budget year trends and information to last year's detailed figures. Suppose, in the budget period, because of a new restaurant in the area, you expect a slight drop in the seat turnover to 3.25. This will be compensated for by an increase in your average check of 12 percent to $13.36. Your budgeted sales are, therefore,

Number of seats		Seat turnover rate		Average check		Days open in month		Total monthly sales
80	×	3.25	×	$13.36	×	30	=	$104,208

This approach to budgeting may require a little more work but will probably provide you with budgeted figures that are more accurate and can be analyzed more meaningfully than would otherwise be the case.

SEVENTEEN

Working Capital and Cash Management

WORKING CAPITAL

You will remember from Chapter 2 where the balance sheet was discussed that (listed under the assets) there is a section called current assets. This includes items such as cash, accounts receivable, marketable securities, inventories, and prepaid expenses. On the other side of the balance sheet is a section for the current liabilities, including such items as accounts payable, accrued expenses, income tax payable, and the current portion of long-term mortgages. The difference between total current assets and total current liabilities is known as net working capital:

Current assets − Current liabilities = Net working capital

Even though this chapter is about cash management, it is not about only the management of cash but also of working capital, that is, all the accounts that appear under the "current" sections of the balance sheet. In cash management, your objective should be to conserve cash, earn interest on it (one possibility), and thus maximize profits.

Money does not always come into a restaurant at the same rate that it goes out. At times you will have excess cash on hand; at others there will be shortages. You need to anticipate both of these events so that shortages can be covered. In this way, your cash balance will be kept at its optimum level.

How Much Working Capital?

How much net working capital does your restaurant need? This cannot be answered in general terms with an absolute dollar amount. For example, suppose it were a rule of thumb that a restaurant should have a net working capital of $5,000. One restaurant might find itself with the following:

253

Current assets	$15,000
Current liabilities	10,000
Working capital	$ 5,000

On the other hand, a large restaurant would have to have larger amounts of cash, inventories, accounts receivable, and other items that are current assets. Also, it would probably have larger amounts in its various current liability accounts. Its balance sheet might, therefore, look like this:

Current assets	$100,000
Current liabilities	95,000
Working capital	$ 5,000

The smaller restaurant is in much better financial shape than the larger one. It has $1.50 ($15,000 divided by $10,000) of current assets for every $1.00 of current liabilities, a comfortable cushion. The large restaurant has just over $1.05 ($100,000 divided by $95,000) of current assets for each dollar of current liabilities—not so comfortable a cushion.

You will recall from the discussion of the current ratio in Chapter 13 that as a general rule a business should have at least $2.00 of current assets for each $1.00 of current liabilities. This means that its net working capital ($2.00 minus $1.00) is equivalent to its current liabilities.

However, this rule is primarily for companies (such as manufacturing, wholesaling, and some retailing organizations) that need to carry very large inventories that do not turn over very rapidly.

Restaurants can often operate with a very low ratio of current assets to current liabilities, often as low as 1 to 1. In other words, for each $1.00 of current assets there is $1.00 of current liabilities. This means that the business has, in fact, no net working capital.

At certain times of the year, some restaurants can even operate with negative working capital: In other words, current liabilities exceed current assets. This might be typical of a seasonal operation. Such a restaurant would have current assets vastly in excess of current liabilities during the peak season, but the reverse situation could prevail in the off-season.

Let us have a look at some of the more important working capital items that constitute cash management.

Cash

Cash on hand (as distinguished from cash in the bank) is the money in circulation in your restaurant. This could be cash used by cashiers and servers as "floats" or "banks" for change-making purposes, petty cash, or just general cash in your office safe. The amount of cash on hand should only be sufficient for normal day-to-day operations. Any surplus cash should be deposited in your bank in savings accounts or term deposits so that it can earn interest. Preferably, each day's net cash receipts should be deposited in the bank as soon as possible the following day.

Cash in the bank in your current account should be sufficient to pay only current bills or current payroll. Any excess funds should be invested in short-term securities (making sure there is a good balance between maximizing the interest rate and the security and liquidity of the investment) or in savings or other special accounts that earn interest.

Accounts Receivable

In certain types of restaurant, there may be extensive accounts receivable. For example, a catering company doing group business might request a deposit prior to handling a function but after the event invoice the hosting organization for any balance due, creating an account receivable. Similarly, many restaurants today accept credit cards in payment for meals; unpaid credit card amounts are accounts receivable until the cash is collected.

Attention to accounts receivable should be focused on two areas: ensuring that invoices are mailed out promptly and following up on delinquent accounts to have them collected. Money tied up in accounts receivable is money not earning a return.

Extension of credit to customers is an acknowledged form of business, but it should not be extended to the point of allowing payments to lag two or three months behind the mailing of the invoice.

Methods of controlling accounts receivable (such as accounts receivable turnover and days sales in receivables) were discussed in Chapter 13. Another way of keeping an eye on your accounts receivable is to prepare a monthly chart showing their age. The following illustrates such a chart:

Accounts Receivable Aging Chart

Age	May 31		June 30	
0–30 days	$59,000	79.5%	$56,400	74.2%
31–60 days	11,800	15.9	8,800	11.6
61–90 days	2,400	3.2	8,600	11.3
over 90 days	1,000	1.4	2,200	2.9
Totals	$74,200	100.0%	$76,000	100.0%

This particular chart shows that the accounts receivable outstanding situation has deteriorated from May to June. In May 79.5 percent of total receivables were less than thirty days old. In June only 74.2 percent were less than thirty days outstanding. Similarly, the relative percentages in the thirty-one- to sixty-day category have increased from May to June. By contrast, in the sixty-one- to ninety-days bracket 11.3 percent of accounts receivable are outstanding in June, against only 3.2 percent in May.

This particular aging schedule shows that the accounts receivable are getting older. If this trend continues, collection procedures will have to be improved. If after all possible collection procedures have been explored an account is deemed to be uncollectible (a bad debt), it is then removed from the accounts receivable and recorded as a bad debt expense on your income statement. The decision about its uncollectibility should only be made by you as owner.

Marketable Securities

Generally, any surplus cash not needed for immediate purposes should be invested in some type of security. Investments could be for as short a period as one day but are usually for longer periods, although seldom more than a year. If you had surplus cash for periods of a year or more, it might then be wise to seek out long-term investments, such as building a new restaurant or expanding your present one, because the return on those investments over the long run could be expected to be greater than for investment in short-term securities.

Most restaurants, particularly those that rely for much or all of their trade on seasonal tourists, have peaks and valleys in their cash flows. You should invest surplus cash from peak-season flows in short-term securities until it is necessary to liquidate them to take care of low, or negative, cash flows during the off-season. Sometimes it is necessary to build up surplus cash amounts to take care of periodic lump sum payments, such as quarterly tax or dividend payments. These built-up amounts can well be invested in marketable securities until they are needed for payment of these liabilities.

In times of high interest rates, many restaurants find it profitable to invest all cash in excess of day-to-day needs in the most liquid of marketable securities: that is, those that can be converted into cash quickly if an unanticipated event requiring cash occurs.

You must consider two important factors when investing in marketable securities: risk and liquidity. A low risk generally goes hand in hand with a low interest rate. A more risky investment would have to offer a higher interest rate in order to attract investors. Government securities have very low risk and usually guarantee that the investment can be cashed in at full face value at any time. Their interest rate, however, is also relatively low. On the other hand, investments in long-term corporate bonds, with a distant maturity date, may offer a higher interest rate. This type of security is, however, subject to economic factors that make their buy-sell price more volatile. This volatility increases the risk and can reduce the profitability of investing in them if they have to be liquidated, or converted into cash, at an inappropriate time.

Inventories

The level at which inventories should be maintained for food and beverages can be established by calculating the inventory turnover rates for each.

Food Inventory Turnover. The turnover rate for food is calculated as follows

$$\frac{\text{Food cost for the month}}{\text{Average food inventory during month}}$$

Food cost for the month is calculated as follows:

Beginning of the month inventory
+Purchases during month
−End of the month inventory

and average inventory is calculated as follows:

$$\frac{(\text{Beginning of the month inventory} + \text{End of the month inventory})}{2}$$

Assume you have the following figures:

Beginning of the month inventory	$ 7,000
End of the month inventory	8,000
Purchases during month	24,500

The inventory turnover rate is

$$\frac{\$7,000 + \$24,500 - \$8,000}{(\$7,000 + \$8,000)/2} = \frac{\$23,500}{\$7,500} = 3.1 \text{ times}$$

The inventory turnover can be calculated annually, but it is preferable to do it monthly, particularly if monthly income statements are prepared. This is because if the turnover rate at the end of any month is out of line, corrective action can be taken then, instead of only at the year-end.

Traditionally, restaurant industry food inventory turnover ranges between two and four times a month. At this level the danger of running out of food products is minimal; on the other hand, there is not an overinvestment in inventory tying up money that could otherwise be put to use earning interest income. However, despite this range of two to four times a month, there may be exceptions.

Turnover Trends. Perhaps of more importance to your restaurant is not what the actual turnover rate is but whether or not there is a change in this turnover rate over time and what the cause of the change is. For example, let us assume that the earlier figures of $23,500 for food cost and $7,500 for average inventory, giving a turnover rate of 3.1, were typical of the monthly figures for your operation. If you noticed that the figure for turnover changed to 2, this could mean that more money was being invested in inventory and not producing a return:

$$\frac{\$23,500}{\$11,750} = 2 \text{ times}$$

Alternatively, a change in the turnover rate to 4 could mean that too little was invested in inventory and that some customers might not be able to get certain items listed on your menu:

$$\frac{\$23,500}{\$\ 5,875} = 4 \text{ times}$$

In some restaurants, the turnover rate may be extremely low (less than 2). For example, a restaurant at a resort property in a remote location may only be able to obtain deliveries once a month. It is thus forced to carry a large inventory. On the other hand, a drive-in restaurant that receives daily delivery of its food products from a central commissary and carries little inventory overnight could conceivably have a turnover rate as high as thirty times a month. Each restaurant should establish its own standards for turnover and then watch for deviations from those standards.

Beverage Inventory Turnover. Alcoholic beverage inventory turnover is calculated using the same formula as for food but substituting beverage inventories and purchases for food inventories and purchases. The normal monthly turnover rate for beverages is from ½ to 1 turnover a month. Again, however, there are exceptions to this rule of thumb.

Accounts Payable, Accrued Expenses, and Other Current Liabilities

The cash conservation objective with accounts payable, accrued expenses, and other current liabilities is to delay payment until payment is required.

However, this does not mean delaying payment until it is delinquent! A restaurant with a reputation for delinquency may find it has difficulty obtaining food, beverages, supplies, and services on anything other than a cash basis.

If a discount for prompt payment is offered, the advantages of this should be considered. For example, a common discount rate is 2 percent off the invoice total if paid within ten days; otherwise it is payable without discount within sixty days. On a $1,000 purchase that you paid within ten days this would save $20. This may not seem to be a lot of money, but multiplied many times over on all similar purchases made during a year it could amount to a large sum. However, in the example cited you may have to borrow the money ($980) in order to make the payment within ten days. Let us assume you borrowed the money for fifty days at an 8 percent interest rate. The interest expense on this borrowed money would be

$$\frac{\$980 \times 50 \text{ days} \times 8\%}{365 \text{ days}} = \$10.74$$

It would still be advantageous to borrow the money since the difference between the discount saving of $20.00 and the interest expense of $10.74 is still $9.26.

PROFIT IS NOT CASH

One of the most important facts you must remember in cash management and in analysis of income statements is that the net profit amount shown on the income statement is not the equivalent of cash. A reason for this is the accrual nature of the accounting process (discussed in Chapter 1). With accrual accounting, sales are recorded at the time the sale is made, even though you may not receive the cash until some time later.

Similarly, you can purchase supplies on credit. In other words, the goods are received and used but not paid for until thirty days or more later. However, as long as the goods are used during the income statement period, they are recorded on the income statement as an expense.

Also, some expenses may be prepaid at the beginning of the year (for example, insurance expense), yet the total insurance cost is spread equally over each monthly income statement for the entire year. This means that, for example, in January $12,000 may be paid out for annual insurance, yet only $1,000 is recorded on the January income statement as an expense and $1,000 will be shown as an expense for each of the next eleven months.

Another complicating factor is that some items (such as depreciation) are recorded as an expense on the income statement even though no cash is involved.

For these and other reasons, the net profit shown on your income statement cannot normally be equated with cash. If you wish to equate net income with cash (a good idea in most businesses) you must convert it to a cash basis, and one of the ways to do this is to prepare cash budgets. Cash budgets are a major aid in effective cash management.

Cash Budgeting

The starting point in cash budgeting is the budgeted income statement showing the anticipated (forecast) sales and expenses by month for as long a period as is required for cash budget preparation.

In our case we will use a three month period. Assume that the budgeted income statements for Eddie's Eatery for the next three months are as in Table 17.1. In order to prepare the cash budget from these statements, Eddie needs the following additional information:

- Accounting records show that, each month, approximately 60 percent of the sales is in the form of cash, and 40 percent is on credit and collected the following month.
- March sales were $28,000 (Eddie needs this information so that he can calculate the amount of cash that is going to be collected in April from sales made in March).
- Purchases of food (food cost) are paid 25 percent cash and 75 percent

TABLE 17.1

Budgeted Income and Expenses

		April		May		June
Revenue		$30,000		$35,000		$40,000
Food cost		12,000		14,000		16,000
Gross profit		$18,000		$21,000		$24,000
Payroll and related expense	$9,000		$10,500		$12,000	
Supplies and other expense	1,500		1,750		2,000	
Utilities	500		750		1,000	
Rent	1,000		1,000		1,000	
Advertising	500	12,500	500	14,500	500	16,500
Income before depreciation		$ 5,500		$ 6,500		$ 7,500
Depreciation		2,000		2,000		2,000
Net income		$ 3,500		$ 4,500		$ 5,500

credit. The 75 percent (accounts payable) is paid the month follow-ing purchase.

- March food purchases were $11,000. (Again, Eddie needs this infor-mation so that he can calculate the amount to be paid in cash during April).
- Payroll, supplies, utilities, and rent are paid 100 percent cash during each current month.
- Advertising has been prepaid in January ($6,000 cash) for the entire year. In order not to show the full $6,000 as an expense in January (because the benefit of the advertising is for a full year), the income statements show $500 each month for this prepaid expense.
- The bank balance on April 1 is $10,200.

Eddie can now use the budgeted income statements (Table 17.1) and the preceding information to calculate the amounts for his cash budget. The process is simple. His first cash budget month is April and cash receipts and disbursements can be calculated as follows.

Cash Receipts.   The cash receipts for April are

Current month sales $30,000 × 60% cash =	$18,000
Accounts receivable collections March sales	
$28,000 × 40% =	11,200

Cash Disbursements.   The cash disbursements for April are

Current month food purchases (food cost): $12,000 ×	
25% paid cash =	$3,000
Accounts payable for food purchases from previous	
month $11,000 × 75% =	8,250
Payroll and related expense, 100% cash =	9,000
Supplies and other expense, 100% cash =	1,500
Utilities, 100% cash =	500
Rent, 100% cash =	1,000
Advertising: already paid in January (the $6,000 would	
have been shown as a cash disbursement for that	
month)	0
Depreciation: does not require a disbursement of cash;	
it is simply a write-down of the book value of the	
related assets	0

Eddie's completed cash budget for the month of April would then be as follows:

Opening bank balance	$10,200
Receipts	
Cash sales	18,000
Collections on accounts rec.	11,200
Total	$39,400
Disbursements	
Cash food purchases	$ 3,000
Accounts payable	8,250
Payroll and related expense	9,000
Supplies and other expenses	1,500
Utilities	500
Rent	1,000
Total	$23,250
Closing bank balance	$16,150

Note that the closing bank balance each month is calculated as follows:

Opening bank balance + Receipts − Disbursements

Or for April

$$\$10,200 + \$29,200 - \$23,250 = \$16,150$$

Each month the closing bank balance becomes the opening bank balance of the following month. Eddie's completed cash budget for the three month period would be as in Table 17.2.

From Table 17.2 Eddie can see that the bank account is expected to increase from $10,200 to $30,150 over the next three months. When his cash budget for the months of July, August, and September is prepared, it will show whether or not the bank balance is going to continue to increase or start to decline.

Investing Surplus.   From Table 17.2, it is obvious that Eddie is going to have a fairly healthy surplus of cash (as long as budget projections are reasonably accurate) that should not be left to accumulate at no or low interest in a bank account. In this particular situation, Eddie might decide to take $20,000 or $25,000 out of the bank account and invest it in high-interest-rate short-term (thirty-, sixty-, or ninety-day) securities.

Without preparing a cash budget, it would be difficult for Eddie to know that there were to be surplus funds on hand that could be used to

TABLE 17.2

Sample 3-Month Cash Budget

	April	May	June
Opening bank balance	$10,200	$16,150	$22,650
Receipts			
Cash revenue	18,000	21,000	24,000
Collection on accounts receivable	11,200	12,000	14,000
Total	$39,400	$49,150	$60,650
Disbursements			
Cash food purchases	$ 3,000	$ 3,500	$ 4,000
Accounts payable paid	8,250	9,000	10,500
Payroll and related expense	9,000	10,500	12,000
Supplies and other expense	1,500	1,750	2,000
Utilities	500	750	1,000
Rent	1,000	1,000	1,000
Total	$23,250	$26,500	$30,500
Closing bank balance	$16,150	$22,650	$30,150

advantage to increase his net profit and cash receipts. If the cash were taken out of his bank account and invested, the cash budget would have to show this at that time as a disbursement until the securities were cashed in and shown as a receipt.

Similarly, interest on loans, principal payments on loans, purchases of fixed assets, income tax payments, and dividend payouts or owner cash withdrawals would also be recorded on the cash budget as disbursements. If any fixed assets were sold for cash, the cash received would show as a receipt.

Negative Cash Budgets

Seasonal restaurants may find that for some months of the year their disbursements exceed receipts to the point that they have negative cash budgets. By preparing a cash budget ahead of time, however, the restaurant can show that it has anticipated the cash shortage and can plan to cover it, for example, by means of a short-term bank loan. Such a loan will be easier to obtain when your banker sees that good cash management is being practiced through the preparation of a cash budget.

Any loans received to cover cash shortages will be recorded as receipts on the cash budget at that time and as disbursements when paid back.

The cash budget, particularly if prepared a year ahead, can help you in making not only decisions about investing excess funds and arranging to borrow funds to cover shortages but also aids in discretionary decisions concerning such matters as major renovations, replacement of fixed assets, and payment of dividends (in an incorporated company) or cash withdrawals (in a proprietorship or partnership).

EIGHTEEN

Long-term Investments

CAPITAL BUDGETING

This chapter concerns methods of evaluating investments in long-term assets. Investment in long-term assets is sometimes referred to as capital budgeting, but we are not so much concerned in this chapter with the budgeting process as we are with the decision about whether or not to make a specific investment or with the decision about which of two or more investments would be preferable.

The largest long-term investment that a restaurant may have is in its land and building. This is a one-time investment for each separate property. However, this chapter is primarily concerned about more frequent investment decisions for items such as equipment and furniture purchases and replacements.

Differences from Day-to-Day Decisions

Long-term investment decisions differ from day-to-day decisions for a number of reasons. For example, long-term investment decisions concern assets that have a relatively long life. Day-to-day decisions concern assets that turn over frequently. A wrong decision about a piece of equipment can involve a time span stretching over many years. A wrong decision about operating supplies has only a short-run effect.

Also, day-to-day operating decisions do not usually involve large amounts of money for any individual item, whereas the purchase of a long-term asset requires the outlay of a large sum of money that can have a major effect if a wrong decision is made.

CAPITAL BUDGETING METHODS

Four methods of investment decision making will be discussed in this chapter. These are:

1. Average rate of return (ARR)

2. Payback period (PP)

3. Net present value (NPV)

4. Internal rate of return (IRR)

To set the scene for the average rate of return and the payback period methods, let us consider Sarah's, a restaurant that is presently using a manual system for recording sales. Sarah is considering installing an electronic sales register that will eliminate part of the present wage cost and save an estimated $4,000 a year. The register will cost $5,000 and is expected to have a five-year life with no trade-in value. Depreciation is, therefore, $1,000 a year ($5,000 divided by 5). Saving and expense figures are as follows:

Saving—employee wages	$4,000
Expenses	
Maintenance	$ 350
Stationery	650
Depreciation	1,000
Total	$2,000
Saving before tax	$2,000
Income tax	1,000
Net annual saving	$1,000

Average Rate of Return

The average rate of return (ARR) method compares the average annual net profit (after income tax) resulting from the investment with the average investment. The equation for ARR is

$$\frac{\text{Net annual saving}}{\text{Average investment}}$$

Note that the average investment is simply initial investment divided by 2. Using the preceding information, Sarah's ARR is

$$\frac{\$1,000}{\$(5,000/2)} \times 100 = \frac{\$1,000}{\$2,500} \times 100 = 40.0\%$$

The advantage of the ARR method is its simplicity. It is frequently used to compare the anticipated return from a proposal with a minimum desired return. If the proposal's return is less than desired, it is rejected. If it is greater than desired, a more in-depth analysis using other investment techniques may then be used. The major disadvantage of the ARR is that it is based on net profit rather than on cash flow.

Payback Period

The payback period (PP) method overcomes the cash flow shortcoming of the ARR. The PP method measures the initial investment with the annual cash inflows. The equation is

$$\frac{\text{Initial investment}}{\text{Net annual cash saving}}$$

Since the information given earlier for Sarah provides her with net annual saving, and not net annual cash saving, she must first convert the net annual saving figure to a cash basis. This is done by adding back the depreciation (an expense that does not require an outlay of cash). The cash saving figure is

Net annual saving	$1,000
Add depreciation	1,000
Net annual cash saving	$2,000

Sarah's payback period is then

$$\frac{\$5,000}{\$2,000} = 2.5 \text{ years}$$

The PP method, although simple, does not really measure the merit of an investment, but only the speed with which the investment cost might be recovered. It is useful in evaluating a number of proposals so that only those that fall within a predetermined payback period will be considered for further evaluation using other investment techniques.

However, both the PP and the ARR methods still suffer from a common fault: they both ignore the time value of cash flows, or the concept that money now is worth more than the same amount at some time in the future. This concept will be discussed in the next section, after which we will explore the use of the net present value and internal rate of return methods.

Discounted Cash Flow

The concept of discounted cash flow can probably best be understood by looking first at an example of compound interest. Table 18.1 shows, year

TABLE 18.1

Compound Interest, $100 at 10 Percent

	Jan. 1 0001	Dec. 31 0001	Dec. 31 0002	Dec. 31 0003	Dec.31 0004
Balance forward	$100.00	$100.00	$110.00	$121.00	$133.10
Interest 10%		10.00	11.00	12.10	13.31
Investment value end of year		$110.00	$121.00	$133.10	$146.41

by year, what happens if you invest $100.00 at a 10 percent compound interest rate. At the end of four years, your investment will be worth $146.41.

Discounting is simply the reverse of compounding interest. In other words, at a 10 percent interest rate, what is $146.41 four years from now worth to you today? You could work out the solution manually or with a hand calculator, but it can much more easily be solved by using a table of discounted cash flow factors.

Table 18.2 illustrates such a table, and, if you go to the number (called a factor) that is opposite year four and under the 10 percent column, you will see that it is 0.6830. This factor tells us that $1.00 received at the end of year four is worth only $1.00 × 0.683 = $0.683 right now.

Indeed, this factor tells us that any amount of money at the end of four years from now at a 10 percent interest (discount) rate is worth only 68.3 percent of that amount right now. Let us prove this by taking our $146.41 amount at the end of year four from Table 18.1 and discounting it back to the present:

$$\$146.41 \times 0.683 = \$99.99803 \text{ or } \$100.00$$

We know that $100 is the right answer because it is the amount we started with in our illustration of compounding interest in Table 18.1.

For a series of annual cash flows, you simply apply the related annual discount factor for that year to the cash inflow for that year. For example, a cash inflow of $1,000 a year for each of three years using a 10 percent factor will give you the following total discounted cash flow:

Year	Factor	Amount	Total
1	0.9091	$1,000	$ 909.10
2	0.8264	$1,000	826.40
3	0.7513	$1,000	751.30
			$2,486.80

TABLE 18.2
Table of Discounted Cash Flow Factors by Percentage

Period	5	6	7	8	9	10	11	12	13	14	15	16	17	18	19	20	25	30
1	0.9524	0.9434	0.9346	0.9259	0.9174	0.9091	0.9009	0.8929	0.8850	0.8772	0.8696	0.8621	0.8547	0.8475	0.8403	0.8333	0.8000	0.7692
2	0.9070	0.8900	0.8734	0.8573	0.8417	0.8264	0.8116	0.7972	0.7831	0.7695	0.7561	0.7432	0.7305	0.7182	0.7062	0.6944	0.6400	0.5917
3	0.8638	0.8396	0.8163	0.7938	0.7722	0.7513	0.7312	0.7118	0.6931	0.6750	0.6575	0.6407	0.6244	0.6086	0.5934	0.5787	0.5120	0.4552
4	0.8227	0.7921	0.7629	0.7350	0.7084	0.6830	0.6587	0.6355	0.6133	0.5921	0.5718	0.5523	0.5337	0.5158	0.4987	0.4823	0.4096	0.3501
5	0.7835	0.7473	0.7130	0.6806	0.6499	0.6209	0.5935	0.5674	0.5428	0.5194	0.4972	0.4761	0.4561	0.4371	0.4191	0.4019	0.3277	0.2693
6	0.7462	0.7050	0.6663	0.6302	0.5963	0.5645	0.5346	0.5066	0.4803	0.4556	0.4323	0.4104	0.3898	0.3704	0.3521	0.3349	0.2621	0.2072
7	0.7107	0.6651	0.6228	0.5835	0.5470	0.5132	0.4817	0.4524	0.4251	0.3996	0.3759	0.3538	0.3332	0.3139	0.2959	0.2791	0.2097	0.1594
8	0.6768	0.6274	0.5820	0.5403	0.5019	0.4665	0.4339	0.4039	0.3762	0.3506	0.3269	0.3050	0.2848	0.2660	0.2487	0.2326	0.1678	0.1226
9	0.6446	0.5919	0.5439	0.5003	0.4604	0.4241	0.3909	0.3606	0.3329	0.3075	0.2843	0.2630	0.2434	0.2255	0.2090	0.1938	0.1342	0.0943
10	0.6139	0.5584	0.5084	0.4632	0.4224	0.3855	0.3522	0.3220	0.2946	0.2697	0.2472	0.2267	0.2080	0.1911	0.1756	0.1615	0.1074	0.0725
11	0.5847	0.5268	0.4751	0.4289	0.3875	0.3505	0.3173	0.2875	0.2607	0.2366	0.2149	0.1954	0.1778	0.1619	0.1476	0.1346	0.0859	0.0558
12	0.5568	0.4970	0.4440	0.3971	0.3555	0.3186	0.2858	0.2567	0.2307	0.2076	0.1869	0.1685	0.1520	0.1372	0.1240	0.1122	0.0687	0.0429
13	0.5303	0.4688	0.4150	0.3677	0.3262	0.2897	0.2575	0.2292	0.2042	0.1821	0.1625	0.1452	0.1299	0.1163	0.1042	0.0935	0.0550	0.0330
14	0.5051	0.4423	0.3878	0.3405	0.2993	0.2633	0.2320	0.2046	0.1807	0.1597	0.1413	0.1252	0.1110	0.0986	0.0876	0.0779	0.0440	0.0254
15	0.4810	0.4173	0.3625	0.3152	0.2745	0.2394	0.2090	0.1827	0.1599	0.1401	0.1229	0.1079	0.0949	0.0835	0.0736	0.0649	0.0352	0.0195
16	0.4581	0.3937	0.3387	0.2919	0.2519	0.2176	0.1883	0.1631	0.1415	0.1229	0.1069	0.0930	0.0811	0.0708	0.0618	0.0541	0.0281	0.0150
17	0.4363	0.3714	0.3166	0.2703	0.2311	0.1978	0.1696	0.1456	0.1252	0.1078	0.0929	0.0802	0.0693	0.0600	0.0520	0.0451	0.0225	0.0116
18	0.4155	0.3503	0.2959	0.2503	0.2120	0.1799	0.1528	0.1300	0.1108	0.0946	0.0808	0.0691	0.0592	0.0508	0.0437	0.0376	0.0180	0.0089
19	0.3957	0.3305	0.2765	0.2317	0.1945	0.1635	0.1377	0.1161	0.0981	0.0829	0.0703	0.0596	0.0506	0.0431	0.0367	0.0313	0.0144	0.0068
20	0.3769	0.3118	0.2584	0.2146	0.1784	0.1486	0.1240	0.1037	0.0868	0.0728	0.0611	0.0514	0.0433	0.0365	0.0308	0.0261	0.0115	0.0053

Net Present Value

Discounted cash flow can be used with the net present value (NPV) method for evaluating investment proposals. For example, Table 18.3 gives projections of savings and costs for a new microcomputer for Kate's Katering. The computer costs $5,000 and will have a trade-in (scrap) value of $1,000 at the end of its five year life.

The estimate of the future savings and costs is the most difficult part of the exercise. In Kate's case, she is forecasting for five years ahead. Obviously, the longer the period of time, the less accurate are the estimates likely to be. Note that depreciation is calculated as follows:

Initial cost	$5,000
Less: Trade-in	(1,000)
	$4,000

$$\text{Depreciation (straight-line)} \quad \frac{\$4,000}{5} = \$800/\text{year}$$

TABLE 18.3

Calculation of Annual Net Cash Flow

Microcomputer (Investment Cost $5,000)					
	Year 1	Year 2	Year 3	Year 4	Year 5
Saving (wages)	$4,000	$4,000	$4,000	$4,000	$4,000
Expenses					
Initial training cost	$3,500				
Maintenance contract	350	$ 350	$ 350	$ 350	$ 350
Special overhaul			250		
Stationery	650	650	650	650	650
Depreciation	800	800	800	800	800
Total expenses	$5,300	$1,800	$2,050	$1,800	$1,800
Saving less expenses	($1,300)	$2,200	$1,950	$2,200	$2,200
Income tax 50%	0	1,100	975	1,100	1,100
	($1,300)	$1,100	$ 975	$1,100	$1,100
Add back depreciation	800	800	800	800	800
					$1,900
Add scrap value					1,000
Net cash flow	($ 500)	$1,900	$1,775	$1,900	$2,900

Also note that depreciation is deductible as an expense for the calculation of income tax, but this expense does not require an outlay of cash year by year. Therefore, Kate must convert the annual net saving from the investment to a cash situation by adding back depreciation each year. Note also that there is a negative cash flow in year one and that the trade-in value is a partial recovery of the initial investment and is, therefore, added as a positive cash flow at the end of year five in Table 18.3.

The data Kate is interested in from Table 18.3 are the initial investment and the annual net cash flow figures. These figures have been transferred to Table 18.4 and, using the relevant 10 percent discount factors from Table 18.2, have been converted to a net present value basis. Note how the negative cash flow has been handled. As you can see from Table 18.4, Kate's net present value figure from this proposed investment is positive.

It is possible for a net present value figure to be negative if the initial investment exceeds the sum of the individual years' present values. In the case of negative NPV, the investment should not be undertaken, because, assuming the accuracy of the figures, the investment will not produce the rate of return desired.

Finally, the discount rate actually used should be realistic. It is frequently the rate that a restaurant's owners expect the business to earn, after taxes, on the equity investment.

Internal Rate of Return

As you have seen, the NPV method uses a specific discount rate to determine whether proposals result in a net present value greater than zero. Those that do not are rejected.

TABLE 18.4

Conversion of Annual Cash Flows to Net Present Values

Year	Net Cash Flow	×	Discount Factor	=	Present Value
1	($ 500)		0.9091		($ 455)
2	1,900		0.8264		1,570
3	1,775		0.7513		1,333
4	1,900		0.6830		1,298
5	2,900		0.6209		1,801
Total present value					$5,547
Less: Initial investment					(5,000)
Net present value					$ 547

The internal rate of return (IRR) method also uses the discounted cash flow concept. However, this method's approach determines the interest (discount) rate that will make the total discounted cash inflows equal the initial investment.

For example, suppose you decided to investigate renting a building adjacent to your business in order to increase sales. Your investigation showed that it would cost $100,000 to renovate and equip the building with a guaranteed five year lease. The projected cash flow (net profit after tax, with depreciation added back) for each of the five years is as follows:

Year	Cash Flow
1	$ 18,000
2	20,000
3	22,000
4	25,000
5	30,000
	$115,000

In addition to the total of $115,000 cash recovery over the five years, it is estimated the equipment could be sold for $10,000 at the end of the lease period. Your total cash recovery is, therefore, $115,000 + $10,000 = $125,000, which is $25,000 more than the initial investment required of $100,000.

On the face of it, you would appear to be ahead of the game. If the annual flows are discounted back to their net present value, however, a different picture emerges, as illustrated in Table 18.5. Table 18.5 shows that the future flows of cash discounted back to today's values using a 12 percent rate are less than the initial investment by almost $14,000. Thus, you know that if the projections about the venture are correct, there will not be a 12 percent cash return on your investment.

The IRR method can be used to determine the return that you will earn if the investment is made. From Table 18.5, you know that 12 percent is too high. By moving to a lower rate of interest, you will eventually, by trial and error, arrive at one where the NPV (the difference between total present value and initial investment) is virtually zero. This is illustrated in Table 18.6 with a 7 percent interest (discount) rate.

Table 18.6 tells you that the initial $100,000 investment will return the initial cash outlay except for $157 and earn 7 percent on your investment. Stated slightly differently, you would recover the full $100,000 but earn slightly less than 7 percent on your investment. If you are satisfied with a 7

TABLE 18.5

Annual Cash Flows Converted to Net Present Value

Year	Annual cash flow	×	Discount factor 12%	=	Present value
1	$18,000		0.8929		$ 16,072
2	20,000		0.7972		15,944
3	22,000		0.7118		15,660
4	25,000		0.6355		15,888
5	30,000		0.5674		17,022
Sale of equipment and furniture	10,000		0.5674		5,674
Total present value					$ 86,260
Less: Initial investment					(100,000)
Net present value (negative)					$(13,740)

percent cash return on the investment (note this is 7 percent after income tax), then you will proceed with the project.

Nonquantifiable Benefits

In this chapter we have looked at various methods of making investment decisions. We have ignored information that is not easily quantifiable but that may still be relevant to decision making. In practice, however, you should not ignore such factors as prestige, goodwill, reputation, employee or customer acceptance, and social or environmental implications of your investment decisions.

TABLE 18.6

Discount Factor Arrived at by Trial and Error

Year	Annual cash flow	×	Discount factor 7%	=	Present value
1	$18,000		0.9346		$16,823
2	20,000		0.8734		17,468
3	22,000		0.8163		17,959
4	25,000		0.7629		19,073
5	30,000		0.7130		21,390
Sale of equipment and furniture	10,000		0.7130		7,130
Total present value					$99,843

For example, if you redecorate your restaurant, what are the cash benefits? They may be difficult to quantify, but to retain customer goodwill, it may have to be redecorated. Similarly, how are the relative benefits to be assessed in spending $5,000 on restaurant redecoration versus Christmas bonuses for your employees? Personal judgment must play a major role in such decisions.

LEASING EQUIPMENT

We have had a look at various methods of decision making for purchase of assets such as equipment. Another method of obtaining your restaurant's productive assets is to rent or lease, rather than own, them. A lease is a contractual arrangement in which the owner of the asset (the lessor) grants you (the lessee) the right to the asset for a specified period in return for periodic lease payments. Leasing of land and/or buildings has always been a common method used by restaurant operators to minimize the investment costs of going into business. In recent years, leasing of equipment and similar items has also become more common.

Some suppliers of equipment lease directly. In other cases you lease from a company that specializes in leasing. In other words, the lessor is a company that has bought the equipment from the supplier and has gone into the business of leasing to others.

Advantages of Leasing

As a restaurant operator there may be advantages to you to lease rather than to buy equipment and similar assets.

First, you can avoid the obsolescence that you might otherwise have if the assets are purchased outright. However, the lessor has probably considered the cost of obsolescence (a form of depreciation) and calculated it into his rental rates. However, a lease contract that allows you to replace obsolete equipment with newer equipment that comes on to the market can give you an advantage over your competitor.

Second, leasing allows you to obtain equipment that you might not otherwise be able to afford immediately or can purchase only with costly financing. In other words, 100 percent "financing" of leased assets is possible because there are no down payments required and no loan to be repaid with interest. Even if you had the cash available to purchase the assets you need, or a line of credit at your bank that allowed you to borrow sufficient funds, leasing could allow you to use this available cash for investment in more long-lived assets such as land and building that, over time, frequently appreciate in value, whereas equipment generally (if not invariably) depreciates.

Third, income tax can be a consideration. Because lease payments are generally tax-deductible, the lease cost is less demanding on cash flow than it may at first appear. For example, if you lease an item of equipment for $4,000 a year, this $4,000 is tax-deductible, and if your company is in a 50 percent tax bracket, the net cash cost of leasing is only $2,000:

	Item Leased	Item Not Leased
Profit before lease cost	$10,000	$10,000
Lease expense	4,000	0
Profit before tax	$ 6,000	$10,000
Income tax 50%	3,000	5,000
Net profit	$ 3,000	$ 5,000

As you can see by these figures, even though the lease cost is $4,000, the net profit with leasing is only $2,000 less than if the item is not leased.

However, this is an oversimplified situation because, if you owned the asset, you would be able to claim depreciation on it (rather than lease expense) as a tax deduction. Also, if you borrow any money to help finance the purchase of an asset, the interest on that borrowed money is also tax-deductible.

Finally, even though with a lease the lessor is generally responsible for maintenance of the equipment while you use it, the lessor also owns any residual value in the asset at the end of the lease period. The lease contract may give you the right to purchase the asset at that time, at a specified price, or you may have the option to renew the lease for a further specified period.

Because of these variables and the result that each lease arrangement is different, you would be wise to obtain all necessary financial information prior to making the decision to buy or lease any item.

One of the ways to help you to make that decision once you have all the facts is to use the concept of discounted cash flow, discussed earlier in the chapter, to narrow those facts down to a purely financial comparison.

To Own or to Lease?

Assume that Dino (the operator of Dino's Diner) is considering whether to buy or rent new furnishings for his restaurant.

Purchase of the furniture will require a $125,000 loan from the bank.

Cost of the furniture is $125,000. The bank loan will be repayable in four equal annual installments of principal ($31,250 per year) plus 8 percent interest. The furniture will be depreciated over five years at $25,000 per year. It is assumed to have no trade-in value at the end of that period. The income tax rate is 50 percent. Alternatively, the furniture can be leased for five years at a rental of $30,000 per year.

First, with the purchase plan, Dino must prepare a bank repayment schedule showing principal and interest payments for each of the four years (see Table 18.7).

Purchase Cash Outflow.   Next, under the purchase plan he must calculate the net cash outflow for each of the five years. This is shown in Table 18.8. In this figure, note that because depreciation and interest expense are tax-deductible and since the restaurant is in a 50 percent tax bracket, there is an income tax saving equal to 50 percent of these expenses. Thus, in year one, the expenses of $35,000 are offset by the $17,500 tax saving. Dino's net cost, after tax, is, therefore, only $17,500. This $17,500 has to be increased by the principal repayment of $31,250 on the bank loan, and reduced by the depreciation expense of $25,000, because depreciation does not require an outlay of cash. In year one, the net cash outflow is thus $23,750. Figures for the other years are calculated similarly. Note that in year five, because there is no interest expense or bank loan payment to be made, the cash flow is positive rather than negative.

Rental Cash Outflow.   Table 18.9 shows Dino's calculation of annual net cash outflows under the rental plan. Note that under the rental option there is no depreciation expense (because Dino's Diner does not own the furnishings), and there are no interest or principal payments because no money is to be borrowed.

TABLE 18.7

Bank Repayment Schedule for $125,000

Year	Interest at 8%	Principal Amount	Balance
1	$10,000	$31,250	$93,750
2	7,500	31,250	62,500
3	5,000	31,250	31,250
4	2,500	31,250	0

TABLE 18.8

Annual Net Cash Outflow With Purchase

	Year 1	Year 2	Year 3	Year 4	Year 5
Interest expense (from Table 18.7)	$10,000	$ 7,500	$ 5,000	$ 2,500	0
Depreciation expense	25,000	25,000	25,000	25,000	$25,000
Total tax deductible expense	$35,000	$32,500	$30,000	$27,500	$25,000
Income tax saving 50%	(17,500)	(16,250)	(15,000)	(13,750)	(12,500)
After-tax cost	$17,500	$16,250	$15,000	$13,750	$12,500
Add: principal payments	31,250	31,250	31,250	31,250	0
Deduct:					
depreciation expense	(25,000)	(25,000)	(25,000)	(25,000)	(25,000)
Net annual cash outflow (inflow)	$23,750	$22,500	$21,250	$20,000	($12,500)

Discounted Cash Flows. Finally, the net cash flow figures from Tables 18.8 and 18.9 have been transferred to Table 18.10 and discounted by using the appropriate discount factor from Table 18.2. The discount rate used is 8 percent because it is Dino's current cost of borrowing money from the bank. Table 18.10 shows that from a present value point of view, it would be better for Dino to rent in this particular case, because his total present value of cash outflows is lower by $4,450 ($64,339 − $59,889).

Other Considerations. In any buy-or-lease situation there could be other factors to be taken into the calculations. For example, in the purchase option, a restaurant might use some of its own cash as a down payment and borrow less than the full purchase amount required. In such a case, the down payment is an additional cash outflow at the beginning of the first year. Under a purchase plan, there might also be a trade-in value at the end

TABLE 18.9

Annual Net Cash Outflow With Rental

	Year 1	Year 2	Year 3	Year 4	Year 5
Rental expense	$30,000)	$30,000	$30,000	$30,000	$30,000
Income tax saving 50%	(15,000)	(15,000)	(15,000)	(15,000)	(15,000)
Net cash outflow	$15,000	$15,000	$15,000	$15,000	$15,000

TABLE 18.10

Total Present Value (Converted from Figures in Tables 18.8 and 18.9)

	Purchase			Rental		
Year	Annual Cash Outflow (Inflow)	Discount Factor 8%	Present Value	Annual Cash Outflow	Discount Factor 8%	Present Value
1	$23,750 ×	0.9259	= $21,990	$15,000 ×	0.9259	= $13,888
2	22,500 ×	0.8573	= 19,289	15,000 ×	0.8573	= 12,860
3	21,250 ×	0.7938	= 16,868	15,000 ×	0.7938	= 11,907
4	20,000 ×	0.7350	= 14,700	15,000 ×	0.7350	= 11,025
5	(12,500) ×	0.6806	= (8,508)	15,000 ×	0.6806	= 10,209
	Total present value		$64,339	Total present value		$59,889

of the period. This trade-in amount would be handled in the calculations as a cash inflow at the end of the period. In a rental plan, the annual payment might be required at the beginning of each year, rather than at the end, as was assumed in Dino's situation. This means that the first rental payment is at time zero, and each of the remaining annual payments is advanced by one year. Under a rental plan, there might also be a purchase option to the lessee at the end of the period. If the purchase is to be exercised, it will create an additional cash outflow.

Furthermore, terms on borrowed money can change from one situation to another, and different depreciation rates and methods can be used. For example, the use of an accelerated depreciation method will give higher depreciation expense in the earlier years, thus reducing income tax and increasing cash flow in those years.

Because of all these and other possibilities, you must investigate each buy-or-lease situation on its own merits, taking all the known variables into consideration in the calculations before you make your decision.

Computers in Foodservice Management

Throughout most of this book, manual systems of financial control have been discussed and demonstrated. Today, many foodservice operations use computers in this area of management.

In the three decades or so since computers have been commercially produced they have become a major factor in our lives. Despite this, they have been slow to impact the restaurant industry. Initially, this was so because of their high cost and space requirements. For that reason, only chain operations or quite large independent operations used them. Today, however, many restaurants use computerized sales registers to record not only sales dollars but sales per server (for labor productivity analysis) and sales of individual menu items (for menu analysis). Computers have also been put to valuable use to remove much of the drudgery present in manual cost control systems, such as budgeting, inventory control, and recipe costing.

Today the small and low-cost (but still very powerful) microcomputer, or personal computer, has made computers available to even the small independent restaurant entrepreneur. These microcomputers are so low in price that a separate computer can be used cost-effectively by a single department within a large operation. An example of this might be for maintaining storeroom inventory records.

Speed and Accuracy

The main difference between a computerized system and a manual one is the computer's speed and accuracy. Computerized systems, however, cannot do anything that cannot be done manually, and they do not relieve management from the responsibility of decision making once the information is produced.

Computers no longer have to be expensive, take up otherwise valuable space, and require a highly skilled technical person to operate them. No longer is it necessary for them to be operated by specialist computer departments, remote from day-to-day operations and decision making, which produce voluminous reports long after the need for the information they provide is past.

The new, low-cost computers may dictate a change in the way that restaurant managers behave on the job. Competitive survival may require managers to learn to effectively use computer resources and the wealth of information they can provide.

TYPES OF COMPUTERS

Generally, computers can be categorized into three types.

Mainframe Computers

In the early days, computers were very large and required dedicated, air-conditioned rooms and specialist personnel to operate them. They were often remote from the departments that needed the information that they could provide. Sometimes the main computer could be accessed by a terminal located in an individual department, or by an individual operation that was part of a chain. This type of computer is often referred to today as a mainframe computer.

Minicomputers

With the introduction of minicomputers this situation changed. A minicomputer was smaller and cheaper than its mainframe predecessors. A chain organization could now afford to have a minicomputer in each separate operation and still be linked to the head office mainframe. Also, a number of users could be connected through terminals to the minicomputer at the same time. This is known as computer timesharing. As a timeshare user accesses the minicomputer, the computer locates that user's information, receives instructions from the user to manipulate or add to it, and then stores it again until the user next wants it. For a computer to do this with several users, it needs to be programmed so that information from different users is not mixed up and so that each user is treated in turn if several are using the computer at the same time.

The result is that timeshared computers (either mainframe or minicomputer) operate at only about 50 percent efficiency. As the computer gets busier from more users' accessing it, it slows down. Its response time is also irregular, and a user may not know, if the computer does not respond promptly, whether the machine is slowed by heavy use or because the user has supplied information that the computer does not understand and cannot process.

A minicomputer may also need a complicated set of instructions and an expensive communication system, as well as extra levels of security with passwords and protected security levels, to link it with all its users and prevent unauthorized access to confidential information.

Finally, with a large time-shared mainframe or minicomputer, if the computer breaks down every user is out of business unless there is a backup computer linked to the first one.

Despite these shortcomings, mainframe and minicomputers have value where common information must be shared by several users.

Microcomputers

The heart of a microcomputer is the microprocessor. The microprocessor is sometimes referred to as a microcomputer on a chip, but it is actually only a processing and controlling subsystem on an electronic chip (a very small part of the actual microcomputer). Computer chips are so small that 20,000 of them can fit into a briefcase. When the microprocessor was introduced, it dramatically changed the accessibility of computer power and created a major reduction in the cost of this power. Today, a stand-alone microcomputer (or personal computer, as it is sometimes referred to) can cost as little as a few thousand dollars and can be easily placed on a manager's desk or small table. No specialist expertise is required to operate these computers. Indeed, it is no more necessary to know how a computer works in order to use it than it is to know how a car works in order to drive it.

The terms *microprocessor* and *microcomputer* are sometimes used interchangeably, but they do not mean the same thing. A microprocessor is the physical design and structure engraved on the chips that make a microcomputer function. Microcomputers are known as microcomputers because their systems are miniaturized. A microcomputer could, therefore, be simply described as a small computer, although that can be misleading because today's microcomputers, small as they are, are as powerful as much larger computers were twenty years ago. Microcomputers are so independently versatile that it is often better (and cheaper) to buy an extra machine for a special type of job than it is to create a special mainframe or minicomputer time-sharing program that several users can access.

Microcomputers can be operated independently but can also be linked to access the same common information that all their users need from time to time (such as inventory information). This linking of several independent computers is known as networking. As networking capability is further advanced, it may soon be possible for a restaurant operation to have its purchasing needs transmitted by its microcomputer to a network of suppliers' computers.

Also in the future may be electronic funds transfer, in which sales terminals in a restaurant are connected directly to a computer at a local bank, which, in turn, is networked to terminals at other banks. If restaurant customers pay their bills by bank credit card or check, the card or check can be verified by the local bank's computer, which then issues instructions that are transmitted to the customer's bank so that the funds are immediately transferred to the restaurant operation's local bank account. The advantages of this to the restaurant operator are the time saving of one or more days (and the resulting increase in interest income) that occurs and the reduction of losses from dishonored credit cards or NSF (not sufficient funds) checks.

HARDWARE VERSUS SOFTWARE

The hardware of a computer system is the physical equipment that follows a predetermined set of instructions in a self-directed fashion. Instructions are developed by programmers. Once a program (or set of instructions) is placed in the hardware, the computer can carry out those instructions without any operator intervention. Any intelligence that a computer has must be programmed into it, and any weaknesses in that intelligence are the fault of the program.

Software

A computer may be able to operate with many different programs for different jobs. Each program is copied into the computer when it is needed. When a new program is fed in (loaded), the previous program is replaced. When the machine is switched off, any program currently in the machine is lost to it. Thus, because of the temporary nature in the computer of each program, programs are known as software. Software is generally stored on tape or on disks, and when it is loaded into the machine it is not removed from the tape or disk but only copied.

Once information is stored on tape or disk, this storage medium can be used with any other computer of the same type. The information on the disk or tape is read by the computer scanning the magnetic surface and copying the encoded data into the computer's temporary memory (sometimes referred to as random access memory [RAM]). Once the data are in the computer they can be amended, added to, or removed if they are no longer wanted before storing them again on the disk or tape. In other words, software storage tapes or disks are the permanent record of a program.

Good hardware is not hard to find, but good software is the key to a computer system's performance. Software has to be written (contain instructions) in a language, or set of codes, that the computer understands, and it then usually has to convert these instructions into another internal language of its own before it can actually carry out the instructions. There are more than 2,000 different computer languages available to programmers today, and each of these languages may have several dialects of its own.

System Software

Sometimes the word *firmware* or *system software* is used. Firmware is a piece of software that is built right into the computer by its manufacturer. In other words, it is a piece of hardware that behaves as a piece of software. It generally comprises some circuits that load certain instructions into the computer immediately when it is switched on. For example, firmware might contain some identification codes for security purposes so that only users who properly identify themselves can use the computer or use some of its applications, depending on who they are. Firmware is also used for diagnostic purposes such as detection of user errors (for example, using an inappropriate code that the computer does not understand).

Hardware Systems

Computer hardware systems are usually made up of a number of components. Even a microcomputer cannot do much without the aid of some other hardware, or peripheral equipment. The main part of the computer where all the work or manipulation is carried out is sometimes referred to as the central processing unit (CPU). The CPU is often referred to as the brain of a hardware system because it controls all other hardware devices.

The CPU has its own set of built-in instructions in its memory chips that cannot be altered by the user. These instructions are known as read-only memory (ROM), which the user can access and "read" but cannot change. These instructions are specified by the computer manufacturer by using its own codes. Because different manufacturers use different codes, programs from one manufacturer often do not work on competitor computers.

In order to load user programs or instructions into the CPU another hardware device is required. For computers that operate from programs on disks, that input device is known as a disk drive. With some computers the disk drive (or drives, if there are more than one) may be built right into the CPU.

Also needed is another input device so that the user can interact with the CPU as work is in process. This input device is a keyboard, much like a typewriter keyboard. Again, this keyboard is sometimes built into the CPU instead of being a separate item of hardware linked to the CPU.

Another hardware item is the monitor, also known as a screen, cathode ray tube (CRT), or video display unit (VDU). The monitor displays prompts to the user from the CPU, what is input from the keyboard by the user, and the result of the work that is being done. With some computers, the monitor may be built in and be part of the CPU. The keyboard and monitor together are sometimes referred to as input/output (I/O) devices.

Finally, for most work performed a printer is needed. The printer is invariably a separate piece of equipment attached by cable to the CPU. When work performed by the user is printed out, the printed material is often received as "hard copy" to differentiate it from "soft copy," or work that is only viewed on the monitor and may still have further work done on it before a hard copy is needed. For example, when a guest is dining in a restaurant that has a computerized sales system, the server can view the soft copy of the guest's check on the monitor during the course of the meal and add items to it as the meal progresses. When guests indicate that they wish to pay, the accuracy of the final copy of the guest check can be viewed on the monitor prior to printing out the hard copy (guest check) for presentation to the guest.

Obviously, with all these various pieces of hardware comprising a computer system there has to be a high degree of compatibility among them. In addition to compatibility of hardware, the software that is used must have language compatibility with each item of hardware.

Canned Software

The question sometimes arises whether it is better to have software specifically written for an individual restaurant's needs or to buy an already written software package (known as canned software). Specifically written software is far more expensive than a canned program. Also, most restaurants are small businesses that do not have the resources necessary to carry out the systems analysis and program design work necessary to develop their own computer software.

Canned programs have normally been widely tested and any errors (bugs) in them will generally have been detected and corrected. Demonstrations of canned software can usually be viewed before the purchase decision is made. The cost to buy, install, and train employees can also be determined in advance, and any compromises that need to be made between an operation's needs and what the software can do can be made.

A successful canned software package thus represents a proven product obtainable at much less cost than a custom-designed one. In addition, there are now available for the restaurant industry specialized canned software packages in such areas as food and beverage cost control.

Obviously, the benefits of using off-the-shelf software have to be weighed against its disadvantages. A software package written for broad restaurant requirements may not be as easy to use, or as fast, as one that is custom-designed.

Interactive Programs

Software programs can be either interactive or noninteractive. An interactive program prompts the user sequentially step by step. It is thus easier to use because it helps ensure that no information that should be entered by the user is omitted.

A noninteractive program provides no prompts. Thus the user must know exactly what information to enter in correct sequence line by line and in a predetermined format. This requires more user skill (and thus an added training cost). The advantage is that the program is a lot faster.

Integrated Software Systems

In a restaurant, some information is used for more than one purpose. For example, the name of a food item might be used in receiving, storing, issuing, recipes, production, inventory, and sales control.

With a computer system it is feasible, sensible, and advantageous to use software that is integrated. In integrated software systems, the objective is to record an item of data only once and then to use it in every possible way to provide information for planning and control purposes. If the item of data had to be entered into the computer each time it was wanted, errors could be made. Errors cost time and money to correct.

One could consider a restaurant as an entire system and have a completely integrated package of computer software to control and plan every single aspect of its operation. However, a completely integrated software package to handle all this would be costly and complex, would probably incur higher training costs because of its complexity, and would create severe maintenance and data security problems. Further, if one part of the system failed, it would create difficulties in all departments or areas. For these reasons, a small property would find a completely integrated system financially difficult to justify.

Application-oriented Software Systems

At the other extreme is a software system that is oriented to a single application. If software is application-oriented, it is generally designed to handle one specific type of job and does not allow much integration. An example is a payroll system that is not integrated with labor cost budgeting, or a food inventory control system that is not integrated with purchasing and food costing.

Because of their relative simplicity, application-oriented software systems can be easily evaluated to see whether they will perform precisely the limited jobs that they are to do. These systems are cheaper to buy and install and can be introduced into an operation over time as finances allow. An ideal situation is to move from a piecemeal stand-lone set of application systems to an integrated system over time as long as each part can be made compatible with others. In this type of in-house network, each computer system is able to operate on a stand-alone basis but can integrate with all others for transmission of certain data.

Obviously, the more narrow an application-oriented system is, the easier it is to develop and the lower will be its cost. It will also be more efficient and reliable because it controls fewer functions. However, the narrower an application system becomes, the less effective it may be as far as overall control is concerned. For example, if a food inventory control system has to be supported by a separate food cost control system, then two packages of software are required, two different computer hardware systems may be needed, and two sets of user/operator systems have to be learned.

Initially, most computer applications in the hospitality industry were stand-alone applications. But as the power and memory capacity of computers have improved, the software packages available have become less stand-alone and more integrated.

Three common application-oriented software packages are word processing, database managers, and spreadsheets.

Word Processing

Word processing refers to software that is programmed to manipulate words (text). Any small computer can be programmed to handle word processing. Surprisingly, many people do not think that machines that are only used to do word processing are true computers. But if they can be programmed to do word processing, then they can be programmed to do other things as well.

The purchase of a low-cost microcomputer to be used primarily for word processing is a good way to introduce computers into a business. Word processors can be very useful when a large amount of standard correspondence is handled, such as in a catering operation where a standard banquet contract is used and only certain information (such as the number of expected guests, the menu selected, and the price of the meal) has to be inserted.

The main purpose of a word processor is to facilitate text creation and editing, and the ease with which this may be done is a major factor in selection of word processing software. One of the major advantages of using computers rather than typewriters for word processing is that documents can be printed more attractively. For example, with some computer printers a variety of typestyles can be used in the same document.

As well as allowing text editing, more sophisticated word processing software contains spelling checkers with a dictionary of as many as 30,000 words. If a word is typed that is not in the dictionary, it will be highlighted on the monitor. If it is a technical word not found in the regular dictionary, that word can be added to the dictionary so that it will not be highlighted the next time it is used.

Some word processing software also has graphics capabilities, meaning that bar or pie charts can be used to highlight certain types of information such as departmental expense trends.

Database Manager

A database manager is a collection of records such as addresses of regular customers, a food or beverage inventory listing, personnel data, or a file of recipes. These are all records that form a database. A database manager allows quick access to and ready manipulation of the records that are in that database. In other words, it is much like an office filing system where records (files) can be randomly accessed, used as required, and then restored in the same order or rearranged in some other order before storing.

For example, for one application a database of recipes can be stored in alphabetic sequence according to the main recipe ingredient and only recipes containing that ingredient can be printed out. For another application, all recipes can be stored alphabetically, regardless of ingredients, before printing them.

It may be useful to purchase a software package that includes both word processing and a database. For example, it may be necessary for a catering company to send out a standard form letter to all the businesses it regularly deals with advising them of a change in its banquet menu prices. The computer can be programmed to take each business's address in turn from the database, type it on the restaurant's letterhead, type in the letter from the word processor, then move to the next address and letter on a new page until all addresses have been used. All of this can be completed without any user intervention once the process has been started.

Spreadsheet

Spreadsheet software is basically a large electronic sheet with rows down the side and columns across the top, much as one would see on a work sheet for preparing a budget. Most managers have struggled with budgets using pencils and column pads and have become frustrated when they wish to see what happens, for example, if the food cost to sales ratio is altered over a twelve month annual budget. The changes that have to be made to food cost, gross profit, and net profit require thirty-six alterations, considerable erasing and correcting, and a risk that one or more errors will occur. A properly programmed electronic spreadsheet will allow a manager to answer this type of "what if?" question in seconds and print out the results. Indeed, multiple "what if" changes can be made at the same time at rapid speed.

Spreadsheets lend themselves not only to budgeting but also to forecasting. For example, a spreadsheet can have in its memory all the various menu items a restaurant offers, including how many of each are sold on average by meal period and day of the week for each specific month. The spreadsheet can then forecast for the current month, on the basis of past performance, how many portions of each menu item should be produced by the kitchen for each meal period each day of the current month. Spreadsheets also lend themselves well to the following applications:

- Scheduling employees for improved labor cost control.
- Preparing depreciation schedules.
- Calculating percentages (given the dollar amounts) for common-size financial statement analysis.
- Calculating the sales mix and gross profit figures given menu items sold and their cost and selling prices.
- Converting budgeted income statements (given appropriate ratios) to cash flow budgets.
- Using NPV and IRR analysis for long-term investments.
- Preparing budget variance analyses.
- Using break-even analysis for various types of decisions.

Integrated Work Stations

As far as planning and control are concerned, word processing, database manager, and spreadsheet software are closely related. A computer ought to be able to pass data from its database manager to a spreadsheet and then in turn pass the results to a word processor for addition of text and final printing of a report, including graphics where these would be valuable.

Indeed, for many microcomputers today, single-software packages that include all three of these software systems on one disk are available. These are known as integrated work stations.

ACCOUNTING PACKAGES

Another area that lends itself well to an integrated software package is general accounting. Most businesses with a manual system of accounting use an integrated approach for their general ledger, sales, accounts receivable, purchases, accounts payable, payroll, and inventory control. Today, there are integrated software packages available for computerization of this work. In some situations, it may not be feasible or practical to integrate each of these subsystems on the mainframe computer. For example, it may be useful to separate food inventory control so that a specialized software package can be purchased that will do many more things than a general accounting system's inventory control subsystem will do. Some of these additional and desirable features will be discussed later in this Appendix.

Similarly, it may not be practical for a restaurant to computerize its payroll. One of the reasons is that the expense of maintaining computerized payroll software is comparatively high. Each time the laws relating to employment change (such as for minimum wage rates, tax deduction rates, and unemployment insurance rates) the software must be rewritten to accommodate those changes. For this reason, many establishments contract out their payroll preparation to a computer service company that specializes in this kind of work.

ECR AND POS SYSTEMS

For locations where food and beverage sales are recorded, two types of systems are available: an electronic cash register (ECR) and a point of sale (POS) system. Basically, the ECR is a stand-alone electronic register, whereas a POS system links several ECRs together to a separate remote computer and the sales register is primarily a keyboard rather than a separate machine. Unfortunately, the terms *ECR* and *POS* are often used interchangeably. Technically speaking, however, a POS system is much more sophisticated than a stand-alone ECR, even though an ECR can provide a great deal more cost of sales information than its predecessors (mechanical sales registers).

Electronic Cash Registers

ECRs have allowed cashiers to be dispensed with in most establishments because servers can act as their own cashiers and the machine records, among other things, sales by server so that each knows how much cash to turn in at the end of each shift.

Most ECRs have some sort of video display, often just a strip window with space for a limited number of characters. Increasingly larger video displays are appearing on the equipment so that, for example, the entire bill for a group of people at a table can be seen on the monitor. More sophisticated models can have keys that light up to prompt the operator what to do next or have the monitor display messages about subsequent steps to make, or to explain mistakes.

Most ECRs have automatic pricing (eliminating pricing errors), change control features (in some cases linked to automatic change dispensers to reduce losses from change-making errors), and automatic tax calculation for jurisdictions where food and/or beverage sales tax applies.

Computerized ECRs can summarize sales not only by server (broken down into cash and charge subtotals) but also by categories, such as appetizers, entrees, and desserts. In chain operations, this sales information might be networked to the head office computer for further, more detailed processing.

Some ECRs can also be programmed to print out the most popular combinations of appetizer, entree, and dessert that customers choose. This is useful information for menu and sales mix planning.

Some ECRs can also provide inventory control for items that can be easily quantified such as steaks. If it were to be used for complete inventory control, however, the ECR would have to be programmed to remember the recipe of each dish, and that sort of inventory control might be better left to a separate software control system (to be discussed later). Alternatively, the ECR might be linked to another computer and send sales information to this computer so that the food cost control work could be done there.

Some ECRs have time clocks built into them. This allows servers to clock in and out of work on the machine using a magnetically striped employee ID card, thus providing hours-worked information for staff planing and payroll. At the end of each shift or day, summary reports of employee hours worked, by employee and in total, are available. Information can also be accumulated in the ECR for each weekly or biweekly payroll period. A built-in clock can also track patterns of sales by time of day or time of guest arrivals and departures. This could be valuable for staff scheduling, labor cost planning, and kitchen food production planning.

ECRs can also have scales attached to them for automatic calculation of the sales value of items (such as salads) sold by weight.

With most ECR systems it is not necessary to have sales checks preprinted with sequential numbers. Blank standard sales checks can be purchased (at a saving in cost without numbering), and the ECR will print a consecutive number on each when the check is first started. If the same check is used for a reorder, the employee must instruct the machine that a previous check number is being used. If the server does not use the previous number when adding items to an active sales check, the machine will assign it a new number since it assumes it is a brand-new check. If the server collects the full amount of the check from the customer and only turns in the amount of money from the reorder, the first number will show up as a missing check and the dishonesty will be spotted because the register prints a report at the end of each shift or day of the "open" checks—that is, those that have not been closed off—and identifies the employee responsible.

Integrated Point of Sale Systems

Generally a POS system is a series of individual sales terminals (such as ECRs) linked to a remote CPU. Food and beverage POS systems may be used as stand-alone systems for each separate food and beverage outlet but may also be linked to other POS systems in other sales outlets. They can also be linked to other equipment such as a printer in the kitchen that tells the kitchen what has been recorded in the register and needs to be prepared in the kitchen without the server's (who has rung up the item on the register) having to walk to the kitchen. The kitchen may also be able to send messages back to the system's monitor to prompt servers when it is time to pick up prepared food orders.

The most recent device is an electronic server pad (ESP). With an ESP, servers no longer have to write out orders at the customer's table and then go to a terminal to enter them there. They simply punch them into a hand-held computer and the information is beamed to a central computer through low-frequency frequency-modulated (FM) waves. The central computer then relays the information to a printer in the kitchen and/or bar.

Hotel POS systems in food and beverage areas may also be linked to the front office accounting system so that hotel guests charging food and beverage items in the restaurant or bar can have the amounts automatically added to their front office accounts.

In other words, a POS system has a much greater capability than an ECR and can produce a much larger variety of management reports by sales outlet and in total. It is generally a totally programmable system that can be easily modified within the business to accommodate changes in menu prices and many other items.

It can also be linked to a chain head office where data can be analyzed by the mainframe computer, results compared from unit to unit, and data consolidated by region and for the chain as a whole. In some systems, analysis reports for each individual unit can be sent back to the unit in a process known as downloading. Downloading can also be used to provide each unit's computer with new menu pricing and recipe costing information.

The major disadvantage of a POS system is that if the CPU fails, each POS terminal in the entire system fails (because terminals cannot operate independently of the CPU) unless the system is backed up with disk memory or unless the individual terminals can be upgraded to operate in at least a limited way with some memory capability and to produce some reports independent of the CPU.

INVENTORY CONTROL

Computers can be very valuable as a tool in inventory control. They can do the following:

- Prepare purchase orders for suppliers. It is now also possible for computers through networking to place orders with approved suppliers who submitted the best price for the items and quantities needed automatically.

- Prepare lists of items to be received from each supplier so that receiving employees can compare what is delivered with what should be delivered.

- As products are received and product information is recorded in the computer from invoice information, compare this information against purchase orders and specifications for those items.

- Issue appropriate credit memoranda for goods short-shipped or returned to suppliers.

- Produce food and beverage receiving reports for products delivered.

- Maintain a record of all storeroom purchases from information entered from invoices and update the perpetual inventory of each storeroom item.

- Record all issues from the storeroom from information entered from requisitions, use this information to adjust the perpetual inventory of that item, and calculate the total cost of all items issued each day to aid in the calculation of daily food and beverage costs.

- Calculate the cost of items requisitioned by any individual department for any period of time.

- Compare requisition signatures (using a scanner) with a record of those signatures stored in the computer to ensure they are authentic.
- Compare at any time quantity information of actual inventory for any specific item with what the computer-maintained perpetual inventory record is and print out variance reports.
- Let both management and the food buyer know when quantities purchased exceed prescribed limits for storeroom stock.
- Provide each month a list of all items that were short-stocked during that period.
- Issue monthly dead-stock reports showing items that have not moved in a stipulated period, such as thirty, sixty, or ninety days.
- List how many units of each item were purchased from any one supplier and whether that purchase was made at the best quoted price.
- List how many of each item was used during each month and compare this with what should have been used according to actual food and/or beverage sales based on standard recipes and portion sizes.
- Verify supplier month-end statements against receiving invoices and/or receiving reports and issue checks in payment of those statements.

A sophisticated inventory control computer program can also adjust the volume of storeroom inventory required in accordance with the level of business. Thus, instead of leaving it to management to establish a fixed minimum and maximum level of stock for each storeroom item, the computer can adjust the reorder point and the order quantity to the actual usage or sales (which may change over time or by season) for that item. Each day, the computer prints out a list of items to be ordered, quantities needed, and economic order quantity (if this is built into the system). In cases where particular suppliers are under contract to provide specific storeroom items at contracted prices, the actual purchase orders can be prepared for those suppliers.

Bar Codes

One of the recent advances in inventory control is the use of bar codes on product containers. The bar code is a series of parallel black bars of varying width on a white background. The scanners that read the code can be counter level models (such as those found at check-out stands in supermarkets) or hand-held wands (the type most useful in restaurant receiving so that heavy cases do not have to be lifted to pass over the scanner).

A common bar code is the ten-digit Universal Product Code (UPC) system, in which the first five digits identify the manufacturer or processor and the second five digits provide information about the product. It is not necessary for the product to be in a sealed container such as a carton or box. Even open crates of fresh produce such as apples and lettuce can be bar-coded. The bar code information read and recorded by the computer can include the product's name, package size, quantity of the item (from which inventory records can be adjusted), and other desired information. For example, part of the bar code can represent specifications for each product.

The UPC has also been advantageous to suppliers who may have dozens of different qualities and container sizes of a particular product, each of which can be quickly identified by reading its bar code and matching this with the purchaser's purchase order specification.

Where bar coding is used by a restaurant, it offers the following advantages:

- Fast order processing.
- Reduction in purchasing time.
- Reduction in specification misunderstandings between purchaser and seller.
- More accurate purchasing, ordering, receiving, and inventory records.
- Improved food, beverage, and supplies cost control.
- Improved supplier delivery schedules and performance.
- Simplification of receiving procedures.
- Improved inventory and issuing control (as items are issued they can again be passed over the scanner so that perpetual inventory count will be adjusted and proper cost information recorded on requisitions).

Note that bar codes do not contain price information because the code is placed on products by the manufacturer, who usually does not know what the end price of the product will be after it has gone through various distribution levels. Thus, pricing information has to be entered into the hospitality operation's computer from invoices received from suppliers.

FOOD CONTROL SYSTEMS

In Chapter 6 a method of food cost control based on accurate costing of standard recipes using manual means was illustrated. Unfortunately, because of the constant daily changes in food purchase costs, a restaurant with an extensive menu would find revising recipe costs manually a prohibitively time-consuming task. Even a limited-menu restaurant may still find the job too time consuming and not worth the effort.

Recipes as Basis for Control

Computers, however, can considerably simplify this work by using a database software system that operates from a computerized file of standard recipes and their ingredients. As new purchases are made, the inventory (ingredient) quantity and cost information is entered into the computer from invoices. Alternatively, terminals can be equipped with a wand reader at the receiving area to read the UPC codes on containers. If items do not have the UPC codes the information has to be entered manually into the computer.

As new ingredient price information is entered, the computer automatically updates all total recipe costs (using current portion costs or a weighted average, depending on which method management chooses) for any recipes containing any of these ingredients. A report showing what recipes are affected and what the new food cost is in dollars and percentages for that recipe can be printed and possibly flag the need to change the menu selling price.

Food Production Control

Each day before production is started it is only necessary to enter into the computer the name of each recipe item and the number of portions to be produced that day from forecast sales. The computer will print the standard cost for all those recipe items individually and in total, print the recipes with the ingredient list for the required number of portions, and print a requisition listing the ingredients and the quantities required from the storeroom. If more than a required quantity is needed for a particular day (for example, a number 10 can of an item when only half a can is required for production), the computer makes a note of this excess and takes it into account when future requisitions are prepared.

The computer also calculates a food cost for the day based on food produced according to forecast sales.

Inventory Control

As requisitions are printed, the computer also adjusts the storeroom inventory count for period-end stocktaking and can provide a value for items requisitioned but not yet used in production (for example, the half number 10 can mentioned earlier). From time to time a normal storeroom inventory reconciliation must be carried out, comparing the physical count of items actually in stock with the computer listing of what should be there according to production usage.

If bar-coded products are used, inventory taking is further simplified. A manual count of those products is not required. A hand-held bar code reader can be passed over the bar code and count all containers or products and compile the actual inventory (including pricing and total valuation). The computer can also issue a report showing how this actual inventory (either in total or product by product) differs from the computer's perpetual inventory record (compiled from invoices and requisitions) of what should be there.

Taking a physical, or actual, inventory is also easier with a computer even if products are not bar-coded. There are programs that will print an inventory form, complete with current item costs, leaving only the count quantity to be inserted manually. After the count, count figures can be entered into the computer and a final inventory report produced showing extensions (item count times price) for each item and total inventory value.

Management Reports

Finally, management reports showing planning errors such as overproduction of menu items because of poor forecasting can be prepared. A completely comprehensive food cost control system would have built into it (by linking it to POS registers) the actual sales histories of various menu items in combination with other menu items and provide the kitchen with daily food production requirements to minimize such factors as overproduction planning errors.

Other management reports might show operational errors (wastage because standard recipes were not followed) and costing errors (loss of potential revenue in comparison with actual revenue because selling prices have not kept up with increasing food costs). Another report might show cost trends for major purchases to assist in forward menu price planning.

Glossary

Absolute changes: The amount of change in dollars of an item on the income statement from one period to the next.

Accelerated depreciation: A method of depreciation that gives greater amounts of depreciation expense in the earlier years of an asset's life. See also **Depreciation.**

Account: A record in which the current status (or balance) of each type of asset, liability, owners' equity, sale (revenue), and expense is kept.

Accounting equation: Assets = liabilities + owners' equity.

Accounting period: The time period covered by the financial statements.

Accounts payable: Amounts due to suppliers (creditors); a debt or a liability.

Accounts receivable: Amounts due from customers or guests (debtors); an asset.

Accounts receivable aging: Preparing a schedule classifying receivables in terms of time left unpaid.

Accounts receivable average collection period: The number of days the average receivable remains unpaid.

Accounts receivable turnover: Annual sales divided by average accounts receivable.

Accrual accounting: As opposed to cash accounting, a method of accounting whereby transactions are recorded as they occur and not when cash is exchanged; the matching of sales and expenses on income statements regardless of when cash is received or disbursed.

Accrued expenses: Expenses that have been incurred but not paid at the balance sheet date; a liability.

Accumulated depreciation: The total depreciation that has been shown as an expense on the income statements since the related assets were purchased. See also **Depreciation.**

Acid test ratio: See **Quick ratio.**

Adjustments: Entries made at the end of each accounting period in journals and then in the accounts so that the accounts have correct balances under the accrual accounting method.

Allowance for doubtful accounts (bad debts):   An amount established to cover the likelihood that not all accounts receivable outstanding at the balance sheet date will be collected.

Amortization: A method of writing down the cost of certain intangible assets (such as franchises or goodwill) in the same way as depreciation is used to write down the cost of tangible fixed, or long-term, assets.

Asset: An item, a property, or a resource owned by a business.

Audit tape: A continuous chronological record of each transaction recorded in a cash or sales register. The tape can usually only be removed at the end of each day by an authorized person.

Average check: Sales divided by the number of people served during a certain period of time. Sometimes called average cover or average spending.

Average cover: See **Average check.**

Average rate of return (ARR): A method of measuring the value of a long-term investment. The equation is net annual saving divided by average investment.

Average sales per seat: Sales for a period of time divided by the number of restaurant seats.

Average spending: See **Average check.**

Bad debt: An account receivable considered or known to be uncollectable. See also **Allowance for doubtful accounts.**

Balance: The amount of an account at a point in time.

Balance sheet: A statement showing that assets = liabilities + owners' equity. A balance sheet shows the financial position of a company at a point in time.

Balance sheet equation: Assets equals liabilities plus owners' equity.

Bank: See **Float.**

Bank reconciliation: A monthly or periodic procedure to ensure that the company's bank account balance amount agrees with the bank's statement figure.

Beverage cost: See **Cost of sales.**

Beverage cost percentage: Cost of beverages sold divided by beverage sales and multiplied by 100.

Beverage receiving report: A form completed daily or weekly to summarize purchases of alcoholic beverages.

Book value: Initial cost of an asset or assets less related accumulated depreciation.

Bottle coding: Alcoholic beverage bottles coded with a difficult or impossible-to-duplicate mark to identify them as legitimately purchased bottles.

Break-even analysis: An analysis of fixed and variable costs in relation to sales as an aid in decision making.

Break-even equation or formula: An equation useful in making business decisions concerning sales levels and fixed and variable costs.

Break-even point: The level of sales at which a company will make neither an income nor a loss.

Budget: A business plan, usually expressed in monetary terms.

Budget cycle: The sequence of events covered by a budget period from initial budget preparation through to comparison of actual results with budgeted estimates.

Call liquor: A premium liquor usually identified by brand name.

Capital asset: See **Fixed asset**.

Capital budget: A budget concerning long-term, or fixed, assets.

Cash accounting: A method of accounting (as opposed to accrual accounting) whereby transactions are only recorded at the time cash is received or disbursed.

Cash budget: A budget concerned with cash inflows and cash outflows.

Cash disbursements: Money paid by cash or by check for the purchase of goods or services.

Cash management: Cash conservation and the management of other working capital accounts to maximize the effectiveness of the business's use of cash.

Cash receipts: Cash or checks received in payment for sale of products or services.

Collusion: Two or more people working together for fraudulent purposes.

Common shares: A form of stock or share issued by an incorporated business to raise money.

Comparative/common-size statement analysis: Two or more financial statements presented with all data in both dollar and percentage figures.

Comparative statement analysis: Financial statements for two or more periods presented so that the change in each account balance from one period to the next is shown in both dollar and percentage terms.

Contribution margin: The difference between sales and variable costs or expenses.

Contribution statement: A form of income statement presentation where variable costs are deducted from sales to show contribution margin, and fixed costs are then deducted from contribution margin to arrive at profit.

Controllable cost or expense: A cost that is controllable by an individual (such as a department head).

Control state: A state in which the government partly or fully controls the liquor distribution system.

Convenience food: A product that has been partly or fully preprepared by the manufacturer.

Cost: The price paid to purchase an asset or to pay for the purchase of goods or services. Also frequently used as a synonym for *expense*.

Cost management: An awareness of the various types of cost and the effect that the relevant ones have on individual business decisions.

Cost of sales: Generally referred to simply as food cost or beverage cost. Calculated by adding beginning of the accounting period inventory to purchases during the period, and deducting end of the period inventory, adjusting where necessary for items such as employee meals and/or interdepartmental transfers.

Credit: 1. an entry on the right-hand side of an account; 2. to extend credit or to allow a person to consume goods or services and pay at a later date.

Credit invoice: An invoice prepared by a supplier showing, for example, that goods delivered to a company have been returned as unacceptable.

Credit memorandum: A dummy credit invoice made out by a company prior to receipt of a credit invoice from the supplier.

Creditor: A person or company to whom a business owes money.

Current assets: Cash or other assets likely to be turned into cash within a year.

Current dollars: Historic (previous periods') dollars converted to terms of today's dollars for purposes of comparison.

Current liabilities: Debts that are due to be paid within one year.

Current liquidity ratios: Ratios that indicate a company's ability to meet its short-term debts.

Current ratio: The ratio of current assets to current liabilities.

Daily food receiving report: A report that summarizes daily invoice information about food purchases.

Debit: An entry in the left-hand side of an account.

Debt: Money owed to a person or organization; an obligation.

Debt to equity ratio: The amount of debt (liabilities) expressed as a ratio of owners' equity.

Declining balance depreciation: A method of accelerated depreciation in which higher amounts of depreciation expense are recorded in the earlier years of an asset's life.

Demand, elasticity of: See **Elasticity of demand.**

Department budget: An operating budget prepared for an individual department in a multidepartment organization.

Departmental income: The income of an individual department after direct expenses have been deducted from sales; sometimes referred to as contributory income.

Dependent variable: An item that is affected by what happens to another item. For example, labor cost is affected by the level of sales; labor is the dependent variable.

Depreciation: A method of allocating the cost of a fixed asset over the anticipated life of the asset, showing a portion of the cost, for each accounting period of the life, as an expense on the income statement.

Derived demand: The business that one department has as a result of business in another department, for example, cocktail lounge sales resulting from customers' having drinks while eating in the dining room.

Direct cost or expense: An expense that can be distributed directly to an operating department and is generally controllable by that department.

Direct purchases: Food purchases that are put directly into production either in the kitchen or in a sales area. See also **Storeroom purchases.**

Discount: A reduction of the amount paid on a purchase because of prompt payment.

Discounted cash flow: A method of converting future inflows and/or outflows of cash to the value of today's dollars.

Discretionary cost or expense: One that could be incurred but does not have to be at the present time.

Dividend: An amount paid out of profit after tax to shareholders as a return on their investment in the company.

Double-entry accounting: An accounting procedure that requires equal debit and credit entries in the accounts for each business transaction to ensure that the accounting equation is kept in balance.

Drawings: See **Withdrawals.**

Earnings statement: See **Income statement.**

Elasticity of demand: The effect that a change in price has on demand for a product or service.

Employee orientation: A formalized procedure of introducing each new employee hired to his or her job.

Employee turnover: The loss and replacement of an employee.

Exit interview: A procedure of meeting with each employee who leaves employment to try to determine the reason he or she is leaving.

Expenditure: Payment in cash for purchase of a product or service, or incurrence of a liability for purchase of a product or service.

Expense: Products or services consumed or used in operating a business.

Financial leverage: A method of financing where the amount of debt (liability) is increased in proportion to equity (owners' investment).

Financial position: The financial condition of a business as indicated by its balance sheet.

Financial statements: A balance sheet and an income statement and, where appropriate, a statement of retained earnings and other supporting information.

Fiscal period: An annual accounting period that may not coincide with the calendar year.

Fixed assets: Assets of a long-term or capital nature that will be depreciated over a number of years.

Fixed cost or expense: A cost that does not change, in the short run, with changes in volume of business.

Float (or Bank):   An amount of money advanced to an employee for change-making purposes.

Food cost: See **Cost of sales.**

Food cost percentage: Cost of food sold divided by food sales and multiplied by 100.

Franchise fee or cost: The cost to purchase the right to use the name and/or services of another organization.

Full-bottle replacement: A bar control procedure in which bartenders are only given full new bottles of liquor for an equivalent number of empty used ones.

Goodwill: The value of an established business, based on its name or reputation, above the value of its tangible assets.

Gross profit: Sales less cost of sales.

Happy hour: In a bar, a period when drink prices are reduced.

Historic cost: The cost of something at the time it was paid for, not adjusted to current cost.

Horizontal statement analysis: See **Comparative statement analysis.**

Income statement: A financial statement showing money earned from sales of products and services for a period of time, less the expenses incurred to earn those sales; sometimes referred to as the profit and loss statement.

Income and expense statement: See **Income statement.**

Incorporated company: A legal form of business operation that differentiates it from a proprietorship or partnership.

Independent variable: An item that is not affected by what happens to another item. For example, restaurant sales are not affected by labor cost; sales are the independent variable.

Indirect cost or expense: A cost not allocated directly to a department. See also **Direct cost.**

Integrated pricing: An approach to pricing so that product prices in one department are compatible with those in a related department.

Interest earned ratio: Profit before interest and income tax divided by interest expense.

Internal control: A system of procedures and forms established in a business to safeguard its assets and help ensure the accuracy of the information provided by its accounting system.

Internal rate of return (IRR):   A method of measuring the value of a long-term investment using discounted cash flow. See also **Discounted cash flow.**

Inventory: Products (generally food and beverages) purchased but not yet used to generate sales. See also **Physical inventory.**

Inventory turnover: Cost of sales for a period of time divided by the average inventory for that period.

Invoice: Document prepared to record the sale of products or services and giving details about the transaction and the total value of the sale.

Jigger: A measuring device for portion control of small quantities of beverages used in cocktails. See also **Shot glass.**

Job description: A description of what a job entails, the tasks that must be performed, and when those tasks must be performed. See also **Task procedures.**

Job rotation: Training employees at different jobs so that they can easily be moved from one to another when the need arises.

Joint cost or expense: One that is shared by more than one department.

Journal: Accounting record summarizing business transactions as they occur prior to posting the information to the individual accounts.

Kickback: Cash or merchandise given to a purchaser by a supplier to encourage the purchaser to favor that supplier.

Labor cost percentage: Labor cost divided by sales and multiplied by 100.

Labor productivity standard: A predetermined level of employee productivity, such as the number of restaurant customers to be handled per server during a meal period.

Lapping: A method of fraud that can occur when an employee has complete control of accounts receivable and payments received on these accounts.

Leasehold improvements: Architectural and/or interior design changes made to rented (leased) premises.

Ledger: A book of accounts in which business transactions are entered after being recorded in journals.

Leverage: See **Financial leverage** and/or **Operating leverage.**

Liability: A debt or an obligation owed by a business.

License state: A state in which the government has little or no control over the liquor distribution system.

Liquidation: The closing of a business by selling its assets and paying off its liabilities.

Liquidity: The financial strength of a business in terms of its ability to pay off its short-term or current liabilities without difficulty; a healthy working capital position; a good current ratio.

Loan: An amount borrowed; a debt; a liability.

Loan principal: The repayment of the initial amount borrowed on a loan is a principal payment as distinct from interest that is in addition to principal payments.

Long-term asset: See **Fixed asset.**

Long-term budget: A budget for a period of time generally in excess of one year.

Long-term liability: A debt or obligation to be paid off more than one year hence.

Loss: An excess of expenses over revenue.

Marketable securities: Investments in government bonds or similar securities that can be readily converted into cash.

Market quotation sheet: A form used to record suppliers' quotes so that prices for food products to be purchased can be compared.

Market value: The current value of an asset, sometimes known as its replacement value.

Markup: The difference between the cost of an item and its selling price.

Matching principle: A principle of accrual accounting relating expenses to the revenue earned during a period regardless of when the cash was received or the expenses paid.

Memorandum invoice: A temporary dummy invoice prepared in the absence of a proper invoice.

Monopoly state: See **Control state.**

Mortgage: A long-term debt or liability generally secured by using long-term assets (such as land and/or building) as collateral.

Net assets: See **Net worth.**

Net book value: See **Book value.**

Net income: Total revenue from sales and other income less total expenses.

Net present value (NPV):   A method of measuring the value of a long-term investment using discounted cash flow. See also **Discounted cash flow.**

Net working capital: Current assets less current liabilities.

Net worth: Total assets less total liabilities; owners' equity.

Noncontrollable cost or expense: Costs or expenses that are generally fixed in nature in the short run, such as rent or interest.

Note payable: A liability documented by a written promise to pay at a specified time.

Occupation costs: Costs such as rent, real estate taxes, interest, and depreciation.

Open state: See **License state.**

Open stock: The inventory of food products in kitchens and other areas.

Operating budget: A budget concerned with revenue and/or expenses.

Operating cost: See **Expense.**

Operating leverage: The relationship between fixed and variable expenses; high fixed expenses compared to variable expenses indicate high operating leverage.

Order form: A form completed daily summarizing what has been ordered from each supplier, the quantity ordered, and the price quoted.

Outstanding check: A check issued in payment of a debt that has not yet been cashed in by the payee or has been cashed in but has not yet been deducted from the payer's bank account.

Owners' equity: Total assets minus total liabilities; net worth.

Par stock: The maximum amount of stock that should be on hand at any time for each inventory item.

Partnership: An unincorporated business owned by two or more persons.

Payback period: The time it takes to recover an investment; initial investment divided by net annual cash saving.

Perpetual inventory card: A form that is used to record the movement of all items in and out of storage rooms; one card is used for each item.

Petty cash: A fund of money controlled by an individual from which minor purchases of products or services can be paid.

Physical inventory: The actual counting, recording, and pricing of assets.

Portion cost factor: An equation used to simplify the calculation of a menu item's cost when the supplier changes the price; calculated by dividing the portion cost by the supplier's price per pound.

Portion size: See **Standard portion.**

Post off: A supplier's discounted price for an alcoholic beverage product.

Preferred shares: A form of stock or share issued by an incorporated business to raise money, generally ranking before common shares with reference to dividends.

Prepaid expense: An expense paid for and shown as an asset until it is matched up with related revenue and shown as an expense. See **Matching principle.**

Present value: See **Discounted cash flow.**

Product differentiation: A method of presenting a product or service in a different way from competitors, for example, by creating a unique ambiance or providing superior service.

Productivity standard: See **Labor productivity standard.**

Profit: See **Net income.**

Profit and loss statement: See **Income statement.**

Profit center: A department where the department head is responsible for the sales and control of costs in that department.

Profit margin: See **Profit to sales ratio.**

Profit to sales ratio: Profit divided by sales and multiplied by 100; also known as profit margin.

Proprietorship: An unincorporated business owned by a single individual.

Quick ratio: The ratio of quick assets to current liabilities.

Ratio: The relationship of one item to another. For example, $2,000 of current assets to $1,000 of current liabilities would be a 2:1 ratio.

Ratio analysis: The use of various ratios to monitor the ongoing progress of a business.

Receiving report: A form, completed daily, listing all goods received for the day.

Receiving stamp: A stamp placed on each invoice and initialed in the appropriate place by each person responsible for control procedures for products received.

Recipe: See **Standard recipe.**

Relative change: The change for each item on an income statement from one period to the next expressed in percentage terms.

Relevant cost or expense: One that is important and to be considered in a particular business decision.

Requisition: A form, completed by an authorized person, requesting that needed items be issued from the storeroom.

Retained earnings statement: A financial statement used by an incorporated business to show accumulated net incomes less accumulated losses less any dividends paid since the business began. See also **Statement of capital.**

Return on owners' equity: Profit after income tax divided by owners' equity.

Revenue: Money earned from sales and/or income received in exchange for products or services.

Sales: See **Revenue.**

Sales check: A document used by restaurants to record the sales of food and beverages.

Sales mix: The ratio of what people select from various menu items offered.

Scrap value: See **Trade-in value.**

Seat turnover: The number of guests served in a restaurant during a period of time divided by the number of seats available.

Semifixed or semivariable cost or expense: One that has both fixed and variable elements and is neither entirely fixed nor entirely variable in relation to sales.

Share: See **Common shares** and **Preferred shares.**

Shift schedule: See **Stacked schedule.**

Short-term budget: A budget prepared for a period of time generally less than a year.

Short-term liability: See **Current liability.**

Shot glass: A measuring device for portion size control of standard bar drinks. See also **Jigger.**

Solvency: The ability of a company to meet its debts as they become due.

Specification: A detailed description of a product that needs to be purchased.

Spillage allowance: A quantity allowance (such as one drink per bottle) given to bartenders because it is unrealistic to expect that each liquor bottle can be emptied without some "spillage."

Stacked schedule: A stacked, or shift, schedule is an employee schedule used in departments where groups of employees arrive on the job at the same time and then leave together at the end of their shift. See also **Staff schedule** and **Staggered schedule**.

Staff schedule: A schedule, usually prepared in advance week by week, showing which employees will be on duty each day and the hours each one will be working. See also **Stacked schedule** and **Staggered schedule**.

Staffing guide: A form developed for each department showing the number of employees, by job category, who should be on duty to meet various possible levels of business volume.

Staggered schedule: A staff schedule used when individual employees in a department arrive on the job at various times and leave at various times at the end of their shift. See also **Stacked schedule** and **Staff schedule**.

Standard cost or expense: What the cost should be for a particular level of sales or revenue.

Standard portion: The quantity of a food or beverage item that is to be served to a guest to achieve a desired standard cost. See also **Standard cost**.

Standard recipe: A written formula stating the quantities of each ingredient required to produce a specific quantity and quality of a food or beverage item.

Standing order: An arrangement with a supplier to provide a predetermined quantity of a particular item or items on a daily or other periodic basis without having to contact the supplier each time.

Statement of capital: Statement used by a partnership or proprietorship to show the status of each owner's investment in the business. See also **Statement of retained earnings**.

Statement of operations: See **Income statement**.

Statement of retained earnings: A statement used by an incorporated company showing previous balance sheet figures, plus net income for the period, less any dividends paid during the period, to arrive at current period-end retained earnings.

Stockholder: An investor who owns common and/or preferred shares (stock) in an incorporated business.

Stockholders' equity: See **Owners' equity**.

Storeroom purchases: Purchases of food products that are controlled in a lockable storeroom. See also **Direct purchases**.

Straight-line depreciation: A method of depreciation in which equal portions of the amount paid for an asset are shown as an expense during each accounting period of the life of the asset.

Strategic budget: A long-term budget for periods generally in excess of one year.

Sunk cost or expense: A cost incurred that is no longer relevant and cannot affect any future decisions.

T account: A simplified form of account in the shape of a *T*, with account title on top, debit on the left, and credit on the right.

Task procedures: Detailed step-by-step procedures, preferably in writing, of how a particular task is to be performed.

Trade-in value: The scrap or cash value of an asset at the time its useful life is over or when it is exchanged with cash for a new asset.

Transaction: A business event requiring an entry in the accounting records.

Trend index: In a series of periods of operating results, the result for the first (base) period is given the value of 100; subsequent period results are then given a number higher or lower than 100 to reflect each period's change relative to the base year more accurately.

Trend results: Business operating results compared for a number of sequential periods.

Turnover ratios: Ratios that measure the activity of an asset during an accounting period, such as inventory turnover.

Units of production depreciation: A method of depreciation basing depreciation expense on the number of units used or produced by the asset during an accounting period.

Upgrading: A method of fraud practiced by suppliers who deliver a lower-quality product and invoice for a high-quality product actually ordered.

Variable cost or expense: One that increases or decreases in direct or linear fashion with increases or decreases in the related sales or revenue.

Vertical statement analysis: See **Comparative/common-size statement analysis**.

Volume: Level of sales expressed in dollars or units.

Well liquor: Nonpremium lower-cost liquor. See also **Call liquor**.

Withdrawals: Monies taken out of a business by individual owners in a proprietorship or partnership (similar to dividends in an incorporated company).

Working capital: Current assets less current liabilities.

Working capital management: See **Cash management**.

Index